Brian Ke

The Footloose American

Following the Hunter S. Thompson Trail Across South America

Praise for **THE FOOTLOOSE AMERICAN**

"Brian Kevin has written a marvelous travel romp following the *Proud Highway* of Hunter S. Thompson through Latin America. Kevin is a helluva good writer, and if the Gonzo King were alive he would give *The Footloose American* a thumbs up."

—DOUGLAS BRINKLEY,
author of *Cronkite,* CBS News historian, and
literary executor of Hunter S. Thompson's estate

"Brian Kevin has achieved a miraculous first with this brilliant travelogue that follows Hunter S. Thompson's journeys through South America shot into the prism of the modern traveler's aesthetic. The vividness of Kevin's writing makes for great reading, and his stories bring to life the immediacy and romantic allure of the Latin experience."

—ANDREW ZIMMERN,
creator of *Bizarre Foods* on the Travel Channel

"Brian Kevin's journey through South America in the footsteps of gonzo journalist Hunter S. Thompson is a tour de force. He has brought back a wonderful kaleidoscope of unforgettable characters and keen insight, wrapped in frequent moments of hilarity. This is the work of a first-class writer from whom we will be hearing a lot more in the years ahead. I look forward to every page."

—SCOTT WALLACE,
author of *The Unconquered: In Search of
the Amazon's Last Uncontacted Tribes*

"Is there a point to another 'in the footsteps' narrative? Emphatically yes. Brian Kevin's decision to follow the journey that created the perspective of one of the seminal writers of our time, Hunter S. Thompson, does more than offer a needed understanding of Thompson's origins. Kevin's journey through South America reconsiders what it means to be a journalist, a traveler, a gringo, and an American. Plus, it's a great travel narrative on its own."

—SCOTT HULER,
author of *On the Grid* and *No-Man's Lands*

"In this meticulously rendered quest, Brian Kevin reveals that before the screeching bats and blood-sucking lizards, Hunter S. Thompson was an earnest, quixotic—even innocent—young writer trying to learn how the world worked. *The Footloose American* illuminates how Thompson's sharp eye for truth, honed on the back roads and in the back rooms of South America, would soon fall on fissures in his own country as they cracked wide open in fear and loathing."

—MARK SUNDEEN,
author of *The Man Who Quit Money*

The Footloose American

The Footloose American

Following the Hunter S. Thompson Trail Across South America

BRIAN KEVIN

B\D\W\Y

BROADWAY BOOKS

NEW YORK

Published in the United States by Broadway Books,
an imprint of the Crown Publishing Group,
a division of Random House LLC,
a Penguin Random House Company, New York.
www.crownpublishing.com

BROADWAY BOOKS and its logo, B\D\W\Y, are trademarks of
Random House LLC.

Chapter two previously appeared in abridged form as "After the Time of
Cholera" in Wend magazine (September 2010).

Grateful acknowledgment is made to Villard Books for permission to reprint
an excerpt from The Proud Highway by Hunter S. Thompson. Copyright
© 1997 by Hunter S. Thompson. Reprinted by permission of Villard Books,
an imprint of Random House, a division of Random House LLC.
All rights reserved.

Library of Congress Cataloging-in-Publication Data
Kevin, Brian.
    The footloose American : following the Hunter S. Thompson trail
across South America / Brian Kevin.
       1. South America—Description and travel. 2. South America—Politics
and government. 3. South America—Social conditions. 4. Indians of South
America—Social conditions. 5. Thompson, Hunter S.—Travel—South
America. 6. Kevin, Brian—Travel—South America. I. Title.
F2225.K48   2014
980—dc23   2013038287

ISBN 978-0-7704-3637-7
eBook ISBN 978-0-7704-3638-4

Printed in the United States of America

Book design by Barbara Sturman
Map by Joe LeMonnier
Cover design by Cardon Webb
Cover photographs: (top) courtesy of the Hunter S. Thompson Collection
     © The Estate of Hunter S. Thompson, used by permission of The Wylie
     Agency LLC; (bottom) Bruno Fert/Picturetank
Author photograph: Jamil Roberts

10 9 8 7 6 5 4 3 2 1

First Edition

To Elsa,

who moved the whole house while I was away

Contents

The Footloose American

CHAPTER ONE

Weekend at Bernie's

As I came over the brink of the cliff, a few children laughed, an old hag began screeching, and the men just stared. Here was a white man with 12 Yankee dollars in his pocket and more than $500 worth of camera gear slung over his shoulders, hauling a typewriter, grinning, sweating, no hope of speaking the language, no place to stay—and somehow they were going to have to deal with me.

—*National Observer*, August 6, 1962

I

The moment that South America first became real to me, I was tearing across the roadless desert in the back of a jostling beer truck. Exhaust fumes hung heavy on the air. Mirage ponds quivered in the distance. From the truck's shuddering chassis, a blast beat echoed across the flats, muffling the clink of contraband bottles, a death-metal soundtrack to the rawbone panorama of sand and sky.

We were crossing the Guajira Peninsula, a desolate nubbin of yellow dirt that juts like a fist off the very top of South America. Until that moment, it had all been prologue, the familiar rites and venues of an orderly arrival abroad: customs lines and cab stands, sterile hotel hallways, clumsy introductions in an unfamiliar tongue. Now the Colombian outback was screaming past me on both sides, hazy behind a sandstorm of our own making. With every turn, the photographer and I braced, clinging tightly to the truck-bed's wooden rails, holding on to keep from being thrown onto the flats.

This felt real because it felt dangerous, I thought. And fairly or unfairly, danger was what I'd come to Colombia expecting to find.

At the wheel of the truck was Bernie José, the jovial, elfin proprietor of a nameless pool hall in a remote Colombian fishing village called Cabo de la Vela. Bernie, for the moment, was my guide. Together with my photographer companion, I was crouched in the back of Bernie's pickup truck, surrounded by twenty-one cases of Venezuelan beer that clattered as we roared past cactus clusters and thatched-roof homesteads. Before we'd set out that morning, Bernie had dolefully recalled for us the day he'd flipped his truck while driving across a dry riverbed, breaking a leg and permanently disfiguring his passenger in the process. Now he waved at us periodically in the rearview mirror, flashing a grin and a thumbs-up whenever we hit a particularly kidney-rattling bump.

In 1962, the American writer Hunter S. Thompson described a similar ride across the peninsula as "punishing both truck and passengers unmercifully." Thompson would later become known for his fondness for hyperbole, for liberally sprinkling his prose with adjectives like "savage," "brutal," "terrible," and "fearsome." In this instance, though, his description seemed apt. Truck suspensions have come a long way in the last fifty years, and yet each time Bernie's Toyota walloped the dry, packed earth, I found myself wondering how my own whiplash must have compared to Thompson's.

Hunter S. Thompson was a young and decidedly unknown reporter in 1962. He had come to Guajira in search of smugglers, researching a story for an American newspaper about the region's brisk trade in bootlegged goods. I, in turn, had come to Guajira in search of Thompson. The smugglers I encountered more or less by accident.

Seventy-two hours earlier, I had stepped off a plane in Barranquilla, a jumbled Colombian metro on the country's muggy Atlantic coast, only to find that I had no baggage. It was a double-whammy of arrival shock. To a denizen of the dry Montana Rockies, stepping out of the airport into coastal Colombia is like getting bludgeoned with a sack of wet laundry. The equatorial humidity is just so complete, the saturation so overwhelming, that the lungs simply give out on you, withering in the swelter like damp paper bags. As I'd staggered out of the passenger terminal, trying hard to jump-start my jangled respiratory system, I had studied the slip of paper handed me inside. On it was a phone number, a hotline to call in order to find out whether the one small rucksack I'd packed for my six-month journey across the continent might eventually be located. Naturally, my luggage had been lost, because this is how all good trips begin—with adversity.

Hunter S. Thompson had it worse. In May of 1962, on the eve of a yearlong hitch across the continent, he described his circumstances grimly in a letter to a friend. "My situation is as follows," he began.

> I am in Aruba with $30. Tomorrow afternoon I have a free ride to Colombia, aboard a small sloop that will also carry a load of contraband whiskey. I may be in jail within 48 hours—a Colombian jail. If I get to Barranquilla, my goal, I will have no more than $5; what happens then is up to god.

By comparison, my situation was cushy. For starters, I was already in Colombia, and getting there had been easy-bordering-on-impulsive. Some months earlier, I'd sat in front of a laptop in my local coffee shop in Missoula, Montana, feeling listless and depressingly bourgeois. I was twenty-nine years old and functionally unemployed, recently divorced, and more recently awarded a flimsy master's degree in the humanities. On something like a whim, I'd traded a few years' worth of airline miles for a ticket to a country that I associated mostly with drug kingpins and guerrilla armies. It took about ten minutes, six mouse clicks, and zero smugglers' boats.

Upon my arrival in Barranquilla, I had several hundred dollars and only a vague itinerary. In the absence of my rucksack, I also had the clothes on my back, a half dozen Nature Valley granola bars, and one dog-eared copy of

The Proud Highway, Thompson's first volume of collected correspondence.

Like a lot of people my age, I first encountered Hunter Thompson via director Terry Gilliam's 1998 film adaptation of his most popular book, *Fear and Loathing in Las Vegas.* The film was kind of a dorm-room standard in the late 1990s, a surrealist take on Thompson's classic and quasifictional 1972 account of a drug-fueled search for the American Dream. I remember watching *Fear and Loathing* in my dormitory basement with a passel of stoned freshmen, giggling at the trippy visuals and at Johnny Depp's comic portrayal of Raoul Duke, Thompson's profligate alter ego. For those unfamiliar, *Fear and Loathing* is essentially a psychedelic buddy comedy. The protagonists are the journalist Duke and his bad-mannered Samoan lawyer, Dr. Gonzo (an overweight, mustachioed Benicio del Toro). The two of them spend 118 minutes wandering around Las Vegas in an LSD fog, wreaking havoc on hotel rooms, halfheartedly reporting on a big-purse motorcycle race, and lamenting the inevitable decline of the California counterculture. To an audience of Clinton-era undergrads at a state college in small-town Wisconsin, the movie's mind-altering milieu was as foreign as anything Fellini might have cooked up.

I read the book shortly thereafter. In its day, *Fear and Loathing in Las Vegas* was a bestseller, published a year after it was serialized in the pages of *Rolling Stone.* At the time, Thompson was a literary up-and-comer, known mostly for his reporting on the popular politics and subcultures of the 1960s, and *Fear and Loathing* was a deranged blend of fact and fiction that made his name. The *New York Times* called it "a custom-crafted study of paranoia, a spew from the 1960s and—in all its hysteria, insolence, insult, and rot—a desperate and important book." I read it cover to cover one afternoon, stealing pages between mozzarella-stick deliveries during a slow shift at the Applebee's where I waited tables.

From the get-go, Thompson's writing style got its hooks in me—his sense of humor, his exaggerated descriptions, the raw confessional tone with which he describes a fragmenting American society. He famously referred to his work as "gonzo journalism," and I admired his gall for brazenly branding his own technique, like a boxer or an avant-garde painter. His writing was indeed subversive for its day, blending old-fashioned immersion reporting with literary techniques more reliably found in fiction—tools like scene, dialogue, and point of view that had mostly been the domain of novelists and short-story writers. Critics in the early '70s referred to this style as "the New Journalism," and Thompson was considered one of the genre's standouts, alongside now-canonized writers like Joan Didion, Norman Mailer, and Truman Capote.

Not that his prose style is necessarily what Thompson is remembered for. In the popular consciousness, Thompson's name and his "gonzo" brand are more immediately associated with the flamboyant drug use and crazed antics that eventually came to complement or cloud his literary reputation, depending on whom you ask. From his early fame as a *Rolling Stone* contributor in the 1970s to his suicide in 2005, he built a pop-culture legacy around his unconcealed fondness for Wild Turkey, cocaine, and LSD. He invited camera crews onto his homestead near Aspen to watch him fire automatic weapons and detonate explosives. In 1970, he ran for Aspen's county sheriff on the Freak Power ticket. In the '80s, he was a regular patron and honorary manager at San Francisco's storied O'Farrell Theatre sex club, and in 1990, police raided his home to seize an apothecary of illegal drugs, along with several sticks of dynamite. When he shot himself at age sixty-seven, he left behind a madman's legacy and a note that read, "No More Games. No More Bombs. No More Walking. No More Fun."

But long before any of that, Thompson was just a twenty-something kid with thirty bucks trying to hitch a ride off of Aruba. Which is why *The Proud Highway* made up the bulk of my carry-on. The book is one of the few pieces of Thompsonalia to pre-date the emergence of the author's loose-cannon public persona. It's a collection of letters that Thompson sent in the late '50s and early '60s, back when he was just an eager and anonymous young freelancer, and included within are eighteen letters he wrote during a single year spent wandering across South America.

Outside the Barranquilla airport, I reached into my bag to feel for the book, patting it with one hand while I waved down a cab with the other. As I arrived in Colombia, clueless and luggageless, those eighteen letters were the closest thing I had to a guide.

"Goddamn," said the photographer a few hours later, looking at me from across the table of a Barranquilla pub. "This might not be the ugliest city I've ever seen, but it is a *hella* strong contender."

The two of us were seated in a strip-mall sports bar in a bland commercial stretch of the city. I took a sip from my beer and looked out the window, where a column of beige and boxy office towers hemmed us in. The palms along the road seemed to wither in the evening heat, and my sweat-soaked shirt clung like a cobweb to the back of my vinyl chair. I let the cool bottle linger against my lips, a momentary antidote to the swampy humidity. Beer consumption on this trip was going to be high, I thought.

My drinking companion was photographer Sky Gilbar, a California expat living in Panama and an accomplished Associated Press photographer who'd worked extensively in Latin America—though not so extensively he wasn't still prone to grating Cali-isms like "hella." In the weeks after buying my impromptu plane ticket, I had surfed the social networks for some travel advice, and Sky and I were introduced online by a friend of a friend. "Colombia is a stunningly beautiful country," he wrote in an e-mail, "with the warmest people you are likely to find anywhere on Earth. Did I mention the most beautiful women on the planet?" I was going to have a great trip, Sky assured me, although he wasn't so sure about my proposed itinerary. Barranquilla, for starters, was nothing but a "hot and bland port city." Of all the sunny, sexy destinations in Colombia, why would I want to go there?

I asked Sky whether he was familiar with Hunter Thompson. Sure, he said, *Fear and Loathing in Las Vegas,* right? In fact, he was a big fan. So I decided to tell him everything I knew about the Hunter S. Thompson Trail across South America.

It's not a part of Thompson's biography that gets much attention, but from May of 1962 to May of 1963, the future "gonzo journalist" was a freelance South American correspondent for a since-defunct newspaper called the *National Observer.* At the time, he was twenty-four years old, still a starving unknown looking to make a name for himself as a writer. He'd been churning out short stories since he was in high school and, for a couple years, doing some small-time freelancing, contributing short, newsy features to papers like the *Louisville Courier-Journal* and the *New York Herald Tribune.* In 1960, he'd spent a few months working in Puerto Rico—a decidedly non-glamorous job at an English-language bowling magazine—and after returning home broke, he'd started work on a novel about licentious American drifters living in San Juan, called *The Rum Diary*. But Thompson was restless, looking for his big break.

A Kentuckian by upbringing, he was living on the California coast when his South America plan materialized. He'd spent most of 1961 shacked up in the pastoral, bohemian enclave of Big Sur, hunting wild boar, working on the novel, and rubbing shoulders with folks like Henry Miller and Joan Baez. From well-traveled local luminaries like Miller, he'd heard tales of the expat life, and he'd done just enough island-hopping the year before to get a taste of it. His travels in the Caribbean had taken him within a few hundred miles of the South American mainland, and in Thompson's imagination, the continent was "the last frontier," an unspoiled outback brimming with untold stories, where the field of freelancers was thin and the biggest story of the era—the Cold War—was playing itself out daily in the streets. In South America, Thompson figured, a hungry reporter could make a name for himself. Such a trip, he wrote in a letter, may be "my last chance to do something big and bad, come to grips with the basic wildness."

Thompson's plan happened to coalesce with the launch of the *National Observer,* an upstart newspaper founded in February 1962 by the Dow Jones Corporation. The *Observer* was an early experiment with the concept of a national newspaper, a sort of precursor to *USA Today*. It was a weekly paper aimed at an educated readership, with an emphasis on in-depth reporting and analysis that the quick-turnaround dailies couldn't match. At around 200,000 readers, its initial circulation was smallish (Dow Jones's flagship paper, the *Wall Street Journal,* reached nearly 800,000 at the time), but the novelty of a weekly national newspaper attracted a lot of attention in media circles, so the *Observer* was widely read and discussed among influential writers and editors at other publications.

The fledgling paper was actively seeking contributors, and when Thompson wrote about the prospect of submitting a few articles from South America, the *Observer*'s editors encouraged him to send whatever seemed like a good fit. It was all the invitation that Thompson needed.

"I am going to write massive tomes from South America," he declared in a letter just three days after the *Observer*'s inaugural issue. "I can hardly wait to get my teeth in it."

All of this I explained over e-mail to Sky, who wrote back that he'd had no idea Thompson was once a foreign correspondent. This, I said, wasn't surprising. The year that Thompson spent down south is a period in his life that his biographers have all but ignored. In the years since the author's death, dozens of "lost interviews," biographies, and remembrances have offered glimpses of Thompson the man, but most tend to focus on his later career and the eccentric character he came to adopt. To some degree, this neglect of Thompson's South American reportage is understandable. He is, after all, a writer whose name has become synonymous with the oddities and ugliness of US culture. Thompson famously proclaimed his beat to be "the death of the American dream," and outside of those few early letters, his own writing rarely mentions his young adventures abroad.

But Thompson's South American pilgrimage shaped, in no small part, the edgy journalist who came to national attention not long after his return to the States. Before setting out for South America, Thompson was a wannabe novelist and photographer, a post-Beat dilettante more concerned with short stories than social movements. He fervently identified with Lost Generation writers like Hemingway, Fitzgerald, Faulkner, and Dos Passos, and he often looked down his nose at the grind of workaday journalism, dismissing it as a soul-sucking task to be undertaken only for a paycheck.

The Hunter Thompson that America came to know—the freewheeling correspondent, the caustic social chronicler—*that* Hunter Thompson was born in the streets of Rio de Janeiro, the mountains of Peru, and the black-market outposts of Guajira. It was in South America, in fact, that Thompson developed his razor-edged understanding of the dying American Dream.

"After a year of roaming around down here," he wrote at the end of his journey, "the main thing I've learned is that I now understand the United States, and why it will never be what it could have been, or at least tried to be."

That line had puzzled me since I first read it in *The Proud Highway* nearly a decade before. Just what did Thompson mean by this? It's a declaration that stands in stark contrast to another that he made about five months before the trip. In January 1962, Thompson wrote to a friend in Europe, scoffing at the idea that travel might meaningfully alter one's perspective on the United States.

"I doubt that a man has to go to Europe, or anywhere, for that matter, to understand the important things about this country," he wrote. "Maybe he has to go to Europe to be prodded into articulating them, or before they seem worth talking about, but I think we have enough space and perspective over here so a man can step off into a corner and get a pretty good view."

But Thompson found something in South America that dramatically reshaped his views on home—that dramatically reshaped *him*. The Thompson who left for the continent in 1962 was a self-identified seeker and escapist. The one who came back a year later was a narrow-eyed critic of American political culture and social ritual. If *The Proud Highway* became one of my favorite books as a college student, I think it's because it offered a tantalizing glimpse at the nomad who came in between, and I wanted to better understand that transition. When I first read it, I was twenty years old and still reeling from my own first exposure to international travel, a relatively tame semester in suburban Scotland. I was gripped by the notion that travel could confer the same eagle-eyed clarity that Thompson seemed to enjoy, and I told myself that I would go abroad again as soon as possible.

But I never did, and ten years later, I found myself still wondering about that act of transformation, about how you could leave home one day and come back with a clearer understanding of your own world and your place in it.

So a couple of months before purchasing my Colombia ticket, I dug up all of Thompson's South American reportage from a dusty microfiche archive of the *National Observer*. In total, there are eighteen stories. A few were reprinted in Thompson's 1979 collection, *The Great Shark Hunt*, but most have been out of print for more than fifty years. The majority of the articles revolve around the Cold War drama of American foreign policy, the triumphs and travails of a Kennedy-era idealism that sought to remake South America in its own capitalist image. Others offer "slice of life" portraits of societies colored by corruption, violence, and political intrigue. The stories offer glimmers of the "gonzo" style that Thompson would later develop. They're gritty and shrewd, and most impressively, they're keyed into a number of social issues that still affect the continent today.

Reading Thompson's *Observer* stories and letters from

the continent, I got the impression of a bright and driven young writer—a bit of a hell-raiser, sure, but one with a clear voice and an emerging interest in democracy and world affairs. Thompson the vagabond reporter came off as worldly and inquisitive, with a lightning-quick wit and a budding sense of injustice. It was, in many ways, a template for the sort of writer—for the sort of *person*—I wanted to be. Poring over the columns of old newsprint, my face lit up by the glow of the microfiche reader, I found it impossible not to layer my own voice over Thompson's, not to feel a sense of kinship. Both of us had come out of flyover country and settled in the American West. We shared a love of the outdoors and a nascent interest in politics. And we were, it seemed to me, both at a similar place in our lives. I too felt the now-or-never urgency that the young Thompson had described, that looming sense of a "last chance to do something big and bad, come to grips with the basic wildness."

But instead of traipsing around South America, I had spent my twenties settled into a classroom, a desk job, and a premature marriage. I looked with a kind of wistful admiration to the younger and hungrier Thompson whom no one seemed to know—much, I suppose, as Thompson had once looked to Hemingway, Faulkner, and his other literary heroes. Something in South America changed Hunter Thompson, and I wanted to know what it was, to figure out how the experience of a foreign culture had so altered his relationship with his own. In truth, I wanted some of that transformation for myself. At twenty-five, Thompson returned home from South America with a new understanding of journalism, injustice, and the American Dream. I, on the other hand, was staring down the barrel of my thirties with two useless degrees, no job, and a failed marriage, the ink on the divorce papers still wet. And I didn't understand a damn thing.

———

M y e-mail exchange with Sky paraphrased all of this, though I played down my existential angst about transformation, the American Dream, and so forth. My plan, I told him, was to retrace Thompson's route across the continent, and this is what explained my offbeat itinerary. Barranquilla—hot, bland, or otherwise—was my starting point.

Sky was intrigued. "I am totally game to join you for a leg or two of your journey," he offered. Would I have any interest in a partner for the first few weeks of the trip? Someone who knew his way around Colombia and spoke far better Spanish than my rudimentary child-speak?

Sí, I told him, *absolutamente.*

So there we were a few months later, in Barranquilla, getting to know each other at the Colombian equivalent of a TGI Fridays.

"Yep," Sky said again, setting down his beer. "This is easily one of the ugliest cities I have ever seen."

I couldn't disagree. My taxi ride from the airport had given me my first real glimpse of Latin American urban poverty, a suffocation of sheet-metal shanties that seemed to characterize much of the city's outskirts. Traffic in Barranquilla was a lawless, laneless contest of cabs, donkeys, and moto-taxis, all competing against the gaudily painted, repurposed school buses that served as mass transit. The shopping district surrounding our hotel seemed inoffensive enough—densely packed avenues of concrete, neon, and litter—but I'd come through several seedier sectors on my way into town, passing whole blocks of morning-time drinkers and what looked to be an impressive number of whorehouses.

"So all of this out here," I asked, gesturing at the tired

palm trees and mausoleum-like office buildings, "this is not typical of a Colombian metro?"

"Man, not at all." Sky shook his head. "Much more drab than Medellín or Cartagena. Colombians are actually super-passionate about their architecture. Art Deco is big. There's a ton of colonial preservation. But this place?" He shrugged. "I don't know, dude."

Sky gave a quick side-nod toward an adjacent table, and I looked over to where a trio of cute uniformed nurses sat, chatting over their cocktails in clipped Caribbean Spanish. He leaned over his place mat conspiratorially.

"On the other hand," he said, "there are things that don't change no matter where you go in Colombia." He sat back in his chair and grinned slightly, raising his bottle in a mock toast. "At least the women of Barranquilla are still beautiful." Then he took a long swig and exhaled in satisfaction. "Hey, did you know this is Shakira's hometown?"

Sky was a tall, tanned thirty-year-old with a goatee and the kind of nondescript, close-cropped haircut that's justifiably popular in equatorial climates. More often than not, he wore a camera around his neck and a leather satchel over one shoulder, heavy with lenses and other tools of his trade. Over beers that afternoon, he regaled me with stories of his time on the continent, waxing romantic about his fondness for Colombia, which in large part seemed to stem from his fondness for Colombian women. Sky was clearly a bit of a playboy, a good-natured soldier-of-fortune type who could segue onto the subject of women from seemingly any unrelated topic. He also kept up with my beer consumption, which I admired, and he seemed just as passionate about South American politics and social movements as he was about the Shakira look-alikes coming in and out of the bar. I liked him instantly.

"So our first stop is Guajira, then?" Sky asked as the bartender brought another round.

"La Guajira," I confirmed. "The land of the Wayuu, where Thompson first touched down in May of '62."

I had mailed Sky photocopies of Thompson's *Observer* stories, including his first article from the continent, entitled "A Footloose American in a Smugglers' Den." The piece opens on Thompson as he disembarks from the bootlegger's boat in a tiny village at the tip of the peninsula. He had managed to hitch the ride there from the Dutch island of Aruba, about ninety miles out to sea, where he'd stopped en route to the continent after visiting friends in Puerto Rico. From the *Observer* story, Sky and I had gleaned what little we knew about Guajira: (a) that it was a desert, and (b) that it consisted largely of reservation land for Colombia's indigenous Wayuu tribe. Some cursory Internet searching hadn't revealed much more. Like many Latin American countries, the Colombia of the Internet reflects mostly those areas of interest to visiting tourists, and Guajira isn't a region that sees a lot of gringo traffic—or any kind of traffic, really, since the whole peninsula is largely without roads.

"The problem is," Sky said, "I don't know any smugglers with boats. So how are you supposing we get out there?"

I unfolded a map that, thankfully, I'd been using as a bookmark. "We can take a bus as far as Riohacha," I said, pointing to a town some 125 miles east of Barranquilla. Riohacha is the capital of the La Guajira department (the Colombian equivalent of a state) and effectively the gateway to the peninsula. Near it on the map was a small blue icon of a beach umbrella, indicating *la playa*. Where there was *la playa*, I figured, there would be some kind of tourism infrastructure. From Riohacha, then, I hoped we could rent a truck or some other sort of off-road conveyance.

Sky laughed. "That simple, huh? Then we just tear off into the desert, full speed ahead?"

I nodded.

"And what are we looking for exactly?"

I shrugged. "Stories, I guess. Adventure. Ghosts."

We both laughed at how little we'd planned anything beyond that moment. At least in this, I thought, we had something in common with Thompson. When the nurses at the neighboring table got up to leave, Sky's eyes followed them to the door.

"You know what they call speeding in Colombia?" he asked, turning back to me. "*Ir a toda mierda,* which basically means 'going full shit.'"

I laughed again and finished my beer. The two of us stayed at the pub for a couple more hours that night, poring over the map and sketching back-of-the-napkin itineraries beneath posters of scantily clad Aguila beer models. By the time we teetered back to our hotel, feeling chummy and intrepid, my backpack was waiting for me in the room. On one of the plastic clasps, the airline had tied a short note. *Buen viaje y buena suerte,* it read. So long and good luck.

II

"It's good that you should see a Colombian mall," Sky said the next morning as we nursed our hangovers with fried eggs and guava juice. "They're no different than American malls, really, but Colombians love them because they combine two of their favorite things: shopping and air-conditioning."

The Muzak and fake foliage of the Portal del Prado shopping center wasn't the rugged, romantic setting I'd pictured for my first full day in South America, but simply "going full shit" into the wilds proved more difficult than I'd envisioned. There were errands to run and bus tickets to buy, and in Colombia, these kinds of seemingly straightforward tasks can sometimes occupy one's entire day. Simply put, America's quintessentially Protestant emphasis on efficiency has never gained much of a foothold in Latin America, where any number of commonplace tasks and routines can seem needlessly swaddled in layers of tail-chasing and bizarre, paradoxical frustrations.

Consider the phenomenon of Colombian cell phones. Before setting out for Guajira, Sky and I needed to gather a few things: some nonperishable food, cash, batteries, a couple of bags of "goodwill" candy for any kids we met along the way. But most important and time-consuming was the task of acquiring a couple of cell phones. It had never occurred to me that I might carry a cell in South America. For starters, I was accustomed to a messy system of contracts, carriers, and expensive plans back home. Moreover, I hadn't expected to find much service outside of the major cities. So the ubiquity of cell phones and cellular coverage in South America was the first of many misconceptions about the developing world that would evaporate for me in the coming months.

This is not to say that Colombian cell phone usage makes any sense. Dirt-cheap and available on every street corner, most Colombian cells operate on a counterintuitive arrangement in which minutes are prepaid and incoming calls are free. The result of this, Sky explained on our way to the mall, is a Kafka-esque scenario in which everyone owns a cell phone but no one ever has any minutes. So rather than waste their own, most callers will simply dial their intended target, then wait for a single ring before hanging up, hoping that the recipient will call back on his or her own dime.

Which, for lack of minutes, no one ever does. Consequently, the streets of most Colombian towns are crowded with vendors charging customers to use fleets of non-depleted cell phones, which they keep tied to chains like pens at the bank. In even the smallest Colombian villages, you can't throw a rock without hitting a sign that advertises these *minutos,* posted in corner-store bodegas, on street carts, and even in private homes.

But we didn't want to rely on *minutos,* and we figured there'd be times when we'd need to call each other, so we squared away our phone situation at Portal del Prado, enjoying some Arctic air-conditioning in the process. Sky's Spanish was vastly superior to mine, so he mostly handled the transaction, flirting mercilessly with the round-eyed, tube-topped attendant at the kiosk. Funny, I thought, how easy it is to recognize playful innuendo, even when you're fighting to understand the language.

The rest of our supplies we picked up at the Colombian equivalent of a Walmart anchoring one end of the mall. Unlike American big-box stores, however, this particular retailer employed several conspicuously armed security guards, which I learned when one of them chased me down to ask gruffly that I check my backpack in a locker. From the short-barreled rifle hanging at his side, I guessed that gringos with illicit backpacks were the least of his potential problems. So there's at least one difference between American and Colombian malls, I thought. In Colombia, the mall cops get to carry guns.

We were further delayed at the bus terminal, where a smooth-talking driver duped us into leaving Barranquilla on the local rather than the express, which meant stopping for a pickup at every no-name village along the way. It's an easy mistake to make in Colombia, where every shifty-eyed counter agent will assure you that *his* is the only nonstop route. We stuck out the bus ride for several hours, covering all of seventy miles before switching at another terminal to a *puerta-a-puerta*—a "door-to-door" shuttle van that carries a dozen passengers for a few pesos more than bus fare. Our particular conversion van was packed with middle-aged men and smelled faintly of diesel, and when it finally pulled away from the station, it was clear we had zero chance of reaching Riohacha before nightfall. But at least Barranquilla was in the rearview mirror, and the rest of the continent spread out in front of us like a dashboard map.

"Jesus Christ is coming back! *Jesús Cristo va a regresar!*" I heard the bearded and wild-eyed street preacher before we'd even stepped out of the *puerta-a-puerta*. It was an uncharacteristically cool evening in the beachside village where we stopped for dinner, and a handful of locals were loitering around an open-air market, sipping *refrescas* and trying to ignore the ragtag prophet howling in the street. At our driver's urging, we filed out with our fellow passengers, lining up at a street-corner grill for some cheese-stuffed corn pockets cálled arepas, the de facto national street food of Colombia.

"He is bringing you his blood!" yelled the preacher, addressing no one in particular. *"Jesús Cristo le ofrece su sangre!"*

Sky looked at me and rolled his eyes. The air was heavy with the buttery scent of frying arepas. In line in front of us, a stocky middle-aged guy who'd been riding shotgun in the van turned around and pointed none-too-subtly at the preacher.

"You see that guy?" he asked in Spanish. *"That* guy is an asshole."

I blinked and begged his pardon.

"He's an *asshole!*" said the guy again, a little louder this time. "He used to be a hit man for the cartels, and now he stands out here screaming about salvation."

In the road, the street prophet was literally thumping his Bible with a fist, his knees bent and back arched like a soccer goalie in his stance. He looked like a cross between Cesar Romero and how I'd always pictured John the Baptist, his elastic face hidden behind a bird's nest of a beard. He looked ready to tackle someone.

"These fucking guys," our companion snorted dismissively. He shook his head. "All these evangelicals, these born-again guys? They're the ones who used to do the really bad things."

We paid for our arepas and piled back into the van, passing the preacher as he waved his arms and moaned. His pupils were grotesquely dilated, a pair of total eclipses, swallowing the light. As the van pulled away, the shotgun guy leaned out the window for a parting taunt.

"Hey, asshole!" he yelled. "Killed anybody lately?"

The preacher turned to face the van, nostrils flaring above a wild tangle of a mustache. For an instant, I pictured him opening his Bible, retrieving a pistol from the hollowed-out compartment inside, and firing on the van with an assassin's deadly precision. Instead, our driver widened his eyes and hit the gas. As the van screeched away, the preacher shook his fists and yelled back that we were all sinners and all going to die. I decided to take this as an ontological prediction rather than a personal threat.

The instigator up front introduced himself as Alex, and the rest of the way to Riohacha, he told us about his own messy history with the cartels. As a teenager, he'd fallen in with local drug smugglers and helped move cocaine up and down the coast in a speedboat, which eventually led to a stint under house arrest in his twenties. He was surprisingly nonchalant about this, discussing it as if everyone in the van had been in the cocaine biz at one time or another. And for all I knew, this might have been true. When the three of us stepped out at Riohacha a couple of hours later, Alex offered us a ride and invited us to join his family for dinner.

We met up with his wife and twentysomething daughter at a beachside boardwalk, and the five of us ate cups of shrimp salad from a row of vendor stalls. Riohacha seemed charming, its boardwalk bustling with families and couples holding hands. The city sits at the base of the Guajira Peninsula, a Caribbean vacation town for middle-class Colombians and a hub for a booming industry in offshore natural gas. Alex and his family led us on a brief tour of the waterfront, all palm trees and wide parkways lined with Wayuu artisans and their woven baskets. The air smelled like salt water, and the seaside district seemed to be enjoying some prosperity. At one point, we passed a brand-new museum sponsored by Chevron, dedicated entirely to the wonders of natural gas. It was closed, but La Sala Interactiva Étnica del Gas looked like a lovely and modern facility, despite a name that translates awkwardly to "The Interactive Ethnic Gas Chamber."

It was Alex who introduced us to Bernie, the truck-driving barkeep. Recently, Alex said, a few small ecotourism companies had popped up in Riohacha, leading travelers onto the peninsula on guided 4 x 4 tours. He wasn't sure where to find any of them, though, and anyway, he knew a guy who could do it cheaper. So following our post-dinner stroll, we drove with Alex's family to an unlit, residential part of town. Alex borrowed my cell on the way over (his was out of minutes) and chatted to someone in a diphthong-heavy language that I imagined to be Guajiro.

We pulled up in front of a small cinder-block home with a dirt bike out front. Bernie was waiting for us outside. He was a fit-looking Wayuu in his mid-forties, with the dark eyes and slight build characteristic of his people. When we hopped out of Alex's truck, he smiled at us warmly and shook hands.

Bernie had spent most of his life on the peninsula, Alex said, by way of introduction. He owned a pool hall in a coastal village called Cabo de la Vela and occasionally moonlighted as a guide. Sure, Bernie said, he'd be happy to show us around Guajira. He'd been meaning to restock his beer cooler up there anyway. At that moment, his truck was with a mechanic in a town called Uribia, about a quarter-way up the peninsula, where the paved road ends. But if we could meet him there the next morning, we could head out from there, and Bernie said he'd even let us crash at his place in Cabo. Alex offered to arrange our ride to Uribia with a taxi-driver friend, and the next thing we knew, we were hashing out a fee, shaking hands once more, and piling back into the truck. Sky and I barely said a word during the entire negotiation.

By the time we finally checked into a hostel that night, our heads were spinning at how fast the whole thing had come together. We'd been prepared for much worse. In "A Footloose American in a Smugglers' Den," Thompson wrote with frustration about Guajira's severe inaccessibility. Trying to get anywhere on the roadless peninsula, he said, "can turn a man's hair white. You are simply stuck until one of the Indians has to run some contraband." But with next to no effort on our part, Sky and I were all set up, ready to go full shit into the heart of contraband country.

Thompson paddled up to the tip of South America in a small rowboat, tossed by the waves and overburdened with luggage. He'd have cut a strange figure coming ashore:

a bedraggled would-be foreign correspondent humping an
unwieldy typewriter and a mess of camera gear. The Aruban
smugglers had put him ashore at a village called Puerto Estrella, where he'd spend the next several days with confused
Wayuu natives before making his way inland. He described
the village in the *Observer* as having "no immigration officials and no customs." He continued:

> There is no law at all, in fact, which is precisely
> why Puerto Estrella is such an important port. It
> is far out at the northern tip of a dry and rocky
> peninsula called La Guajira, on which there are
> no roads and a great deal of overland truck traf-
> fic. The trucks carry contraband, hundreds of
> thousands of dollars worth of it, bound for the
> interiors of Colombia and Venezuela.

Guajira does indeed have a long tradition of both smuggling and general lawlessness. Throughout the colonial era,
the obstinacy of the Wayuu people kept the Spanish coloniz-
ers more or less at bay. Missionaries infiltrated in the early
twentieth century, but up until then, the peninsula was essentially a no-man's-land, off-limits to non-indigenous Colombians. Even after the Department of La Guajira was
formally created in 1964, the area stayed effectively autono-
mous, and to this day, it's still something of a frontier. The
vast majority of the peninsula is inside Colombia, but the
Venezuela border slices across its southeast corner, bisecting
the Wayuu's traditional homelands. As a result, tribal members enjoy dual citizenship and can cross the border freely,
avoiding established checkpoints. This arrangement, combined with hard-to-police coastlines and an overall lack of

state authority, is why Guajira has historically been a "smugglers' den."

Cheap consumer goods are routinely carried over by the Wayuu from Venezuela, who pay only a token tariff and sell them on the peninsula at a markup. Other Venezuelan products come across via clandestine overland truck routes, bypassing customs agents along the established roads. Cheap Venezuelan gasoline is routinely smuggled across the porous border. Still other goods arrive by cargo boat from free-trade zones like Panama and Aruba, to be unloaded in sparsely regulated backwater ports like Puerto Estrella. Of course, some of this trade is legit. In the 1990s, the Colombian government took an adaptive approach and abolished the tariffs on certain goods intended for local use. But even much of that merchandise eventually finds its way into mainland Colombia via desert routes or bribes to customs and police. In 2012, those agencies seized around $128 million worth of smuggled goods, but the government estimates that 90 percent of contraband in Colombia still goes undetected.

Whatever its origin, then, chances are good that any product you purchase in Guajira has found some way to evade import taxes. And on our way to meet Bernie, Sky and I asked our taxi driver to stop off at the Chicago Stockyards of this desert smuggling scene, a dusty metropolis called Maicao, about ten miles from the Venezuelan border.

The sprawling street market in Maicao is a sort of a contraband Costco, filled with shoes, clothing, cigarettes, liquor, dog food, bike parts, and kids' toys—most any imaginable consumer item under the sun, all sold by Wayuu merchants at ridiculously cheap prices. While Sky wandered around shooting photos, I browsed the stalls and chatted up vendors. I noticed quickly that communication in Maicao was easier for me, since many of the locals spoke equally rudimentary

Spanish, preferring instead their native Guajiro, a Caribbean Arawak language that Thompson described as being "a bit like Arabic, which doesn't ring well in a white man's ear."

For the price of a latte, I bought a bottle of Scotch from a teenaged girl who giggled as she gave me my change. Despite the contraband status of the merchandise, the bazaar at Maicao had the same warmly chaotic atmosphere as your average Saturday-morning farmers' market back home. It was bustling with people. A band in the center square played *vallenato* music, a favorite Colombian mixture of accordion, sappy lyrics, and African hand drums. On a side street, a row of fifty live goats lay bleating, their legs tied up, each one stacked atop the next like a row of fallen dominoes. Behind all this was the ubiquitous urban soundtrack of car horns and idling engines—although, as Sky pointed out, even the street traffic was unique.

"You see these cars?" he asked as we met up by the goats. "Land Cruisers? F-150s? That's the kind of car you drive only if you have access to cheap gas. You would never see huge cars like this on the streets of Bogotá or Medellín." And indeed, on our way out of town, our taxi driver pulled over to buy gas from a ten-year-old boy on the side of the road, a wide-eyed Guajiro-speaker who sold it by the gallon from fluorescent plastic jugs.

Thompson had also noted the trappings of affluence around the otherwise hardscrabble Puerto Estrella. To a description of the natives' poverty and simple style of dress, he added this wry postscript: "A good many of the men also wore two- and three-hundred-dollar wristwatches, a phenomenon explained by the strategic location of Puerto Estrella and the peculiar nature of its economy." Had F-150s been available in 1962, he probably would have spotted a few parked conspicuously around the village.

But after a decades-long and fairly benign run, smuggling in Guajira has become a source of controversy. When Colombia's "law-and-order president," Álvaro Uribe, came to power in 2002, his government started cracking down on the region's black markets for essentially the first time in Colombian history. Lost tax revenue was one motivation, but Guajira's smuggling biz has also developed a more sinister aspect in the years since Thompson's visit. In recent decades, Colombia's perennially active left-wing guerrillas and right-wing paramilitaries have exploited Guajira's geography and lax regulation to smuggle drugs, run guns, and skim off the top of the Wayuu's smuggling profits via extortion. While the country's main paramilitary group, the United Self-Defense Forces of Colombia, or AUC, has been officially disbanded since 2006, mafioso-like former "paras" have increasingly taken over the most profitable smuggling rackets. In 2003, the Colombian government helped set up Wayuu petrol cooperatives, hoping to undercut smugglers by enabling the tribe to legally import Venezuelan gasoline. Over the next few years, though, one co-op board member was murdered while numerous others resigned under duress. The co-op's tankers have been bombed and customs agents killed in encounters with both guerrillas and former paras. Today, Guajirans like Bernie will likely tell you that the latter group essentially controls gasoline imports, and accounts of smuggling-related violence seem to crop up in human-rights bulletins every few months.

All of this helps earn Guajira its Wild West reputation, but it also raises difficult questions about the Wayuu's relationship to the rest of their country. Reports by indigenous advocates and international aid groups tend to paint Guajira as a victimized region, a place where the troubles of an often-violent country have "spilled over" to affect the unaligned natives. And certainly, the smuggling biz hasn't much empowered the Wayuu. Guajira is one of Colombia's poorest departments, where, according to the country's National Planning Department, some 65 percent of its households find their basic needs unmet. Of the roughly 150,000 Wayuu living on the Colombian side (there's a slightly higher number in Venezuela), maybe 10,000 or so draw paychecks from multinational energy companies—mining natural gas for Exxon or coal at a large open-pit mine south of Maicao, called Cerrejón. The rest are mostly pastoralists, getting by on some combination of goat-herding, sales from contraband, and seasonal migrations for temporary work in the cities.

On our way out of Maicao, we saw a testament to the Guajiran subsistence mentality. A few miles outside of town, our taxi passed a Wayuu driver whose dented Honda had just hit and killed three goats. By the time we pulled over to offer some help, the driver was already tossing one of the carcasses into the rear of his hatchback. "I'm taking them with me." He shrugged without smiling. "It's money, right?"

As I watched that driver shoulder his road-kill goats—or the somber, brown-skinned kid pouring gas into the taxi—it might have been easy to accept this notion of a Wayuu people who've been shoved somehow from an aboriginal state of grace. This seems to be our default, twenty-first-century narrative about indigenous people, after all, and not without good reason. But arriving for the first time in South America, the mid-twentieth-century Thompson didn't see things this way. His account muddies the waters a bit, portraying the Wayuu as willing accomplices in Guajiran vice, complicit in the peninsula's underworld going back at least half a century.

"It would not be fair," he wrote obliquely, "to say that the Indians arbitrarily take a healthy cut of all the contraband that passes through their village, but neither would it be wise to arrive and start asking pointed questions."

As Sky and I approached the end of the paved road in Uribia, I wondered which Guajira we would find on the other side—the lawless twenty-first-century outback or the primitive paradise lost.

I t took a few tries to start Bernie's ancient blue Toyota, but eventually we shuddered out of the mechanic's yard in Uribia and down the road to a bodega, where Sky and I helped load twenty-one cases of impossibly cheap Venezuelan beer. Far from being flush with the profits of illicit smuggling, Uribia was kind of a dump. The town's dusty streets were littered with ragged plastic bags, so many that it seemed impossible for the tiny desert outpost to have produced them all. On the way in, we passed a dry creek bed filled with bags. They fluttered like prayer flags on the cactus fences and got caught underneath the tanker trucks that supply Uribia with fresh water. Many of the bags had been sun-bleached to pale pastels that bordered on colorlessness. In fact, the most vivid colors in the seemingly all-beige town came from the bright patterned frocks of the Wayuu women, called *mantas guajiras,* which looked a little like burqas but more festive and without the veil. The men, on the other hand, dressed like cowboys in blue jeans and Stetsons. It was a far cry from the borderline savages that Thompson described: Wayuu villagers wearing nothing but neckties as loincloths. "I decided that at the first sign of unpleasantness," he wrote, "I would begin handing out neckties like Santa Claus—three fine paisleys to the most menacing of the bunch, then start ripping up shirts."

Within an hour, Bernie, Sky, and I were going full shit through the Guajiran desert, racing along a thoroughly rutted jeep track with nothing on the skyline but a shimmering blue mirage that I initially mistook for the Caribbean. As Bernie's Toyota hammered its way across the scrub, Sky and I gave up pretty quickly on trying to drink the beer, concentrating instead on staying grounded in the truck bed. The thunder of Bernie's engine made it impossible to be heard, and my tailbone rattled with every hummock, but I felt for the first time like we were really traveling in Thompson's footsteps, and I could see from his grin that Sky did too. In my head, I played back Thompson's exhilarated description of driving across the peninsula, "roar[ing] through dry river beds and across long veldt-like plains on a dirt track which no conventional car could ever navigate."

Bernie wanted to make two stops en route to Cabo de la Vela. The first was pure tourism, a trip to the Salinas Manaure salt mines along the coast north of Uribia. You'll see them in the distance, he said proudly, and sure enough, the desert landscape was flat enough to spot the mines from a couple of miles out—a cluster of glistening piles that swelled on the horizon like bleached dunes. As we drove closer, the desert clay beneath us gave way to a stretch of blinding ivory, crystal flats dotted here and there with dirty white mounds. We parked next to another old pickup near a trickle of a creek, its water the color of skim milk.

Bernie played tour guide as we climbed shakily out of the truck, gesturing grandly and giving us some background on the mines. For centuries, he explained, the Wayuu had worked the Manaure flats, harvesting small amounts of salt by hand and fishing in saltwater lagoons. Then, in the early 1970s, the tribe ceded much of the land to the government in exchange for housing and development programs that most Wayuu agree never materialized. The government industrialized salt production, while a few small Wayuu cooperatives kept on manually harvesting the outlying plots. For decades, he said, the Wayuu and the government clashed over market prices, vanishing benefits, and ancestral territory. More recently, though, government reps and tribal operators formed a joint company to run the mines, and today the Wayuu own 76 percent of it. They still mine a quarter of the flats the old-fashioned way, using hand tools and wheelbarrows, patience and brawn.

Sky and I walked out across the flats to where half a dozen Wayuu workers were scattered around a fifteen-foot pile of salt, a rust-eaten dump truck and a Bobcat loader parked alongside. Underfoot, the salt crystals were crunchy and jagged, and the sun was nearly blinding, glinting off every imaginable surface. The Wayuu workers were equal numbers men and women, flanked by a yard sale of pickaxes, chisels, and wheelbarrows. They stared at us a bit coolly as we approached.

"Buenos dias," I said, and one of the older men offered a hesitant half wave. He was shirtless. A single gold tooth glittered in the sunlight.

"Sorry to interrupt," Sky said in Spanish. "We were just hoping to see how you worked."

The crew seemed unmoved, but they warmed up a bit when I pulled a couple of water bottles out of my backpack. Despite the intense heat, they seemed to have no water at all, and they nodded gratefully as we passed the bottles around. Sky asked whether he could take a few photos, and that seemed to be the magic icebreaker. The request sent most of the crew into giggles.

While Sky turned on the charm, expertly cajoling the workers into posing, I tried to strike it up with one of the women standing on top of the pile. She wore a deep red *manta guajira* that stood out against the landscape like a splash of spilled wine. I asked how she could possibly work the flats all day without wearing sunglasses, and she just laughed.

"Tengo mucha resistencia," she said quietly, pointing to and then averting her dark eyes. Her name was Ana Maria, and we shared my water bottle while we watched Sky lining up shots of her coworkers against the endless plane of the flats.

"So why do you not use the big machines?" I asked in my clunky Spanish.

Ana Maria shrugged and explained, slowly, that it was important for her family to use traditional methods for salt harvesting, never mind the seeming inefficiency. Artisan salt production at Manaure yields about 60,000 tons of salt each year, compared with 350,000 tons from industrial production. According to her, though, the manually harvested plots kept hundreds of Wayuu employed, while the labor force required to run the mechanical harvesters was minimal. As the seawater filled and then evaporated in one salt lagoon, the Wayuu workers moved over to harvest another. Following this pattern, most Wayuu salt miners could expect to bring home about $200 a month. It wasn't a perfect system, but it kept her people employed until the community could figure out how to use the profits from their newly formed company to create more jobs. And besides, Ana Maria shrugged again, this was their tradition.

As I stood there in that alien landscape, watching Ana Maria's robe flap in the breeze, it really did feel like we were witnessing a vanishing traditional lifestyle, something exotic and segregated from the outside world. If you looked at it one way, a scene of stereotypical aboriginal poverty was playing out all around us, with grim Wayuu laborers pushing wheelbarrows beneath an unrelenting sun. Clutching their pickaxes and dressed only in shorts, the men around the salt pile could almost have been the loincloth-clad primitives that Thompson had sketched in the *Observer.*

So it was a welcome reality check when Ana Maria asked if we'd send her copies of Sky's photos.

"How can we do that?" Sky asked. "Is there a post office in Manaure?"

She stared at us blankly.

"You guys aren't on Facebook?" she asked. Then she reached out for my notebook and scribbled her e-mail address.

O ur second stop on the road to Cabo felt a little more Third World. After leaving the salt flats, Sky and I squished in alongside Bernie in the truck's front seat. His accent was hard to understand, and I relied on Sky for a lot of translating, but Bernie struck me as a genuinely kind and cheerful guy. He seemed not the least bit put off by my frequent questioning, and he smiled easily—a Cheshire-cat grin that said he was enjoying our company, if not taking our Q&A all that seriously. Most of the villagers in Cabo were related to him somehow, he said, although he didn't always know just how. Wayuu families are grouped into vast matrilineal clans, and family ties could get pretty tangled. Bernie lived part-time in Riohacha with one of his wives and part-time on the peninsula with another. When I asked how many kids he had, he just grinned playfully and stared straight ahead. "A lot," he said, and shrugged.

As we drove, Bernie explained a few Wayuu traditions, talking about the creator god Mareywa, who was said to live near Cabo de la Vela, and about the tribe's reparations-based justice system, which employs "Wayuu lawyers" called *putchipuutos* to negotiate monetary settlements between victims and offenders. He took great pleasure in teaching us a couple of words in Guajiro, including the declarative *"Ho!"*—evidently, the Wayuu equivalent of *"Vamos!"* or "Let's go!" When I told Bernie about efforts in the United States to preserve dying indigenous languages, he just smiled in puzzlement and shook his head, like he couldn't understand why anybody would stop speaking their own tongue.

After another suspension-busting hour, we pulled up to a thatched-roof shack so small and dilapidated, I wondered at first whether someone hadn't erected an outhouse in the middle of the desert. Bernie killed the engine. *"La casa de mi novia,"* he said, calling his second wife by the less formal "girlfriend." Goats and small children wandered the dusty yard, and a few of the latter stopped to stare at us as we stepped out of the truck. Underneath a tattered awning, three men seemed to be napping in a triangle of woven hammocks, threadbare ball caps pulled down over their eyes. I scanned the horizon. In any direction, the shack was the only visible manmade structure. It felt a little like pulling up to Ben Kenobi's hut on Tatooine, the barren desert planet in *Star Wars*—except that Obi-Wan, by comparison, had a much nicer pad.

Bernie called out, and a girl in her mid-teens appeared in the doorway, wrapped in a blue patterned frock with a matching cloth tied around her hair. On her feet, she wore a pair of plastic flip-flops that accentuated her adolescent appearance. *"Mi novia,"* Bernie said again, and the girl smiled bashfully before lowering her eyes. He didn't introduce us, but walked over and embraced her, speaking affectionately in Guajiro. She stood barely to his shoulders. If she'd have been clutching a teddy bear, I thought, it wouldn't have looked out of place. She turned to walk back inside and Bernie followed, asking us in Spanish to please wait out in the yard.

Whatever look I gave Sky must have betrayed my ethno-centric chagrin, because he raised his eyebrows at me and shrugged. "The age of consent in Colombia is fourteen, dude," he said, already adjusting his light meter to shoot in the dying desert sun. Indeed, some months after I returned to the States, newspapers reported that a Wayuu girl of ten had become one of the youngest living mothers on record.

As the kids in the yard gathered around us, I won-dered which, if any, of them were Bernie's. Two of the boys looked as old as ten, but a third boy and a grinning girl were only toddlers. The older pair spoke mostly Guajiro, so Sky and I did our best to communicate with gestures, pass-ing out some of the candy we'd picked up in Barranquilla. They smiled shyly at first for Sky's camera, then gradually cut loose and started mugging, posing like Pelé with a half-deflated soccer ball.

Eventually, their laughter roused the men in the ham-mocks, who one at a time lifted their ball caps to gaze in our direction. The oldest one looked like he was in his six-ties, leather-faced and graying, while the others were no older than me and Sky. We nodded hello, and the old one extended a callused hand, motioning for us to come over. As we walked toward him, I smelled the sweet stench of the liquor before I even noticed the unmarked bottles beneath the hammocks. All three men smiled groggily. The oldest muttered something I couldn't understand, either in Gua-jiro or a heavily accented Spanish, and I turned to Sky for a translation.

"I think he wants us to sit down," he said.

The younger men sat up in their hammocks and scooted to the side. Awkwardly, we climbed in next to them. As I set-tled into the woven cot, a little off-balance, I set it to swing-ing, and all three of the men laughed out loud. My hammock buddy put his arm around me and leaned in close, muttering what I assumed to be "hello" in Guajiro. The smell of the booze coming off his breath was overpowering, and his thousand-mile stare suggested that the three of them were a good deal more than tipsy. He said something else, with a leering grin, but I couldn't understand him, and Sky only shrugged.

"*Gracias, amigo, gracias,*" I said, thanking him feebly for hammock space, and this too touched off a chorus of addled guffaws and backslapping. Behind the laughter, though, I heard a slight note of menace and, exchanging glances with Sky, I could tell that he heard it too. "We should probably be careful here," he said in English, smiling and trying to sound chipper. I nodded and smiled back.

The oldest man grabbed his bottle and started sloppily pouring into a fistful of plastic medicine cups. He passed them out and then pantomimed a toast. Together, we drank. The clear, thin liquor tasted like an awful combination of Karo syrup and rubbing alcohol. It burned terribly going down, as much from the sweetness as from the obviously high alcohol content. I tasted it up in my sinuses—rotten, terrible stuff. But as I handed the cup back to the old man, I managed an approving smile.

"*Gracias,*" I said again, pathetically, and asked him slowly in Spanish what the drink was called.

"*Chirrinchi,*" he muttered, already pouring another round. "*Chirrinchi, chirrinchi, chirrinchi.*"

As Bernie would later explain, *chirrinchi* is Guajira's trademark moonshine, a fermented sugarcane drink distilled in handmade stills and sold at prices rivaling even the plentiful bottles of bootlegged Scotch. The second shot burned as badly as the first, and I barely had it down before the old man was waving for my cup to pour a third. My hammock mate put his arm around me again and swayed unsteadily. No one spoke. I thought of the Afghans and what little I could remember about their allegedly customary three cups of tea. Perhaps this was some kind of time-honored friendship ritual? Something about it didn't seem cordial, though, just tense and a little bit sinister, like a too-friendly stranger on a dark and deserted road. As the next round was dispersed, Sky caught me glancing apprehensively at my cup.

"You have to drink it, man," he admonished me.

"I know," I said. And smiling through my teeth, I poured the syrupy *chirrinchi* down.

The hard-drinking culture of Guajira was something that Thompson had described, so I shouldn't have been surprised to find myself thrust into it. In Puerto Estrella, Scotch had been the liquor of choice. "It continued all that day and all the next," Thompson wrote, recalling one village drinking binge:

> They tossed it off straight in jiggers, solemnly at first and then with mounting abandon. Now and then one of them would fall asleep in a hammock, only to return a few hours later with new thirst and vigor. At the end of one bottle, they would proudly produce another, each one beautifully wrapped in cellophane. . . . It is bad enough to drink Scotch all day in any climate, but to come to the tropics and start belting it down for three hours each morning before breakfast can bring on a general failure of health. In the mornings we had Scotch and arm-wrestling; in the afternoon, Scotch and dominoes.

Even at twenty-four, Thompson was a pretty accomplished drinker, having come up as a young hooligan running with pals from Louisville's liquor-soaked country-club scene. A year in the Air Force hadn't hurt his tolerance any, and before coming south, he'd spent a few months swilling straight rum beneath a Puerto Rican sun. I was no slouch myself, raised in a sudsy Wisconsin drinking culture, but on the day we sat down for our impromptu *chirrinchi* session, my shot-pounding college years were a decade behind me.

By the time that Bernie finally emerged from the shack, we'd traded some half dozen shots of the stuff. The old man was mumbling in rudimentary Spanish about kicking the Colombian government out of the Guajiran Peninsula, and I was holding my liquor well enough to nod at what seemed like appropriate times. For reasons he was too drunk to articulate, he held the state responsible for Wayuu poverty. Meanwhile, the guy next to me kept showing me the soles of his shoe, staring at me expectantly, then laughing coarsely and slapping me on the back. He was, I think, trying to ask for money.

When Bernie stepped out and cried *"Ho!"* we were quick to jump up from the hammocks. We exchanged quick handshakes with our unsought drinking buddies and piled into the truck's front seat. Bernie threw it into reverse, waving to the kids in the yard and ignoring altogether the drunks beneath the awning. Just another frosty relationship with the in-laws, I thought. As we pulled onto the rutted jeep track, Bernie paused for a moment to sniff at the air in the cab. *"Chirrinchi?"* he asked. Then he shook his head at us and laughed, and we headed out into the desert once more.

III

F or the next two days, we roamed across Guajira like vacationers, rumbling in Bernie's Toyota from one destination to the next, from a local hill with views of the sea to a
sheltered harbor where rickety skiffs bobbed like flotsam on
the tide. Cabo de la Vela was one long street of wood-and-
concrete structures, a village of a few hundred overlooking
a calm Caribbean bay. Like the rest of town, Bernie's place
had dirt floors and no utilities, but he cooked fresh lobster
on a propane stove and strung hammocks for us in a palm
gazebo overlooking the beach. There used to be palm trees
out back, he explained, but a decade of rising sea levels had
killed them off. Maybe, I thought, or maybe it was the village's many gazebos. All the same, the ocean view was arresting, and we sipped Scotch outside in the evenings, feeling
as pampered as at any seaside resort.

After dinner on the second day, swinging in our hammocks and watching pelicans swoop for fish offshore, I
daydreamed out loud about hanging my own hammock
someplace like Cabo and simply letting the sea provide. The
lack of electricity and running water actually made the place
feel less isolated and disadvantaged than self-sufficient and
resilient.

"We could just stick around out here and live the simple
life," I suggested, reaching down to give my hammock a lazy
shove.

"You think so?" Sky asked. "It's pretty quiet up here,
Mr. Journalist. You think it'd be gonzo enough for you?"

I snorted. "I am not that gonzo of a guy," I said.

"Yeah? You could have fooled me, dude," Sky joked. "I
saw you putting back the *chirrinchi* yesterday." We laughed

and watched a tiny sand whirl meander its way along the
waterline.

"Seriously, though," he asked. "Why all the Hunter
Thompson stuff, then? What's the appeal of all this for a
non-gonzo guy?"

It was a fair question. My admiration for Thompson had
never had much to do with his Berettas-and-blow hijinks, or
with the counterculture caricature he became later in life.
I like his early bestsellers, 1966's *Hell's Angels* and 1973's
Fear and Loathing: On the Campaign Trail '72—lurid snap-
shots of the biker gangs, student marches, and turbulent
political movements that shaped my parents' generation. I
came to Thompson for the cultural criticism and stayed for
the acid trips, as it were.

Not that I have anything against recreational drugs or
flying one's freak flag. I've done my share of both. But the
Thompson I identified with was the gung-ho freelancer of
those early letters. I was in a similar boat when I first read
them, just out of college and hustling magazine articles to
make the rent. I related to the Thompson on those pages.
His letters were thoughtful and funny, a series of brash little
manifestos on art, sex, youth culture, and the social and political changes that defined the era. Put simply, I geek out on
that stuff. I wanted to understand my own increasingly chaotic and divided country in the way that Thompson seemed
to understand his. He wrote that he'd acquired his understanding by traveling in South America, and I wanted some
of that seemingly mystical insight. And so there I was.

It seemed like a simple enough explanation, but I had a
hard time articulating it to Sky.

"I'm in it for the history and culture," I said finally, and
I sounded to myself like a sightseer on a tour bus. I tried
again. "I want to put America in some kind of context, I

think, to be able to draw some informed comparisons with the rest of the world. Hunter Thompson just makes a convenient guide."

"What kind of comparisons?"

"Social comparisons, political comparisons, economic comparisons. I'm just kind of a wonk for all that."

"A what?" Sky asked.

"A wonk."

He paused. "I have never heard that word before, dude."

"Somebody who obsesses over some field or another," I explained. "A nerd for facts and details."

"I see," he said, and we were quiet awhile longer. The breeze blew more tiny sandstorms down the shore. The cries of the gulls came in and out with the waves. History and politics and economics all seemed very far away.

"Yep," Sky said eventually. "The rest of the world could end out there, and these guys would just carry on."

Before the weekend was over, we were reminded twice that what struck us as Guajira's Edenic seclusion from the outside world was a bit less romantic for its full-time inhabitants. First, Bernie drove us to a barren hillside about ten miles outside of town, where several dozen wind turbines stretched their gleaming blades across the sky. The wind farm had sprouted a few years earlier, he explained, a joint project of Colombia's government-owned energy utility and a German company (which Bernie simply called "gringo"). Initially, many of the Wayuu were skeptical, since other attempts at resource development—like the Cerrejón coal mine to the south—had resulted in multinational companies displacing Wayuu villages. But in a region where most of the population has only sporadic access to electricity, the prospect of cheap power was appealing. So the tribe sold the land, and afterward, the mayor of Cabo erected a stretch of utility poles between the town and the newly built transfer station.

Sky, Bernie, and I picked our way through the rocks that littered the base of the giant towers, serenaded by the eerie whoosh of the turbines and the bleating of obliviously wandering goats. Near a fenced-in jungle of transformers, a crude wooden mast was the last in the long line of utility poles, reaching like a row of thin dominoes back in the direction of Cabo. There were no lines hanging from the poles, however. A public-private Wayuu utility company had been slow to get off the ground, and while villages in La Guajira carried on without power, the electricity from the new project was all being sent in the opposite direction, to the grid in Medellín. Those empty poles were a testament to the Wayuu's frustrated efforts at altering the very circumstances that Sky and I found so idyllic.

That evening, in the truck bed again, we jostled back toward the paved road in Uribia. We were taking a detour to visit a coastal lagoon, a place where Bernie said great flocks of flamingos sometimes gathered in the summer. Without the beer cases, Sky and I leaned up against our backpacks, our bandanas pressed to our faces to keep out the dust. Up front, Bernie was characteristically chipper, blasting a *vallenato* tape with his windows down and occasionally singing along.

"Esta bien?" he yelled back, and we waved.

We hadn't seen another vehicle all day when a red pickup suddenly materialized behind us, emerging from the scrub in its own cloud of dust. It was closing in fast, and Bernie pulled off the rut we'd been following to let it pass. Except that it didn't pass. The truck was a smallish Toyota with three men in the bed and two riding in the cab, and as it pulled up alongside us, it slowed to an idle.

The other driver was dressed like the Marlboro Man and had the cigarette to match. He motioned for Bernie to roll down his passenger-side window, and from the driver's seat, Bernie leaned over to comply. The man said something laconic in Guajiro, unsmiling, and over the drum of the engines, we couldn't hear Bernie's response. A few feet away, the men in the truck bed were all young Wayuu. One of them had a machete at his side, and all three slouched in various stages of recline around a large and indistinct mound, covered by a blue plastic tarp.

Contrabandistas, I thought. Probably moving goods to Maicao from some illicit port up the coast. Sky and I nodded a respectful hello.

Were the smugglers dangerous? I had never thought to ask. In Thompson's story, mainland Colombians described Guajira as "known to be populated by killers and thieves and men given over to lives of crime and violence." I assumed this was hyperbole, but suddenly I found myself wondering whether we were seeing anything on the flats that we weren't supposed to. In 2004, a nearby Wayuu village was massacred by paramilitary forces intent on wiping out witnesses to a narcotrafficking operation. Some victims were beheaded, while others were burned alive. The paras were disbanded now, but just the week before, a half dozen customs agents were injured by petrol bombs during a skirmish with gasoline smugglers on the road to Maicao. But surely, I figured, most *contrabandistas* were happy to let bystanders look the other way, right?

Other than the machete, the men seemed to be unarmed, although for all I knew they were former paras, with assault rifles hidden beneath that tarp. Even if Bernie hit the gas,

I thought, his beater could never outrun them. The men in the back of the truck nodded back at us impassively. Exhaust from the two engines left a gauzy haze in the air between us.

Sky said nothing. I said nothing. Bernie and the other driver chatted tensely. High above us, some kind of bird of prey was making lazy circles in the cloudless sky, and one of the men tilted his head back to stare, squinting hard against the sunlight. When he looked down again, he caught my gaze and smiled thinly, adjusting his lean body against the truck bed's steel rim.

I noticed then that the men in the back of the truck were ankle-deep in muddy water, which sloshed around their feet as the vehicle idled and shook. The smiling one nodded at me conspiratorially and slid back the tarp just a little, and immediately I realized that these were smugglers of a different kind. Concealed underneath was a giant sea turtle, probably a loggerhead, dead or very close to it. These men were poachers.

I breathed a sigh that was one part relief and one part disappointment. After a few minutes of chitchat with Bernie, the other driver hit the gas, and the Toyota drove off harmlessly. Later, as the three of us gazed at a flock of flamingos preening in the lagoon, Bernie said that the driver was his cousin. He and his fellow poachers were likely on their way to somebody's kitchen, where the turtle could be butchered while still fresh, then packaged for sale in the markets of Uribia and Maicao. Bernie explained this nonchalantly, and it was clear he saw little difference between the sea turtle and the lobsters we'd purchased from some Wayuu fisherman two nights before. A pound or two of meat from an endangered loggerhead fetches around five American dollars in Guajira, and a single animal can yield more than a hundred pounds of meat. The market for turtle meat in the cities was robust, Bernie said, and the Wayuu fishermen poor. With the high price tag, it's easy to understand why they wouldn't be deterred by Colombia's endangered-species laws, which, after all, have next to no enforcement on the remote peninsula. In a place like Guajira, everything is a commodity.

The flamingos staggered by on their twiggy legs, and I asked Bernie whether the Wayuu ever hunted or ate the birds. He shook his head vigorously.

"No, no," he said, *"está prohibido."*

But wasn't it also *prohibido,* I asked, to capture and kill the sea turtles? He thought about that for a while. As we stood there, a family of the gangly, blushing birds tucked their legs underneath them and took off. Finally, Bernie smiled in resignation. I guess so, he said, but the flamingos don't taste as good.

As we drove on into Uribia, it occurred to me that Guajira probably illustrates the complex give-and-take between traditional lifestyles and modern consumer culture as well as any place I'd ever been. It's a relationship that's often oversimplified, presented merely as a clash or a co-opting, a scenario in which a proud and isolated population is tragically infiltrated by the trappings of the industrialized West. The reality, of course, is less neat. In Maicao, you'd be hard-pressed to find a single indigenous Wayuu household with a flat-screen TV, and yet the city's economy depends largely on a black market supplying the country with these and other luxury items. In Manaure, the Wayuu cling to their traditional methods of salt harvesting in the name of preserving jobs, even while crossing their fingers for the kind of economic growth that accompanies industrialization. And while ecotourism is starting to bring the region some welcome economic development, few Wayuu would think twice about poaching an endangered sea turtle to sell for meat in the villages. In Guajira, as around the world, the relationship between traditional and dominant cultures is a messy and not-always-logical mixture of adoption and rejection, adaptation and exploitation.

Thompson seemed to have understood this, and while he sometimes came off sounding less than culturally sensitive, his account of three days among the Rolex-wearing, Scotch-drinking Wayuu dispels any notion of the romantic, noble savage. Then as now, he suggested, native Guajirans were happy to embrace some aspects of the "civilized" world while emphatically rebuffing those they had no use for. The peninsula functions according to the same principle today, with some light tourism and a lingering paramilitary presence thrown into the mix.

Thompson's no-bullshit take on Guajira is actually a fitting precursor to the kind of pull-no-punches realism he would call upon in the rest of his South American reporting. For a traveler more naïve, this shattered mythology of native peoples' primeval innocence might have been jarring—a disenchanting start to a long trip, especially for someone who'd gone off in search of an unspoiled frontier. On the contrary, though, Thompson seemed to find it refreshing. "A week ago I came over from Aruba," he later wrote to a friend, ". . . and spent three days with allegedly savage and fearsome indians. As it turned out, they were the best people I've met."

Back in Uribia, we parted ways with the gracious Bernie José, thanking him earnestly for his services and hospitality. On a dusty, quiet street, the three of us leaned against the truck bed and shared one final round of handshakes and Scotch.

It was late when a cab dropped us off at a cheap beachside hostel back in Riohacha. Sky dialed up Alex from the *puerta-a-puerta,* and the two of them headed out for a night of drinks and girl-watching. I stayed in with my journal and the dregs of the Scotch bottle. I was already too tired for the nightlife, and there was a lot of South America still to go. The room was stuffy, so I lay outside in a hammock, listening to the waves as they lapped against the shore. From time to time I heard the sounds of the revelers downtown, snippets of *cumbia* music and machismo that drifted past like flecks of seawater on the wind.

When I finished the bottle around midnight, I thought of Thompson's closing lines from "A Footloose American in a Smugglers' Den." Arriving in Barranquilla, an exhausted Thompson finds that, as far as the city-dwellers are concerned, Guajira might as well be the moon. "I had the feeling that nobody really believed I had been there," he wrote. "When I tried to talk about Guajira, people would smile sympathetically and change the subject.

"And then we would have another beer, because Scotch is so expensive in Barranquilla that only the rich can afford it."

CHAPTER TWO

After the Time of Cholera

The crew is primitive and vicious-looking
and the captain is an old river toad who
can't understand why I'm here and doesn't
much care for it.

—Personal correspondence, May 26, 1962

The Magdalena River stretches across Colombia's populous Andean region like a wide brown scar, arrowhead-jagged and steeped in symbolism. Like a scar, it's distinguished by its breadth and its permanence, and like a scar, it evokes a messy tangle of concepts: history, pride, damage.

But looking down from an auto bridge back in dumpy old Barranquilla, it just looks kind of muddy and lazy. Sky and I stared at the dung-colored water from a long cable-stayed bridge on the outskirts of town. At its delta, the Magdalena teems with plant life, verdant little bundles torn from the marshlands upstream during high water, and we watched them drifting in great green clumps to where the river meets the sea. Beneath our feet, the Pumarejo Bridge is Colombia's longest at 5,000 feet—longer than the main span of San Francisco's Golden Gate. It could have been one of the country's architectural landmarks, but like the rest of Barranquilla, it is a monolithic and oppressive study in gray, a featureless expanse with even its cables entombed in concrete.

In a sense, the capricious Magdalena is to blame for Barranquilla's tired industrial character. For much of its history, the port city was actually Colombia's foremost trade capital, one of the continent's shining jewels. In the early 1900s, it was a model Latin American metro: modern, cosmopolitan, and enjoying some of the highest standards of living in South America. Then, in the mid-twentieth century, the Colombian government restored and upgraded an old colonial aqueduct called the Canal del Dique. Starting eighty miles upstream, the canal diverted much of the Magdalena's flow from its natural mouth to the neighboring coastal city of Cartagena. With a newer, straighter route to the sea, the locus of commerce shifted, and Barranquilla's star faded in direct proportion to its neighbor's success. Today, historic Cartagena is known not only as the largest container port in Colombia, but also as the Caribbean's capital of culture, art, and tourism. Barranquilla is its ugly stepsister—gritty, crowded, and largely forgotten.

But Barranquilla is still the origin point for one of the world's great river trips, from the Magadalena's mouth to the historic terminus of Girardot, near Bogotá, a route once traveled by grand passenger steamboats and immortalized in the writings of Colombian favorite son Gabriel García Márquez. If you've heard of the Magdalena at all, it may well be through Márquez's novels and stories, in which travel on the river is a recurring theme. It's a fitting setting for the country's beloved Nobel laureate, since the story of the thousand-mile Magdalena is intimately intertwined with the story of Colombia itself.

For four hundred years following Spanish conquest, the Magdalena was the Giving Tree of hydrological features. With its tributaries, it irrigated one of the New World's richest agricultural basins. Cattlemen cleared its forested banks. Bricks made from river sand paved the country's colonial streets, and its currents carried barges of Colombian gold to finance the Spanish empire. For goods and passengers, the Magdalena was a watery superhighway, the primary travel corridor between the coast and the inland capital of Bogotá, Colombia's living artery.

By the time Thompson set out upon the Magdalena, however, the steamboats were only a memory. The last remnant of the fleet had burned to the waterline the year before, and passenger travel on the river had all but vanished. The reasons for this are eloquently explained in Márquez's 1985 opus *Love in the Time of Cholera,* a fifty-year love story in which the deteriorating Magdalena serves as a metaphor for the unrequited love of the book's aging protagonist. When Florentino Ariza, the moony owner of a riverboat company, notices changes along his beloved waterway, one of his captains explains to him the river's ironic undoing: For a half century, Colombians logged the Magdalena's banks in order to fuel their wood-burning ships. Over time, this led to catastrophic deforestation, which, in turn, caused such erosion and sedimentation that the river was no longer navigable for the large steamboats.

So the best Thompson could do in May of 1962 was to barter with a shipping company for passage aboard a small tugboat: in exchange for ten promotional photos of the ship, he rode on a tug pushing seven barges of beer upstream, into the Colombian interior. Bogotá was his goal, and although a bus ride or short flight would have saved him a full week on the river, Thompson's itinerary was dictated by simple thrift.

"I am down to 10 US dollars," he wrote from the boat, "but have developed a theory which will go down as Thompson's Law of Travel Economics. To wit: full speed ahead and damn the cost; it will all come out in the wash."

Thompson didn't write for the *Observer* about his Magdalena journey. In fact, his trip into the geographical and cultural heart of Colombia seemed to hold little romance for him. "There is a definite sense of the Congo here," he wrote in a testy letter on day one. "The fucking bugs are on me in force. I can barely stand it. My balls for a sleeping pill."

Márquez, not surprisingly, evokes the river with more affection. In his memoirs, he writes that "the only reason I would want to be a boy again is to enjoy the voyage once more." At the end of *Cholera,* he ties his characters' destinies to it, closing the book with a moment of magical realism that finds Ariza and his love unwilling to abandon their country's cherished river, resolved to float in an abandoned steamboat forever. For centuries, the relationship between the Colombian people and the Magdalena was one of near-complete dependence. As Sky and I set out to follow Thompson's course upriver—decades after Márquez's eloquent eulogy—I wondered: What was the relationship between the river and its people today?

There are easier ways to see the Magdalena River valley than by boat. Much of the region spent the second half of the twentieth century basically frozen in time, cut off by the end of the steamship era and then rendered off-limits by the drug-trafficking and paramilitary activity that followed. In the last decade, however, many Magdalena River towns have become accessible for the first time by modern paved roads. Buses now reach villages that, a generation ago, were effectively off the map. But wherever possible, I wanted to travel on the river itself, and in the absence of commercial passenger boats, this amounted to fluvial hitchhiking, a gamble that Sky and I could meet and negotiate passage with private boatmen along the way.

At the outset, this proved difficult. From the Pumarejo Bridge, we could see the looming cranes of a shipping terminal, but the only river traffic was a pair of wooden canoes just below us, shuttling straw bales from one bank to the other, presumably to avoid the bridge toll. Barranquilla sits at the crossroads of northern Colombia's highway system, its streets jam-packed with colorful and exhaust-spewing "chicken buses" offering cheap fares to villages upstream. Boat travel in the region is essentially an anachronism. So our hope was either to hire a sympathetic local fisherman or, like Thompson, to talk our way aboard a commercial barge. And we'd been told that the area around the bridge was our best bet for doing either.

Our taxi driver took us down a dirt road in the shadow of the bridge's concrete piers, where a village of tightly clustered lean-tos had sprouted. Their corrugated steel roofs trembled with traffic noise from above, and in the road, a small child used a switch to beat a bewildered-looking mule.

"This isn't poor, you know," Sky admonished me, reading my expression as we drove by. "Around here, this is probably just another working-class neighborhood."

The taxi drove us to a clearing at the river's edge, where a dozen men were busy unloading the canoes we'd seen from above. Most were in their twenties and thirties, milling around and shouting at one another as they tossed straw bales into the beds of two large pickups. Their canoes had flaking blue paint and visibly splintered hulls. Across the side, in fading white letters, one of them read: ASI ES LA VIDA. Such is life.

One of the older men wore a jumpsuit with the logo of the nearby shipping terminal, and when we stepped out of the taxi, he walked over and introduced himself as Julio, extending a hand to each of us. Julio stared impassively while Sky explained our search for a boat, then nodded slowly and turned to consult with some of the other men. I noticed that one of the trucks had a Thundercats decal on the windshield, and I wondered which of these serious-looking workers appreciated the cartoon show from my childhood.

After a moment, Julio turned back to us. Why didn't we just take a bus? he wanted to know. River travel took longer, he said, and besides, it wasn't cheap. He was right on this score, of course. Gas would be a big expense. While Colombia is an oil-rich nation, the majority of its petroleum reserves are tapped for export, and domestic oil sales are heavily taxed. The cost of fueling a motorboat to take us upriver would easily buy us a dozen bus tickets. So we tried to explain our interest in the river's history, our desire to see the Magdalena's farms and villages as someone might have seen them a century ago. But Julio just furrowed his brow and shook his head, clearly dismissing the river as an object of romance. He stared at us contemplatively while a few of his coworkers snickered.

It was understandable, I thought, that the Magdalena wouldn't strike these men as a place of fascination, that the concept might even seem a bit ridiculous. To Julio and his companions, the river was primarily a means of making a living. Sometimes it was an obstacle, something to be crossed with a canoe full of feed. The idea that two gringos would willingly spend a week's wages just to see the countryside as they couldn't see it from the road—I wouldn't blame them if this struck them as absurd. I thought of one of Márquez's characters, the no-nonsense Fermina Daza, willful heroine of *Love in the Time of Cholera,* who scoffs at the notion of a pleasure trip along the Magdalena. "If I go," she insists to her suitor, "it will be because I have decided to and not because the landscape is interesting."

After further cajoling, Julio conceded that it might be possible to find a fisherman willing to take us upriver, but he sure didn't know any. He offered instead to take us to the shipping terminal where he worked. Perhaps there, he said, we could arrange some sort of passage on a commercial freighter. So he joined us in the taxi, guiding our driver through an adjacent shipyard where skinny cattle wandered among the skeletons of old boats, and ten or so minutes later, the four of us piled out at a gated office building still within sight of the bridge. An armed guard at the entrance radioed inside to find out what to do with us.

The man who came out a few minutes later wore a dark blue suit and spoke the brisk English of an international businessman. Benjamin González introduced himself as the commercial director of the Palermo Port Society, a logistics hub for container ships taking cargo into and out of Colombia, and as he gestured us inside the gates, he offered politely to answer any questions we had about trade along the Magdalena. It was true, he said, that commercial river traffic had suffered over the last several decades, in Barranquilla and elsewhere. River erosion and sedimentation were factors, yes, but so were the backroom politics of federal infrastructure projects. By the 1960s, González explained, Colombian leaders had all but abandoned the Magdalena River as a lost cause. Instead, the government funneled money into railroads, road construction, and commercial trucking, shifting resources away from river restoration. Pressure from the American railroad and auto industries probably helped influence this policy, González said, and only recently had some Colombian politicians started advocating for river rehab, citing low emissions and the comparatively low cost of freight shipping.

Rather graciously, considering our out-of-the-blue arrival, González invited Sky and me into a gleaming SUV for a tour of the port. As we drove, he continued to fire off factoids about cargo on the Magdalena River. What everyone agrees on, he said, is that the "roads only" policy is a difficult one to reverse. The Pumarejo Bridge is itself a monument to the pro-asphalt mind-set. It was built without a drawbridge in the 1970s, and as such, it severely limits the size of ships entering the river from the Caribbean. González ticked off the river's major imports—mostly raw industrial materials—and noted its primary exports, petroleum and palm oil. The latter is actually responsible for much of Colombia's ongoing deforestation, since primary rain forest in the middle Magdalena is often cleared to make room for palm plantations.

Unfortunately, González also dismissed out of hand the possibility of hitching a ride aboard a commercial freighter. Such things, he explained courteously, are simply not done anymore.

We cruised in the SUV past sky-high cranes and piles of empty pallets while the shipping exec continued to fire off statistics. When I asked González whether there was any future for Magdalena passenger transport, the buttoned-down businessman turned surprisingly wistful.

"I have thought about it a lot, in a romantic way," he said with a sigh. As a child, González remembered listening to his grandmother's stories about her honeymoon cruise along the river. For the moneyed class, a riverboat trip could be a pretty genteel affair, and González remembered his grandmother's descriptions of chamber musicians on the deck, grand dinners in the ship's dining room, and a visit to the historic river town of Mompós, with its colonial architecture and cobblestone streets. Could that sort of thing happen again? Sure, González said, if someone could make a profit, but he wasn't optimistic.

When we finished our tour, Julio and the taxi driver were waiting for us at the gate. González pulled over the SUV, then looked at us and sighed once more. "I have always wanted to see Mompós," he said. Then he gave us his card and thanked us for our interest in Colombian commerce.

We had struck out on two scores. On our way back to the bridge, we stopped at a roadside bodega, where Sky and I bought Cokes for Julio and the driver. Painted there, on the side of the building, was a mural of a small boy hanging from the limbs of a bright pink tree. At its base, a grinning tiger crouched at the ready, and a snake wound its way through the salmon-colored branches. Just below the dangling boy, a caiman—a South American crocodile—exposed a row of sharp and gleaming teeth. In wavy, dreamlike letters, the mural's caption read: *Que sera del pobrecito Paco?* What will happen to poor little Paco?

In Colombia, Márquez-style magical realism pops up in these sorts of unexpected places. Admiring the mural, I considered the gap between this cultural fondness for the absurd and the pragmatic mind-set of Julio and the men at the bridge. Was it naïve, I wondered, for us to value river travel for its own sake? Benjamin González didn't seem to think so. We sipped our Cokes, and I admired the caiman staring hungrily at poor little Paco. It was the only one I was likely to see, since caimans on the Magdalena have been hunted to near-extinction.

II

The bus that eventually took Sky and me out of Barranquilla smelled of upholstery cleaner and defeat. At least we'd opted for the motorcoach over the chicken bus, so instead of body odor and barnyard noise, we got plush seatbacks, footrests, and a satellite TV showing a live summit of the Union of South American Nations.

UNASUR is an intergovernmental economic council—a bit like the European Union, but with more shouting. And at this particular summit, most of that shouting was directed at former Colombian president Álvaro Uribe. More recently, Uribe has been replaced in office by his own former defense minister, but following two stormy terms as chief executive, he continues to loom large in Colombian politics. In all but the leftiest circles of Colombian political life, he was an exceptionally popular president, thanks to the huge strides his administration made against left-wing guerrillas, particularly the Revolutionary Armed Forces of Colombia.

A little backstory: The guerrilla group known universally as the FARC first emerged in the years just after Thompson's visit. It was founded as a peasant-led, revolutionary socialist army in the late 1960s, and over the next few decades, it came to control much of rural Colombia. Divisions of the FARC clashed violently with both the Army and the right-wing paramilitary groups that were formed to oppose it, but that ultimately came to resemble it. Over time, the group all but abandoned its ideology and committed itself instead to Colombia's profitable drug trade. In the 1990s and early 2000s, the FARC also supplemented this income with ransom money, carrying out ambushes and high-profile political kidnappings that made headlines around the world.

All of this earned Colombia its reputation in the late twentieth century as one of the world's most dangerous countries. When Uribe first came into office in 2002, Colombia was in a state of all-out civil war. It was only following a multiyear military blitzkrieg—heavily subsidized by the United States—that the Colombian Army finally brought the FARC to its knees, pushing remaining cells deep into the jungle on the country's periphery.

The improved security situation dramatically boosted Colombia's economy, and popular support for Uribe soared. In 2006, voters passed a referendum altering the constitution so he could seek a second term. When that was up, Uribe's handpicked replacement was elected by the largest margin in Colombian history.

The United States had a hand in all this: Uribe's success against the FARC was largely the result of a partnership with the United States, which provided helicopters, weapons, training, and close to $8 billion to assist the Colombian military under an initiative called Plan Colombia. And this chummy relationship between Colombia and the United States is nothing new. It dates back, in fact, to the Cold War containment era, and it was the very subject that Thompson tackled in his second South American *Observer* article, a long profile of then-incoming Colombian president Guillermo León Valencia.

Thompson's profile is a little on the dry side—there's nothing gonzo about his descriptions of Colombia's then-recent constitutional crisis—but Valencia cut an interesting figure in South American politics because of his eager cooperation with a Kennedy-era policy called the Alliance for Progress. The Alliance, as it was known, was the geopolitical backdrop to every move that Thompson made in South America, and he referenced it extensively in his letters and articles. The program stemmed from a sociological concept known as modernization theory, which held that certain early industrialized nations could "take off" economically if they were catalyzed by timely injections of foreign aid. That growth, in turn, would breed Western-style democracy and stave off communism.

The Alliance was kind of a carrot-and-stick program, calling for democratic elections, land reform, and competitive market policies in exchange for generous bundles of US assistance. It was the beating heart of the Kennedy administration's policy in Latin America, and Colombia was its first poster child, exhibiting all of what modernization theorists called the "preconditions for take-off": functioning elections, an urban entrepreneurial class, and a budding manufacturing sector. Today, we're more likely to associate Colombia with guerrilla armies or narcoterrorism—and indeed, Thompson would see the country's violent side soon enough—but in terms of development and the democratic process, he accurately described Colombia in 1962 as "one of the most stable countries in South America."

These days, though, Colombia's enthusiastic partnering with the United States doesn't always sit well with the lefty administrations in nearby Venezuela, Ecuador, and Bolivia, whose relationships with the United States are less than cordial. Hence the entertainment value of the UNASUR broadcast. Politicos in Latin America have a well-deserved reputation for impassioned oratory, and as our bus rolled from village to dusty village, Sky and I listened to leaders from each of these countries passionately decrying Colombia's cozy relationship with what former Venezuelan president Hugo Chávez once branded *"el imperio yanqui"*—the Yankee Empire. The main point of contention was a then-new agreement expanding the US military's privileges to operate out of Colombian military bases. The neighbors weren't thrilled at the prospect of having so many uniformed *yanquis* just a short flight from their borders, and while Colombian courts eventually struck down that accord, the debate over the US military presence in Colombia is still one of the continent's most divisive.

So the broadcast held my attention, giving various politicians a chance to show off some of their eyes-to-the-sky, fist-shaking rhetoric. In South America, political actors tend to be large and loud. Writing about Colombia's colorful Valencia back in 1962, Thompson noted that the bombastic personalities of South American leaders can be every bit as important as their meaningful deeds. He might have been describing a modern-day summit when he wrote of Colombian politics, "In the end it is an old story, the problem of turning words into accomplishments—and at the same time, dealing with diverse quirks, jealousies, opinions, and prejudices."

We finally boarded a boat at a town called Magangué, some 120 miles south, where a rusted pontoon ferry shuttles trucks and passengers to the island of Mompós. The river at Magangué looked a lot like it did at the delta, brown and brackish, but with the Barranquilla skyline replaced by a thick forest canopy. The fat, rectangular ferry plowed the wide channel with a diesel roar and all the grace of a bulldozer. Every fifty yards or so, great egrets stared up at us from the banks, and diving cormorants sometimes surfaced in our wake, choking down tadpoles. Fishermen trolled by in long outboard canoes called *jhonsos,* nodding somber greetings to one another as they dragged their nets for catfish.

The island that port executive Benjamin González longed to see is roughly the size of Puerto Rico, although it's always in flux, changing slightly in size and shape as the silt-heavy Magdalena alters its course. For centuries, its namesake town was one of the country's most prosperous. Back then, the main branch of the river flowed eastward around the island, passing the town of Mompós along its right bank. Magangué, meanwhile, was just a speck of a town to the west, on the mainland and separated from the island by only a thin backwater channel. High-masted merchant ships docked in Mompós. The gold trade made it rich, its isolation made it fiercely independent, and the combination prompted South American *libertador* Simón Bolívar to treat the city like his personal ATM. He made eight visits between 1812 and 1830, gathering money and men for his various wars of independence elsewhere on the continent.

After Bolívar, Mompós prospered for another fifty years or so, until the dwindling streamside forests kicked river sedimentation into high gear at the end of the nineteenth century. The Magdalena's eastern flow slowed to a trickle, and the river's main course gradually shifted entirely to the west. Magangué boomed, while Mompós was left stranded, effectively cut off from the outside world. Gold stopped coming to town. Dugout canoes replaced the grand merchant ships. And while the rest of Colombia moved into a new era of industrial modernization and civil war, Mompós stayed behind, its quiet colonial steeples keeping watch over a riverfront where galleons once anchored.

The Model T was still a few years off when Mompós hit the chronological Pause button, and today its brick-lined streets do not comfortably accommodate cars. So our taxi from the ferry terminal dropped us off at a riverside plaza at the edge of town. Stepping out of the cab was like wandering into a historian's hazy daydream. A perfectly preserved sixteenth-century church loomed over the square, bright goldenrod, as if the stucco had been laid just last week. Its domed bell tower was a fairy tale of baroque detailing, while the nave was boxy and simple, more like a rural mission than a grand colonial cathedral. Across the plaza, a silent, gray customs house was ringed with stone-arched walkways, conjuring images of the town in its commercial heyday. Immense ficus trees stretched their branches over the streets, a living awning that gave the whole scene a dim, phantasmic feel of enclosure.

"Mompós doesn't exist," sighs Márquez's Simón Bolívar, making his last pilgrimage down the river in the novel *The General in His Labyrinth*. "Sometimes we dream about it, but it doesn't exist."

We spent the next few days wandering sleepy Mompós, admiring the preserved architecture and chatting up the locals, for whom an encounter with a gringo is still a pretty exotic affair. At its busiest, the pace of life there is languid. The dominant pastimes seem to be playing dominoes and sitting outside in rocking chairs. In fact, as one old-timer explained to me, the rocking chair is such a cultural institution that the local variety has its own nickname: the *mecedora Mompósina*. He was rocking outside of a drugstore when I stopped to admire an unoccupied *mecedora* at his side, and he invited me to try it out.

"Nice, yes?" the old man said, fanning himself with a half-rolled newspaper. And indeed it was—a sturdy red cedar with an easy tilt and a wicker panel on its back, essential for airflow in Mompós's swampy climate. The old man beamed. Mompósino craftsmen have a reputation around the world, he boasted. Fine furniture, carved statues, filigree jewelry—their handiwork was the best in the country.

"It must be a town full of artisans," I said.

Well, the old-timer joked, it's easy to excel at such pursuits when you've had a lot of time on your hands for the last 150 years.

We talked awhile, and the old man advanced a theory about historical preservation in Mompós, although it may be one better suited to Márquez's half-enchanted village. The island rests at the bottom of a deep valley, he explained, making a bowl with his hands. This much is true; it's known to geographers as the Mompós Depression. Well, because of this, the old man said, the winds that gradually wear down the buildings in other towns never blow here, and the sticky humidity of the breezeless afternoon made this seem pretty believable.

"*Los vientos pasan sobre nuestras cabezas,*" he said sagely. The winds pass right over our heads.

There is a second explanation, it turns out. As Sky and I toured the town, we noticed clusters of young men and women at work, wearing yellow jumpsuits emblazoned with the words "La Escuela Taller." As our hostel manager later explained, students at Mompós's "Workshop School" learn hands-on skills like woodworking and metallurgy, which they use to maintain the city's historic infrastructure. They're easy to spot, laying cobblestones or tending to one of Mompós's elaborate wrought-iron gates. Interestingly, much of the school's funding comes from the Spanish government, which has a keen cultural interest in preserving the colonial architecture. It's a peculiar setup—imagine the British paying upkeep on Colonial Williamsburg—but it illustrates how the town's historic vibe, once just a product of its isolation, has now become a legitimate point of pride.

One evening, while drinking beer at a riverside park that seemed to double as an outdoor bar, Sky and I met a pair of local teenagers who, for a fee, offered to take us in their *jhonso* to the nearby Ciénaga del Pijiño. Shallow backwater wetlands called ciénagas are plentiful along the Magdalena, acting as a sort of reserve system that stores water during the spring and fall rainy seasons and returns it to the river during dry spells. They also tend to be strongholds for wildlife, and in giddy, broken English, the would-be teen guides promised us we'd see plenty of "i-gwaah-nahs" and "mung-keys."

In his memoir, Márquez waxes nostalgic about the wildlife-rich river trips he'd taken as a young man, recalling the sound of the manatee's cry and the sky-darkening flocks of herons that would alight at a steamboat's approach. But he also laments the loss of biodiversity along the river since. In *Cholera,* his steamboat captain seethes at manatee-hunters aboard his ship and mourns the birds that seem to have disappeared with the receding foliage. I was curious to see whether and how wildlife along the Magdalena had rebounded.

So the next morning, we showed up at the waterfront and climbed into a long, canopied boat. With our two young guides, we motored up the Magdalena's Mompós branch and turned off at a narrow side-channel. It was an hour-long ride between dense and bushy banks, and the teens spent most of that time sitting in the bow, sharing a large joint and excitedly telling us the Spanish names for various fish and waterfowl. The herons were called *garzas*. The catfish were *bagre*. In the trees, we spotted gray-black hawks called *gavilanes,* and egrets and other waders were abundant in the shallows, their long necks bent like question marks. We did indeed see dozens of iguanas as well, lounging passively on tree trunks, plus a few families of spindly howler monkeys crouching in the canopy. Every so often, one of the guides clapped his hands, laughing as he scared up clamorous flocks of waterfowl.

Fish, meanwhile, literally leapt into the boat. Twice we had to throw back tiny *sardinas* that flopped aboard, sending the guides into fits of giggles. I regretted not packing a fishing rod, wondering what sort of flies would entice the silvery *bocachico* or fat *mojarra lora* that seemed to be a mainstay on dinner menus in Mompós.

The ciénaga itself was a broad, shallow lake ringed with marshy vegetation and small farms. All along the banks were clusters of woody cassava shrubs, grown for their starchy and edible roots, plus small trees crowded with Colombia's peculiar green oranges. Swallows swept here and there across the surface of the lake, skimming the water in small squadrons. After a while, Cheech and Chong killed the motor, and we all stripped down for a swim. It had been a dry few months along the Magdalena, and the water level in the ciénaga was low. At the center of a lake that the teenagers told us was often twenty feet deep, Sky and I found several places to stand with our heads above water.

To me, the whole scene came off as rich and exotic and authentically wild. But of course, in Márquez's day, those farmlands would likely have been thick tropical forest. Colombian biologists estimate that the middle Magdalena rain forest has dwindled by as much as 88 percent since the mid-twentieth century. And those copious *mojarra lora* fish? An invasive species of African tilapia, introduced in the early '90s with disastrous consequences for native species. In fact, the catalog of wildlife I saw that day pales alongside the list of creatures that were absent: critically endangered caimans and manatees; tapirs, foxes, and jaguars that are all but extinct in the Magdalena valley; hundreds of bird, snake, and reptile species decimated by twentieth-century trappers for feathers and skins. This is the insidious thing about species loss—you don't even know what you're missing.

Back at the hostel that night, I heard howler monkeys for the first time, bellowing in the trees outside. If you've never heard the sound, imagine a belching contest between Homer Simpson and Al Bundy, but louder and more menacing. Considering that Márquez and his companions would have heard those howls together with a whole chorus of other primate species, it's a wonder that anyone on those riverboats ever got any sleep. I stayed awake listening for hours, and felt conflicted about allowing my appreciation of "what is" to be tainted by my knowledge of "what was."

Pineapples, it turns out, make less-than-comfortable seat-backs. We left Mompós with a produce vendor named Jaisson, who offered us a lift in his fruit-filled *jhonso* while he made a run to his family farm, about 150 miles upriver. His twenty-year-old boat had only a small outboard motor, so we moved up the slow brown channel at a leisurely pace, reclining amid his crops. The scenery remained unchanged, with tall white *garzas* fishing along the banks and evidence of small farms and ranches onshore—here an acre of corn, there a cluster of cattle. Every so often, we passed an abandoned-looking dugout canoe, pulled up on the beach in an area that otherwise showed no sign of human habitation.

Along the way, we stopped at a pair of tiny villages where Jaisson took orders for pineapples and yuca. His is a disappearing lifestyle, he explained. Although he still has a handful of competitors selling produce along the river, they're far fewer than in decades past. It would actually cost him less, he admitted, to make his deliveries by truck, taking the ferry onto Mompós Island, and I thought, Aha!—another river romantic. But it turned out the initial investment was simply more than Jaisson could afford. Anyway, he said, the ferries were unreliable. The year before, a car ferry on the island's south end had shut down for months when drought rendered the river too low for anything but dugouts and *jhonsos*.

Jaisson let us off in a town called El Banco, where we spent the night before continuing upriver to an industrial port city called Barrancabermeja. From El Banco, fiberglass speedboats called *chalupas* make the three-hundred-mile trip in about eight hours. The *chalupas*—from the same root as the English word "sloop"—constitute a sort of ragtag commuter service along the river's middle section, humble crafts run by co-ops of independent owners. Schedules are notoriously unreliable, but $20 can get you quite a distance upstream, provided you're traveling light and willing to huddle with thirty other people in what is essentially a large motorized bathtub. At one point, our *chalupa* picked up a young man with a small monkey tied to a piece of yarn. He sat behind me, holding the monkey as it screeched, and I spent the better part of two hours waiting for it to leap up and gnaw my ear off.

After a long trip, we were welcomed into Barrancabermeja by the sight of a half dozen looming refinery towers, their torches sending thick columns of smoke into the sky. Barranca, as it's sometimes known, is the nation's petroleum capital and the port of call for many ships sailing inland from the coast. It's a sweltering urban crossroads, and it was here in 1962 that Thompson had to disembark to change boats.

Halfway through his river trip, Thompson seemed to be getting cranky. His letters share exactly none of Márquez's enthusiasm for the journey. If he saw any wildlife at all from the deck of the beer barge, you wouldn't know it from his writings. The only creatures that seemed to warrant coverage were of the six-legged variety. "There is at this moment," began one note, "a beetle the size of god's ass on the table about six inches from the t-writer. It is worse than anything Kafka ever dreamed." Most of Thompson's ink on the Magdalena is devoted to complaints about the bugs, malicious glances from the crew, and the heat—exacerbated by the lack of opportunities to break into the beer cargo. He dismissed Barrancabermeja as just "an oil village on the Magdalena River," but even in 1962 that description would have fallen short. Colombia's first oil field was discovered nearby in 1918, turning Barranca into a sort of boomtown. In 1961, a year before Thompson's arrival, the state-run oil concern Ecopetrol took over the refinery, contributing to the city's cosmopolitan flair by importing workers from around the world. Had Thompson been in higher spirits, it might have been just the kind of rough-and-tumble town he would have enjoyed.

Today, Barranca is a gritty metro of more than 200,000 people, built around the colossal refining facility. It is also a perennial hub of guerrilla violence, once firmly controlled by the FARC, then later by the right-wing United Self-Defense Forces of Colombia, or AUC, the same paramilitary whose former members are muscling in on the smuggling biz in Guajira. Colombia's paramilitaries were initially formed by wealthy landowners as protection from the FARC and other guerrillas, and they often served as an unofficial right hand to the overextended military—a hand less shackled by international treaties on human rights. But as the Colombian conflict continued to spiral, the AUC ran amok, massacring civilians, displacing communities, and themselves dabbling in the drug trade. After years of negotiations with the Uribe administration, the AUC formally demobilized in 2006, but Barranca was the one place in Colombia where Sky and I had nonetheless been warned to stay on guard for paramilitary activity.

More cheerfully, Barranca is also a port of call for a large and colorful boat called the *Florentino Ariza,* a scaled-down, tourist-friendly replica of one of Márquez's cherished steamboats. The boat was christened in honor of *Cholera*'s protagonist by a government agency that works to restore the river's health and navigability. The agency's plan had been for a tourist attraction that could help promote the Magdalena as a natural and cultural resource, running cruises for vacationing Colombians and educational tours for students. And the plan worked—sort of. After the *Florentino Ariza* was launched to great fanfare in the summer of 2005, it operated short tours from the town of Girardot, the same historic terminus that Sky and I hoped to reach. Girardot has some fine surroundings for a cruise, situated as it is on a section of the river where the mountains close in tight, making for some ruggedly beautiful scenery. While the views are lovely, however, the upper Magdalena around Girardot is also lower in volume, and in recent years drought and sedimentation have again hindered navigation for large boats. So Sky and I arrived in Barranca to find the *Florentino Ariza* sailing a sort of "consolation route"—offering scenic cruises alongside the national oil refinery. We bought tickets immediately.

The boat itself looked pretty regal, a double-decker affair with an enclosed cabin below and open-air seating up top. The exterior was a freshly painted white, while the rails, waterwheel, and chimneys were done variously in Colombia's national colors of yellow, blue, and red. Of course, the latter two elements were only for show, as the *Florentina Ariza* is actually powered by three large diesel engines in its stern. Passengers for the Sunday-evening cruise seemed to consist primarily of middle-class Colombian families on holiday, including dozens of pregnant women and young mothers pushing strollers.

The boat shoved off fifteen minutes behind schedule, adhering to the rule that, in Latin America, no form of transportation ever sets out until it has exceeded maximum capacity. We grabbed seats on the upper deck, where a house *vallenato* band played softly as we sailed past tugboats pushing flat-bottom barges. The flatboats, called *planchones,* were probably identical to Thompson's beer barge, but loaded down instead with construction equipment and shipping containers. Some carried oil drums, and on those stood groups of heavily armed Colombian soldiers. Drifting past them was a bit surreal, the fading sunlight glinting off their M-16s while the band cycled through its repertoire of sad Colombian love songs.

The trade-off for Colombia's newfound security is a significantly increased military presence, especially in long-besieged towns like Barrancabermeja. Before we'd boarded, I'd overheard Sky chatting with one of the young soldiers positioned along the waterfront, each one clad in fatigues and shouldering a large assault rifle. Sky had asked him, half-jokingly, what the FARC would want with a rusty old *planchon* anyway, and the soldier had just shrugged. "They want the oil," he said, simple as that. "But it isn't 1990 anymore," Sky had replied. "Isn't the FARC long gone?" The soldier just shook his head and said somberly, "Those sons of bitches just won't die."

Sky wandered around the boat shooting photos, and I settled in against a railing on the lower deck. Dusk was falling, and from the waterline the refinery looked like a city itself, a dark dystopia alive with fiery towers and sweeping searchlights. We floated close enough to smokestacks and derricks to hear the hiss of escaping steam, the hypnotic clanking of metal on metal. Beside me, leaning over the rail, a father and son sipped silently from soda bottles, admiring the whole industrial spectacle. The boy caught my gaze and grinned shyly. *"Es muy bonita, no?"* he asked.

It was pretty, I thought, in a *Beyond Thunderdome* sort of way. The pipelines and fiery citadels had an alluring asymmetry to them, a sculptural quality that I admired. And in fact, Barranca's most recognizable landmark is an eighty-foot Christ statue made to resemble the skeletal framework of an oil derrick. El Cristo Petrolero rises above a ciénaga on the far side of the refinery, his arms raised in benediction, silhouetted against a skyline of distillation towers. I liked how the whole mechanized fortress was juxtaposed against the faux-historicity of the *Florentino Ariza*. In my mind's eye, I pictured the boat from above, its primary colors looking cartoonish among the sooty buildings and the rusted metal barges. The refinery's countless electric lights lit up the waterfront, a constellation rivaling anything in the night sky.

"*Sí,*" I agreed, "*es muy bonita.*"

The boy smiled at me. Then I watched as he and his father threw their empty bottles into the river and walked away down the deck, hand in hand.

III

Over the next several days, we hired a series of private boatmen, each happy to take our pesos, but to varying degrees confused and amused by our motivations. More than once we simply received directions to the bus station. Again and again, I thought of Julio and his serious coworkers beneath the bridge—and of Thompson's unflagging cynicism as he made his way upriver. "Jesus, eight days of this," he moaned in one letter. "You get what you pay for, I guess, and I ain't paid." With each new negotiation, I fought off the gnawing sense that it was callow of us to turn this into a pleasure trip, to approach the Magdalena with a sense of adventure and nostalgia, as Márquez had done. But surely Thompson, for all of his bitching, held a romantic view of travel deep down? Why else does a person descend on Colombia with no Spanish, virtually no itinerary, and $10 to his name?

At least our aqua-hitchhiking was paying off, and we were putting a lot of river behind us. As we ventured farther upstream, the banks gradually took on a Jurassic feel, with broad ferns spreading out beneath a rain-forest canopy. Here and there, the scenery was interrupted by palm plantations, the proliferation of which is responsible for thousands of deforested acres along the Magdalena each year. But there were very few villages, and river traffic was limited to the occasional fisherman in his dugout canoe, his face fixed in a thousand-yard stare. It was tranquil atmosphere, although scenes from *Apocalypse Now* came inexorably to mind. At one point, we passed an olivine military patrol boat no bigger than a fishing skiff, with five uniformed soldiers pressed inside and a machine gun mounted in the bow, unmanned and tilting lazily toward the sky. We spent a night in a military town near one of the largest bases that the Colombians had recently opened to the US military. In another riverside hamlet, our relatively recent guidebook was still suggesting a hotel that had actually been converted to a military installation back in the 1980s—a pretty good indication of the region's popularity with travelers.

Then, in a fishing town called Honda, about a hundred river miles short of our goal at Girardot, we accidentally became local celebrities, and everything started to fall apart.

It unfolded like this: When we'd last had Internet access in Barranca, Sky had reached out on the social networks to a twentysomething stranger in Honda, hoping to find us a friend in town and maybe a free place to stay. The guy's name was Ricardo, and while he didn't have any crash space, he wrote back that he was a technician at the local radio station, where a visiting gringo writer and photographer were apparently enough of a news story to justify some coverage. Would we be willing to do a short interview once we'd arrived in town? Sky wrote back that we were happy to oblige.

We landed in Honda on the same day that Sky and Ricardo had arranged the interview, so the radio station was our very first stop. Honda is a bucolic little town just eighty miles from Bogotá, close enough to attract the occasional weekenders, who come for its scenic bridges and forested foothills. Looming above the city is the post-industrial specter of the abandoned Bavaria brewery, which once employed much of the town before the company consolidated its production and left Honda in the 1990s. When we met Ricardo at the station, he explained to us that the town has been trying to attract tourists ever since, with mixed results—hence the excitement surrounding a pair of nominal gringo journalists.

Ricardo took us into a room lined with CD racks, sat us down in front of a foam-headed microphone, and introduced us to the DJ, a portly and mustachioed man named Tony. As another *vallenato* song faded into silence, he donned a pair of headphones and sat down at a mixer. When a light went on above our microphone, Ricardo gave Tony a thumbs-up, and Tony launched into a string of rapid-fire Spanish that I understood only enough of to know when it was my turn to recite a well-rehearsed explanation of who Hunter Thompson was and why he'd traveled through Colombia. From there, Sky did most of the heavy lifting, and I chimed in periodically with my grade-school Spanish about what we'd experienced so far along the river:

"This region has a rich and significant history."

"The people of the towns are very kind."

"We are seeing many, many animals."

Tony nodded and smiled at me like I was a third-grader, but I closed strong with a three-sentence soliloquy that I'd written down in my notebook, about how more foreign tourists should visit this beautiful area. When we were all through, Ricardo smiled and slapped our backs, and we agreed to meet up for a beer later on.

With the interview wrapped up, Sky and I found a room nearby at the Hotel Turivan, a colonial-style pension with a nice courtyard in the shadow of the old brewery. The name is a portmanteau of *"turismo"* and "Ivan," and we were welcomed inside by Ivan Romero Herrera himself, the hotel's good-humored, thirtysomething innkeeper. Ivan had heard us on the radio, he said excitedly, and boy, had we come to the right place. With a butler's formality, he presented us a glossy Turivan flyer, which announced in bright blue letters that "Honda and the Magdalena River Are My Life" and included a long list of touristic services that Ivan could provide: boat rides, bike trips, ecotourism jeep tours, historic walks around the city, shuttles to nearby towns. Ivan wanted to be a one-man concierge for Honda's expanding tourism economy, he explained earnestly. Then he showed us to our room, at the back of a hotel that was altogether empty, except for his pet duck, Lucas.

We were just unpacking a few minutes later, contemplating showers, when Ivan reappeared in the doorway.

"Sorry to bother you," he said politely, as if he hadn't just left us, "but I think there is someone waiting for you outside."

Lucas the duck followed us back through the courtyard, quacking happily at our heels. The hotel's front door was open, and Tony the DJ was standing outside, rubbing his hands together anxiously, like he was late for something.

"Ah, my friends, please come," he said as we stepped outside. "It is time for you to meet the mayor."

Thus began five long days as the honored gringo guests of the Hondans. Tony marched us downtown and into the mayor's office, where a small, neat man in a sport coat shook our hands and posed with us for pictures in front of a marble statue of Bolívar. We got a tour of City Hall, and Tony introduced us to a handful of local functionaries, all middle-aged men with salt-and-pepper hair and broad stomachs, each one only more pleased to meet us than the last. A walking tour of the city had somehow been arranged, and before we could protest, we found ourselves tromping through the streets with a local historian who pantomimed colonial bayonet duels and insisted on taking our pictures in front of every church, mural, and statue in Honda.

When we finally returned to the mayor's office, the head of the chamber of commerce was waiting there to tell us that our boat ride to Girardot had already been arranged. We would pay only for gas, he said, and the boat would leave in three days' time. Until then, would we please stay and enjoy his beautiful city? Sky and I exchanged looks of weary astonishment.

"Are they going to give us thirty virgins?" he asked.

So we set out to enjoy the beautiful city. Both that night and the next we met up with Ricardo at a bar called Cirrosis—as in "of the liver"—where he introduced us to his nightlife posse. I drank a few beers with the young crowd and excused myself early, heading back to Ivan's to read and sleep, but Sky stayed out and made friends, dancing with the local girls to bone-rattling reggaeton. On the second day, I followed a trail along the river, crisscrossing the bridges and watching the fishermen cast their nets, occasionally returning greetings from strangers who waved to me and cried, *"Hola, periodista!"* The following afternoon, a local news anchor and his wife showed up at Ivan's and practically begged us to join them for lunch. They had once lived in Baltimore, loved all things American, and were eager to spend an afternoon speaking English.

Ivan, meanwhile, was the consummate host. One morning, he drove us in his jeep to some nearby ruins at a place called Armero, where a volcanic eruption had wiped out an entire town in 1985, killing an astonishing 23,000 people. He was thrilled when we mentioned that we'd ridden on the *Florentino Ariza,* the captain of which, he told us proudly, he had once advised on how to negotiate the rapids around

Honda. Ivan genuinely seemed to relish the role of guide. When I came home early from Cirossis one night, he sat up with me in the courtyard, declining a beer and tenderly re-calling his memories of the river as a child. From the time he was about six, Ivan said, he used to ride upstream to visit his grandfather's farm. He remembered the excitement of pil-ing onto a small boat with his auntie, squeezing in among the people, pigs, chickens, and bundles of crops. As a boy, he had always wanted to peer over the edge at the river, and to keep him from leaning out, his aunt had to clasp her legs around him like a vise.

"Sometimes," he said with a chuckle, "we'd show up at my grandfather's and my arms would be purple."

As a young man, Ivan ran a small footwear company for a few years, successful enough that he could afford to buy the hotel. At first he had just wanted to open a bar, he said, but as the region bounced back from the dark days of para-militaries and narcotraffickers, he started to see Honda's tourism potential, and he realized that he didn't much want to sell shoes or tend bar. What he really wanted was to lead tours to the volcano above Armero, to show people the en-dangered river turtles and the rock upstream with the strata in the shape of the Virgin. It's a great job, Ivan told me, and he's never looked back.

Meanwhile, other Hondans' approaches to tourism are still evolving. Back at City Hall, I had flattered the mayor by admiring how pretty the hills were around town, and I'd pointed to a conspicuous cross on top of the largest one, mentioning casually that it must be a lovely hike up, that maybe I would go there to stretch my legs and get an aerial view of the city. I did not expect that on our third morning in Honda I would wake up to find two armed soldiers stand-ing solemnly outside of Ivan's hotel—a courtesy escort for my hike, sent by the mayor. The surrounding hillsides, Ivan insisted, were perfectly safe. The guerrillas and paramilitaries had been gone for years. But while Hondans are proud of their natural resources and eager to attract travelers, even Ivan admitted they were still working to shake off a half century of civil-war mentality. So I spent that morning hiking in the hills alongside the stoic young soldiers. They were quiet and surprisingly out of shape, sweating up the switchbacks in their head-to-toe fatigues and heavy weaponry. At the top, they shared my water bottle silently, and when we'd come back down, they asked to take a picture before striding off into the streets.

When I talked about it later with Ivan, it occurred to me that this kind of cultural pragmatism is pretty understandable, and that maybe it helped to explain the no-nonsense mind-set of Julio and the men at the bridge. In a country where cartel kidnappings and paramilitary violence are relatively recent memories, "adventure" as a concept simply doesn't have much cachet. If Colombians choose to value prudence and *seguridad* over the romance of the trail or the open water, then I suppose, who can really blame them?

On our third and supposedly final evening in Honda, we were drinking shots of aguardiente, Colombia's anise-flavored national liqueur, with some of the town fathers we had met at City Hall. We'd run into them at a downtown tavern, where they offered to teach us how to play *tejo*, a uniquely Colombian bar sport that involves throwing rocks at paper packets filled with gunpowder. The head of the chamber of commerce was there, and after several shots, he casually mentioned that our boat was going to be a little delayed. It would be two more days before we could leave for Girardot. Three at the most. Possibly four. But he was working on it, he assured us, and he would stop by Ivan's as soon as he had an update.

I wasn't thrilled about the delay, but up until then, we'd been hiring our boats in accordance with Thompson's Law of Travel Economics, paying steep fees to boatmen who had no reason to travel upstream except for two gringos who were inexplicably opposed to bus travel. It was all starting to take its toll on my finances, and the prospect of paying only for gas was too good to pass up. If it meant a few more days loitering in laid-back Honda, I decided, I would just have to grin and bear it.

Sky, meanwhile, had no qualms about sticking around. That evening, one of Ricardo's friends was opening a new nightclub, and we had been invited to the inaugural debauch. I was hesitant, but after all the hospitality we'd been shown, Sky had convinced me that it would be rude not to go. So the plan had been to make a brief appearance, then head back to Ivan's, ready to hit the river bright and early the next morning. Now, with the chamber head's revelation, the night was comparatively young. What's more, Sky had taken a shine to a lady friend of Ricardo's—an absolute bombshell who had flirted with him mercilessly at Cirrosis and looked like a cross between Natalie Wood and Salma Hayek. Needless to say, she would be in attendance at the club's opening night. So off we went.

The nightclub Las Tecas—which translates roughly and grandiosely to "The Archives"—looked like a discarded set piece from *Miami Vice,* bedecked with fake palms and so much neon that the room hummed audibly during the brief gaps between earsplitting reggaeton anthems. A sign above the backlit bar proclaimed that tonight's party would feature BIUTIFUL STREEPERS. We settled into a nook with Ricardo's crew, surrounding a table on which the proud new club owner had set an unopened bottle of aguardiente and a tray full of shot glasses. When that bottle was empty, he produced another one, and another after that. And that's pretty much how things went for the couple of hours I managed to stick out the party, mostly chatting with Ricardo about American pop music in a pidgin of his bad English and my bad Spanish.

I left the party around the same time that a topless blond woman came walking across the bar, spraying a mystery liquor into people's mouths with a squirt gun that looked like an AK-47. I thanked Ricardo and the club owner, shared a round of cheek kisses with the women at our table, and told Sky that I'd see him the next day at Ivan's.

Except when I woke up late the next morning, Sky wasn't at Ivan's.

Look at you, Don Juan, I thought admiringly, and I left him a note before heading out to find coffee and an arepa.

I spent much of that day sitting at a sidewalk café, drinking bad instant coffee and working my way through a long magazine article in Spanish about the international flak that Colombia was taking over its military-base agreement with the United States. There was still no sign of Sky when I walked back to the hotel in the midafternoon. His cell number went straight to voice mail, and Ivan said that he hadn't come around. I laughed it off, but after a couple more hours and a few more unanswered calls, my amusement started to drift into concern. I didn't have Ricardo's number, I realized, but somehow I had ended up with the club owner's from the night before.

He answered after a few rings. Our conversation was stilted, but he told me that he'd last seen Sky and Ricardo getting into a cab together sometime after dawn. Was I sure he hadn't come back to the hotel? Positive, I said.

"Then I'll come get you," the club owner told me. "We can go look for him."

A half hour later, he pulled up to Ivan's in a silver Camry with a prominent spoiler, which I'd seen parked outside the night before. In the passenger seat was a girl who'd sat at our table. Both of them looked worried. I hopped in, and they tried to reconstruct for me what they remembered of the wee hours. They spoke quickly and talked over each other, and it was hard for me to keep track of their pronouns. Sky had danced with a girl who they both agreed was crazy. Or maybe her boyfriend was crazy, I wasn't quite sure. At some point, somebody had been slapped—possibly Sky, possibly the girl sitting in the front seat. Everyone was drunk, they said, and things got a little tense. That much I understood.

"*Dios mio,*" the girl up front kept muttering, which made me more nervous than I had been. You don't understand, she said, fingering the beads on her necklace—some people here will take advantage of a drunken gringo. Kidnappings still happened from time to time, and it occurred to me that everyone in town knew who we were, the famed traveling American journalists. "*Dios mio,*" the girl repeated. "*Dios mio.*"

The club owner drove in what seemed like arbitrary circles, stopping occasionally to ask acquaintances if they'd seen a tall gringo matching Sky's description. No one had. The two of them made a half dozen phone calls on my cell (the only one with minutes), asking revelers from the night before whether they'd been with Sky or Ricardo after the club emptied out. No dice there. After an hour of this, we headed back to Ivan's and simply stood outside, deliberating. By now it was after seven p.m. We decided that I would wait through the night, and if we still hadn't heard from

Sky by morning, we would go to the police. No one had any better plan.

The potential seriousness of the situation began sinking in with me, and two thoughts passed through my head in short succession: *I may not be leaving Honda anytime soon.* Followed closely by: *And when I do, it might be without Sky.*

And that, of course, was the moment that he and Ricardo chose to come wheeling around the corner.

"Heeey!" the two of them cried, clearly still in the waning throes of the previous night's party. Both were disheveled, with dark bags under their eyes and overdue for a shower, but otherwise no worse for wear.

"Dios mio!" cried the girl from the club.

"Dude, where have you *been*?" I asked.

"Hanging out with Ricardo, man." Sky shrugged. He sat down on the hotel stoop with an exhausted grunt and ran his hand through his hair. "We ate some food, took a nap for a while, hung out at his place. Then we went and played pool. What have you been doing?"

I shook my head apologetically at the club owner, who was going through some version of the same thing with Ricardo in Spanish. Sky exhaled shakily, and undid a button on his dress shirt, which was already half-unbuttoned and stained with twenty-four hours of sweat.

"Bro, I need some sleep," he said with a laugh, leaning back on his palms. "Oh, and also, I think I lost my cell phone."

Ricardo must have sensed my exasperation, or he'd maybe just been told that we were several hours away from calling the police. He walked over and gripped my shoulders in a way that was meant to be reassuring, looking me squarely in the eyes.

"I am with him all of the day," he said in English, his tone somber. He shook his head slowly. "I am never stop watch-ing him."

Then he and the others climbed into the metallic Camry, and with a farewell honk they sped off, leaving the illustri-ous gringo journalists slumped outside of the Hotel Turivan.

IV

"Mr. Brian?"

Ivan's voice woke me from a sound sleep the next morning. He was standing again in the doorway to our room.

"Sorry to bother you, but I think there is someone wait-ing for you outside."

I opened my eyes groggily. Oh, sweet Jesus, I thought, not again. It was Groundhog Day, and I was Bill Murray, and I was never, ever leaving Honda.

Lucas waddled behind me as I shuffled to the front door, where the head of the chamber of commerce was standing with his hat in his hands, the morning sun reflecting off his bald head. He wore round glasses and had a white mustache that drooped a little at the corners, like a Latino Wilford Brimley.

The chamber head wished me good morning and asked if Sky was also available. Still sleeping, I told him, without adding that Sky would probably be sleeping all day. So the chamber head spoke slowly, knowing that my Spanish was far inferior to Sky's. He had made a mistake, he said, and he was very sorry. The boat to Girardot was actually going to cost roughly three times the amount he had quoted us. He sincerely regretted his error. It was a very nice boat, how-ever, and it could leave in two days' time. Possibly three.

The sun was a huge exposed bulb that protruded from the

grain silo of the shuttered old brewery. I squinted and shaded my eyes as I thanked the man, took his cell phone number, and said I would discuss it with Sky. The minute that I shut the heavy wooden door, Thompson's words from the beer barge rang in my ears: "You get what you pay for . . . and I ain't paid." Both he and Márquez made their journeys up the Magdalena inside of eight days. Sky and I had been following the river for two weeks now, and there was no telling when we would get back on the water. A bus ticket to Girardot, meanwhile, cost less than another night's stay at Ivan's hotel, and it could get us there by lunchtime. I sat down in the cool of the courtyard and asked Lucas what to do. He tucked his beak into his mottled brown feathers and sighed.

"Mr. Brian?" Ivan came around the corner from the front room, where he'd overheard my conversation with Wilford Brimley. "I can help you get to Girardot."

Ivan understood the quest, he said. Who wouldn't want to float the historic passenger route of the Magdalena? He had a small wood-and-fiberglass lancha, better suited for scenic spins around Honda than a hundred-mile journey upriver and back, but it would be his pleasure to make the trip with us. He would charge us only for the gas, he said, and leave his housekeeper behind to staff the hotel and feed Lucas. We could leave the very next morning.

It was an act of pure generosity, and I was touched. When I shook Ivan's hand, a broad grin spread across his face, like he'd been nervous I was going to say no. Thank you, I told him. We couldn't ask for a better guide. He was happy to do it, Ivan said. It would be an adventure.

It wouldn't be fair to blame everything that happened next on Sky's Casanova gallantry—or on the mesmeric curves of his Honda heartthrob—but both of them got us off to a late start the next morning. While Ivan and I stood holding our bags, Sky put us off for two hours while he ran around town, arranging to have flowers delivered and a song dedicated to his crush on Ricardo's radio station. I tried to keep the wait in perspective: after five days in Honda, if one flurry of last-ditch courtship was the price of a ticket out of town, then I was happy to pay it.

It was past noon by the time we lifted anchor, but the day was cool and clear. All three of us were in high spirits, never mind the delay. Ivan brought along a boy he called Sardino to help him man the boat, and Sky and I laughed while we answered Sardino's wide-eyed questions about *los estados unidos*. The tiny motorboat bucked like a rodeo mule as we plowed through Honda's rapids, and by the time we reached the city limits, we were all soaked and a little bit giddy.

A few hours upstream, we stopped for gas at a riverside village called Ambalema. Near the docks was a ramshackle cerveza stand, and the three of us sat down for beers while Sardino went off to fill a half dozen gas canisters. Ivan pointed across the water to the far shore.

"On that side of the river was my grandfather's farm once," he said, "before the *narcotraficantes* came in the 1990s."

This whole stretch of river was effectively a war zone then, Ivan said, and as we slaked our thirst, he told us candidly about the bad old days of the '90s and beyond. Industry might have abandoned the Magdalena around the time of Thompson's journey, but the narcotraffickers who came to prominence afterward still saw the river's value as a transportation corridor. One of Pablo Escobar's closest captains controlled this stretch for a time, Ivan explained. When he died, there were rumors of money and weapons hidden around Ivan's grandfather's farm. Some pretty unsavory types passed through, searching for loot that was never found. Then the paramilitaries came in, and they picked up where the narcos left off, taking over abandoned farms and moving money and drugs up- and downriver. Ivan had an uncle who hung on to the family farm for as long as he could, until the only people left in the area, Ivan said, "were all full of nerves and delusions." Finally, the uncle gave in and sold the farm cheap.

The bartender chimed in as he passed out another round, remembering a time when he wouldn't have crossed the river for fear of his life. Ivan nodded. President Uribe had gotten rid of the narcotraffickers, he said admiringly, and anyone who criticized the US–Colombia alliance didn't understand the difference this had made in the lives of many rural Colombians. Both Ivan and the bartender had enthusiastically supported the amendment permitting Uribe's second term, and had it been possible, they said, they would have given him a third term too.

Our couple of beers turned into three or four, and the bartender brought over a complimentary round of aguardiente. Ivan bought a beer for Sardino, who laughed and tried to tell us he was seventeen, then admitted to being fifteen, then twelve. When I asked Ivan why we hadn't encountered any of the vicious insects that Thompson had described so vividly, he grinned and told us that Uribe had gotten rid of those, too. We laughed and traded shots. All around us, the peaks of the Cordillera Oriental rose up amber against the sky.

By the time we got back on the water, everyone was feeling great. Sky's wooing and our impromptu happy hour had put us hours behind, so Ivan cranked the outboard, and we sped upriver in the fading sunlight, enjoying the encroaching mountain scenery. At our approach, the elegant *garzas* rose up from their perches among the reeds and came to rest on the nearby branches, drifting upward with all the grace and urgency of tissue paper caught in the wind.

We were fifteen miles shy of Girardot when Ivan's engine suddenly made a sound like something out of a blacksmith's workshop, and the boat went into a full-tilt clockwise spin. Sardino scrambled to kill the motor. Sky and I reflexively grabbed the oars. Mine barely skimmed the surface of the water as the lancha leaned hard to starboard, listing skyward at a forty-five-degree angle. Ivan grunted loudly at the wheel as he tried to straighten us out.

"Towards the shore!" he yelled. As the boat slowly regained its equilibrium, Sky and I paddled hard across the current, straining to keep the fast-moving water from sweeping us back downstream.

After a tense few minutes, we dropped anchor next to a rocky beach, where everyone simply sat still for a while, catching their breath. A transom bracket had cracked, leaving the outboard motor dangling uselessly from the stern. As Ivan and Sardino examined the damage, Sky and I clambered ashore, shaking off the river spray and our aguardiente fog. He could fix it with rope, Ivan said eventually, but our speed was going to suffer something fierce. Late as it was, there was no way to make Girardot by nightfall.

The map suggested a small village nearby, but no one could remember whether we'd passed it already, so we motored a short distance upstream, keeping our eyes on the banks. Instead of a village, we came to a small farm plot on the east side of the river, where a somber papaya farmer and his family were sitting outside in the encroaching dusk. They eyeballed us silently as we approached and dropped anchor. None of them seemed to know quite what to make of the ragtag crew disembarking from this tiny boat. Sky and I nodded hello, and Sardino offered a tentative wave.

Ivan waded ashore and consulted with the farmer for a few minutes, then came back to say we'd been offered food and hammocks for the night. We all clambered out of the boat and shook hands, changing into dry clothes and settling in with the family on a set of wooden benches and mismatched patio furniture.

The farmer's wife brought us coffee and plates of *pollo con arroz,* and we tried to make chitchat while we ate. Our host was a large, impassive man, and heavily inked. On one arm I saw a graceful Pegasus taking flight; on the other was a hairy and grotesquely detailed spider. He'd been in the Colombian military once, he explained slowly, but now he raised papayas here on the Magdalena and drove a cab a few days a week in Girardot for extra cash. A handful of related families lived there on his farm, a sort of *cooperativa.* When Sky asked why he left the military, he was quiet for a moment, chewing on a forkful of rice. *"Violaciones de derechos humanos,"* he finally muttered. Human-rights violations. And that pretty much put an end to that conversation.

Still, he and his family were kind to let us stay. We could sputter into Girardot in the morning, we decided, where a friend of Ivan's could retrieve him, Sardino, and the boat. So we settled into our hammocks beneath the stars, the gurgling river within earshot. Around midnight, the skies suddenly opened up with a tropical storm, and we all roused sleepily to settle inside on the farmer's dirt floor. No one thought much about the boat anchored up along shore, covered only partially by a fiberglass awning and filling slowly with rainwater.

The next morning, I learned what it was like to see the river as an obstacle, robbed of its romance. The sunrise sight of Ivan's submerged boat was as surreal as anything from Márquez, and twice as disquieting as Thompson's gruesome bugs. I woke up and walked outside shortly after Ivan, and I found him just standing on the lawn, looking out sadly at the river, from which only the rear half of his small boat was protruding. The rain was still coming down hard, and that part was disappearing fast. Ivan and I looked at each other for just a moment. Then he ran toward the river as I turned back to wake Sky and the others.

Within minutes, I was fully immersed in the dark swell of the Magdalena River, breath held and heaving against the fiberglass hull of Ivan's half-submerged boat. Somewhere to my right was Ivan, and I could feel the force of him as we strained against the current to keep his lancha from capsizing completely. The shouts of the men onshore sounded thin beneath the gasoline-contaminated water. My nostrils stung. My sinuses burned.

The irony of the situation struck me while my hands blindly scoured the river bottom for one of the full gas canisters we'd had on board. Sky and I had set out upon the Magdalena hoping in part to gauge its ecological health. Now here we were, just miles from our terminus, leaking fuel into it at an alarming rate. When I came up for air, I saw my reflection, wavering and distorted on the water's oily surface. I heard the swish of the rain through the long-leafed palms. Then I shut my eyes and plunged back underwater.

Don't think of this as a catastrophe, I told myself. *Think of it as a rite of passage. Think of it as a baptism.*

We worked for hours to pull the lancha up from the current—Sky and the farmers all heaving at ropes, Ivan and I straining underwater against the hull. It was early afternoon before we recovered enough of the boat to start bailing. Sky's hands were lacerated, and I reeked of petroleum.

Ivan, however, kept his cool throughout, and as I watched

him take charge of the situation that day, I felt myself coming to an understanding about the Magdalena and its people. As was probably true in both Márquez's day and Thompson's, most *magdalenos* seem to regard the river simply as an entity in flux, something to be enjoyed one day and struggled against the next. For better or for worse, life along the Magdalena just seems to foster more stubborn will than it does romantic appreciation. It's an adaptive mind-set, and the ecosystem occasionally suffers for it, but it's an outlook that fortifies people, that helps them to function in a sometimes violent and capricious society.

Hours later, a friend of Ivan's arrived with a pickup, and Sky and I slumped into the truck bed with Sardino, riding in defeat the last ten miles into Girardot. For the second time in two days I found myself identifying with Thompson's bleak disposition—specifically with his river-weary assertion that "if I ever get to Bogotá, I may never leave." He wrote nothing at all about the end of his journey on the Magdalena River, but somehow I imagined that it was more jubilant than ours.

Girardot itself looked bland as we drove into town, passing big-box stores and cheap-looking resorts for vacationing Bogotans. We parted too hastily with Ivan at a downtown intersection, grateful for the time we'd shared but feeling awkward about the damage to his boat. By then, we'd all run out of things to say anyway, and Ivan smiled with resignation as we told him good-bye—a smile that said, *Well, I guess I got myself into this.* Sardino was wearing a shirt that I'd loaned him after our battle with the sunken boat. It had been my grandfather's, but I didn't have the heart to ask for it back.

That evening, Sky and I stood on a railroad bridge, too tired to drink the celebratory champagne we'd bought in

Honda. Beside us was a historic depot that once welcomed steamboat passengers to board the seventy-five-mile train ride to Bogotá. We looked away from the bridge to the south, where the Magdalena ascended another 250 miles to its source in the Colombian Massif. I imagined skimming the surface of the water for the length of that trip, hovering above it as it grew fast and shallow in the Andes, then watching as the river reclaimed its youth, dwindling away into a thin mountain stream, a trickle, and then nothing.

CHAPTER THREE

Sex, Violence, and Golf

Somewhere below us, in the narrow streets
that are lined by the white adobe block-
houses of the urban peasantry, a strange
hail was rattling on the roofs.

—*National Observer*, August 19, 1963

I

Sky and I passed our remaining time together riding out a few additional small crises. By sunset in Girardot, we both felt sick with headaches and chills. I chalked it up to having spent our morning submerged in a cold and angry river, and we spent the night wallowing in our motel room, eating pizza and watching a Jeff Bridges movie that turned out to be about a sinking boat.

By morning, I'd made a full recovery, but Sky looked rough—pale and jittery, with bags beneath his eyes. On the short bus trip into Bogotá, he coughed and groaned, too tired and achy even to point out the attractive women seated nearby.

"I had better not have the swine flu," he croaked, slouched against the Plexiglas window. "I have a plane to catch, and if they don't let me on, I'm going to be in real trouble."

It's hard to remember now, but at the time, swine flu was the international apocalyptic disease du jour, and we'd been hearing about it regularly since Barranquilla. Former president Uribe had been diagnosed with the H1N1 virus just three weeks earlier, after falling ill during the same UNASUR conference we'd watched on the bus. Since then, we'd heard rumors that Colombia's whole cabinet was afflicted. Then it was the whole legislature. It was a brutal pandemic, warned the sporadic TV news we'd seen along the way, and it was sweeping unstoppably across Bogotá. But we didn't put much stock in such reports, since Colombian media is in no way above American-cable-news–style sensationalism, and since ratings-wise, contagious respiratory diseases rank right up there with earthquakes and blond-girl kidnappings.

Our bus shuddered up the steep grades into Colombia's

high-mountain capital, and by the time we found a cheap hostel in the colonial district, Sky was bleary-eyed and incoherent. I was helping him carry his bags into our dorm room when we both noticed the large-print poster stapled to the door:

SWINE FLU IS DANGEROUS AND HIGHLY CONTAGIOUS!
SYMPTOMS INCLUDE SUDDEN ONSET OF FEVER,
CHILLS, COUGH, SORE THROAT, CONGESTION,
AND BODY ACHES.

"Well, shit," Sky said slowly, sounding a bit dazed. His face had lost its remaining traces of color. "Dude, am I going to die?"

I tried to sound upbeat. "Probably not," I said. But the symptoms did seem to line up, and I imagined he was right about the airlines taking swine flu seriously.

So we opted to play it safe, and within a few hours of arriving in the cold, gray capital, we were standing outside of an even colder, grayer hospital, watching ambulances fight their way up the crowded street toward the ER.

I have never cared much for hospitals. I grew up just down the street from one, and looking back, it seems like someone I knew was always in it—an uncle following a stroke, my dad with a kidney stone, a classmate after a near-fatal asthma attack. The hospital's boxy brick exterior loomed oppressively over our neighborhood, and it made for a steady stream of sad-looking people pacing up and down the block. Today, as a perennially uninsured adult, I've come to think of hospitals as strongholds of disease rather than places where I might receive treatment for one.

That everyone pacing outside Bogotá's hospital wore a surgical mask only heightened my unease. This is a creepy thing to see in any town—a crowd full of half faces, noses and mouths hidden behind paper muzzles of pale green. I felt sick just looking at the place.

Sky was already a goner, I decided, but there was still hope for me. If I hadn't already contracted swine flu from a month of close quarters with the photographer, I would sure as hell pick it up in there. I grasped Sky's shoulders in what I hoped was a brotherly manner and gave him an encouraging send-off.

"Best of luck in there, buddy. I'll be in the café across the street."

If you must seek medical treatment abroad, you can do a lot worse than Colombia. Statistically speaking, Sky was just one of 15,000 or so foreign visitors who see the inside of a Colombian medical facility each year, and the great majority of these actually schedule their own appointments. Medical tourism is big business in Colombia, where the expertise of doctors is high and the costs (compared with Europe and the United States) are staggeringly low. A hip replacement that might set you back $50,000 in the United States costs only around $9,000 in Colombia. A gastric-bypass surgery in Colombia runs around $15,000, compared with ten times that in the States. According to Colombia's Trade Ministry, about half the country's medical tourists come for either bypasses or heart surgery.

Of course, Colombia is probably more famous for the 10 percent who come seeking plastic surgery. It is this sector, in any case, that the country's tourism industry seems most eager to promote. During my time in Bogotá, headlines there trumpeted the construction of a brand-new cosmetic tourism facility on the city's glitzy north side. When completed, the $19 million Bosque Beauty Garden will be

Colombia's first hotel/surgical center, appealing to those who seek both lofted luxury and lifted brows.

That plastic surgery is popular in metro Colombia is not a fact that requires much support from government stats or medical journals. In certain neighborhoods, the signs and billboards for boob jobs seem almost to outnumber the total number of available boobs. And if the advertising doesn't tip you off, the suspiciously high number of suspiciously round buttocks probably will. Colombians take beauty and body image very seriously, and it's their proud reputation for superficiality that attracts so many nose-job nomads. Sky had actually explained this to me during our very first meeting back in Barranquilla, during an opening soliloquy about the virtues of Colombian women, and I'd seen plenty of evidence since. Yes, there were the ubiquitous ads for plastic surgery, but there was also the country's conspicuous obsession with beauty pageants. I'd flipped past half a dozen of them on motel TVs and seen pictures of winners splayed across every supermarket newsstand we'd run across. On Mompós, we'd caught the tail end of a parade dedicated to the town's *reinas*—pageant-winning "princesses," all dolled up like child victims of reality-TV moms and carted around on streamer-lined floats. Even as I settled into the café across the street from the hospital, it was hard not to notice how explicitly sexualized were the soda posters and the ice-cream ads—collagened lips pressed against Coke bottles, buxom young women simulating fellatio on their cones.

Even fifty years ago, Thompson had noted approvingly that Colombia had a "wholly different sexual climate" from the United States. It was, in fact, one of the things he'd most admired about the country's Caribbean coast. In his letters, he writes admiringly about "the fine, lusty tension in the air" in what he'd seen so far of Latin America. In general, Thompson's letters from the continent exhibit a healthy libido. He writes candidly, for instance, of·having visited a brothel in Barranquilla, but he also seems to have a sociological interest in sex that transcends the mere chasing of tail. With anthropological detail, his letters describe the relationships among Colombian men, their formal prostitutes, and their informal mistresses. Then as now, prostitution was legal, but its legality conferred none of the borderline respectability enjoyed today by sex workers in progressive enclaves like, say, the Netherlands. It was one thing to legally patronize a working girl, Thompson explains, but quite another to be seen in public with one. The mistresses, meanwhile, were considered "nice girls"—debutantes who kept their bedroom exploits clandestine. Specimens from either group, Thompson told an editor, "will knock your eyes out."

Sipping a beer in the café and trying not to ogle the ice-cream models, I thought, not for the first time, of how much the young Thompson reminded me of Sky, and I realized how much I was going to miss the rakish photographer when he was gone.

When Sky emerged eventually from the hospital's creepy rotating doors, he had a paper mask stretched across his face.

That's it, I thought. So much for the Thompson Trail. They're going to quarantine us with the legislature, for sure.

But Sky, it turned out, did not have the swine flu. After a long wait and an hour of poking and prodding, the doctors had diagnosed him with a workaday respiratory infection. They shot him up with penicillin, tied a mask on him, and sent him on his way. His total fee for the consultation, a blood test, and the drugs? About $30. Slightly less than the cost of our bus tickets from Girardot.

B ut there were, as they say in the medical community, complications. That night, we had a date planned with three of the lovely belles of Bogotá. One was a friend of a friend, a born *bogotana* and commercial filmmaker who, like me, had once spent a summer working in Yellowstone National Park. We'd arranged to have a drink, and she'd invited friends—because you don't, I suppose, go to a bar alone with two strange foreign men. Sky took an afternoon nap at the hostel, and by the disco hour, his penicillin seemed to be working its magic.

We met the girls at a dim Italian bar down the street. They were a smart and curious bunch, all in their thirties and fluent in English, and the conversation flowed easily. We talked first about politics (I was learning that Colombians love to talk politics, especially with Americans), then about places we'd traveled, then about security and violence across Colombia.

We were actually just delving into the topic of Colombian sexuality when Sky started looking uncharacteristically ill at ease. The girls (all three beautiful) were describing the pressure they'd felt even as teenagers to take seriously the prospect of plastic surgery. It was pitched, they said, as a sort of career option—an investment for Colombian women in their future success and security. I was fascinated and a little appalled. Sky, meanwhile, just looked distracted. He started tugging at his collar and rolling his neck, like his clothes had suddenly become too tight. We were on the verge of ordering another round when he leaned over and muttered to me.

"I'm sorry, dude," he said. "Stay and have fun, but I have to go back to the hostel."

"Why?" I asked, surprised. "Come on, we've earned a night off, and I think everyone's having a good time."

"It's not that," he said, now clearly wincing. "I think I'm allergic to whatever kind of shot they gave me back at the hospital."

The doctors had indeed asked him about this. He'd mentioned it to me on the taxi ride back to the hostel. Bleary as he had been, he could only remember that, yes, he was allergic to some kind of antibiotic, but he couldn't recall whether it was penicillin or something else. He had guessed "something else." It was penicillin.

So we bid our dates a hasty good night, and I followed Sky back to the hostel out of a sense of moral obligation. For the next several hours, he writhed and itched on the couch in the common room. I tried plying him with the celebratory champagne that we hadn't drunk in Girardot, but he wouldn't take any, and for all I know, alcohol and antibiotic allergies don't mix anyway. So I fed him a handful of over-the-counter allergy pills from my first-aid kit, and eventually they knocked him out.

When Sky left for the airport the next day, he was a shell of a man, groggy and exhausted, but at least his skin was no longer on fire. We waited outside for a taxi as squads of young *bogotanos* whizzed by on motor scooters, and we kept our good-byes businesslike. I thanked him sincerely for everything—for tagging along on an adventurous impulse, for his superior Spanish and his sense of humor, for dragging me out to bars in Honda when I'd rather have stayed inside with Ivan and his duck. He gave me some parting advice about choosing the right buses, promised to keep in touch, and reminded me that the girls in Cali—my next stop—were among the most beautiful in the world. When the cab pulled up, we shook hands. Then he was in it and away.

A few hours later, I got an e-mail, sent from his laptop. "I am in the Bogotá airport in some state," it said, ". . . a sleep-deprived, caffeinated soft reality. I felt compelled to write you. I want you to know that this trip was an incredible experience for me, and the experiences we had I will cherish for a long time.

"Your friend and fellow wonk, Sky."

II

Hunter Thompson did not much care for Bogotá. The place seemed dull and sterile, bereft of that crackling, sultry tension he'd felt along the coast. He complained of "a sexual deadness in the air that makes me feel I might be locked up for looking at women on the street." Everyone around him wore a coat and tie, he groused, and they seemed always to be on some kind of official business. He hated his hotel, an Art Deco monster called the Imperial that looked out across the street at Colombia's presidential palace. It had no hot water, the staff hassled him about his casual attire, and the block was surrounded by churches with constantly ringing bells—"a mad clanging every five or ten minutes." To top it off, he was suffering through his first case of dysentery, a malady that would make anyone grumpy. His perpetual digestive troubles would actually become a running theme (no pun intended) in all of his letters from South America.

The pale yellow building that used to be the Imperial Hotel sits on a corner of two cobblestone streets in the heart of Bogotá's government district. It's a three-story building that went up in 1928, with arched doorways and rounded corners, and today it houses the offices of the Ministry of Culture. Since the presidential palace is just across the road, the whole block is gated and patrolled by armed soldiers, scrutinizing pedestrians and checking bags. It's off-limits to cars, and the sidewalk is closed as well, deemed too close to the palace and lined with more grim-looking soldiers. People walking past the Imperial Hotel today are no longer wearing coats and ties, but it's still a pretty joyless stretch of the city.

One block north of the former Imperial, the Plaza Bolívar is the center of Bogotá's historic district, a windswept concrete square where the pigeons tend to outnumber the people. I strolled through on my first afternoon alone in Bogotá, after scouting out Thompson's old hotel. A few dozen government workers were loitering there on their lunch break. A couple of old men played chess on a blanket, and one lonely harlequin mime was halfheartedly shaking balloon animals at passing families. Like much of Bogotá, the Plaza Bolívar is regal but none too colorful. It's paved with slate-gray tiles and crowded with dusty gray pigeons. On all sides are imposing, historic buildings—the Justice Palace, the Senate chambers, Bogotá's City Hall, and the towering Catedral Primada—and each one of these is its own mottle of grays, browns, and beiges. Stately and impressive, yes, but uniformly drab.

So my eyes were drawn immediately to a scatter of neon splashes on the cathedral facade. It's a breathtaking building, a two-hundred-year-old neoclassical relic designed by a Spanish mason-turned-monk named Domingo de Petrés. Petrés is to grandiose churches in Colombia what Frank Lloyd Wright is to weird rich people's houses in the United States. He's responsible for dozens of landmarks all around the country, but the Catedral Primada is his masterwork, an ornate stone structure with pedestaled statues and a pair of symmetrical 140-foot towers. There's an exquisite grace to

the swoop of the stone between the towers and the upper facade. It's a stirring sight really, especially to a guy who grew
up attending boxy Protestant churches with all the architectural flair of suburban post offices. The Catedral Primada
is striking and imposing at the same time, looming over the
square like a beautiful but austere librarian—you can almost
hear it whispering *sshhh!* to pedestrians in the plaza.

So the festive, hypercolor paint splotches were pretty
conspicuous. There were at least thirty of them, spaced out
at irregular intervals from the front doorway to the feet of a
stone Virgin perched fifty feet above. On the steps out front,
a young military police officer stood at attention, his orders
apparently to hold a large gun and scowl. In my politest
gringo stutter, I asked him what was up with the paint stains.

"Ah, señor," he said, and his scowl gave way to a kindly
look of surprise, "how long have you been in Bogotá?"

Not long, I admitted.

"Well, these marks are from paintball guns," he said,
briefly shouldering his assault rifle in a rather alarming pan-
tomime. "You see, the students gathered here in the square
to protest, oh, several months ago. There were many, many
people. And some of them, well"—he shrugged and smiled,
gesturing back at the cathedral—"some of them get excited."

That turns out to be an understatement. Months earlier, student protestors had effectively brought Bogotá to
a standstill, organizing weeks of massive demonstrations
that brought as many as 30,000 people into Bolívar Square.
The issue at hand was a set of proposed education reforms
that many saw as opening the door to the privatization of
Colombia's university system. As it is, only about a third of
Colombia's college-age population is enrolled (compared
with more than two-thirds in the United States), and protestors feared that more private-sector involvement in higher

ed would raise education costs while weakening standards. More than 500,000 students and some educators boycotted classes for over a month, effectively halting the Colombian academic year. Roadblocks by students and sympathizers stopped traffic all across the capital, and solidarity strikes by taxi drivers worsened the gridlock. And yes, as the soldier explained, there was quite a bit of vandalism. Mostly your garden-variety graffiti, the kind that already covers every blank surface in Bogotá, but also the paintball guns. He wasn't sure whether the stains could be removed.

"Did things get violent?" I asked.

Mostly no, he said. Here and there the police used tear gas and water cannons to disperse the crowds, but only after protestors started throwing rocks. For the most part, the police just stood by and watched. "Over there and over there," he said, pointing to the steps of the Justice Palace and the Senate building, on either side of the square. Turning around, I tried to imagine 30,000 people crammed into the sleepy plaza. A pair of Japanese tourists was quietly tossing corn kernels to the pigeons nearby. The chess players had assembled a small audience of geriatric onlookers. It was hard to envision a mob scene, but there was no denying the fluorescent scars it had left on the cathedral.

"So what happened?" I asked. "Where is everyone now?"

"Back in school," the soldier said. I heard a trace of condescension in his voice, perhaps because college enrollment in Colombia allows young men to avoid their otherwise compulsory military service. "The students won, you see. The government backed down." Then the whiff of condescension descended on me. "Colombia is a country where the government *listens* to its people."

Over the next couple of days, I noticed fading protest graffiti all over town: EDUCACIÓN POR TODOS! (with an anarchist's circle-and-slash around the *A*). ESTUDIANTES RE-SISTE! On the bus one afternoon, I passed the headquarters of the national oil company, Ecopetrol, itself the site of recent protests. It looked positively tie-dyed, speckled with paint-ball bursts in every imaginable hue. In Colombia, I figured, this must be a fairly common form of civil disobedience.

Of course, large-scale strikes and protests are hardly a new phenomenon in Bogotá. They were, in fact, keeping Thompson awake in his drafty room at the Imperial fifty years back. On June 6, 1962, Thompson looked out his hotel window to see a horde of students demonstrating outside the presidential palace. They were striking in solidarity with students in Barranquilla, who'd been agitating for weeks in favor of university autonomy and the right to form student councils. Student leaders had been expelled, prompting street riots in the coastal city that left several hospitalized. Thompson read in the paper about tense standoffs there between protestors and law enforcement.

"[Yesterday] in Barranquilla," he wrote, "the army tackled a student protest march with clubs and gas, and it was only because the students fled that nobody was shot."

In Bogotá, the demonstration outside Thompson's window became a mob, with protestors throwing rocks at the archbishop's palace and various newspaper offices before police managed to disperse the crowd. Several unions around town were also striking in support of the students, and within a week, workers from a pair of unrelated textile and retail strikes would take to the streets as well.

"One strike after another," Thompson wrote, after several days in the capital. "Students, busmen, bondsmen— forever striking, and it is all I can do to wander around in the mobs and get photos that nobody will ever use."

For all his griping, that quote actually reveals Thompson

as a pretty ballsy young reporter. Colombian street protests in 1962 were no joke, seeing as you didn't have to look back far for instances where police were as likely to use rifles as tear gas. At the time, Colombia was just emerging from a bloody decade and a half known as La Violencia, a period of savage conflict between those who identified with the country's Liberal and Conservative parties. Between 1948 and 1964, more than 200,000 Colombians were killed, mostly (and most gruesomely) by death squads in the little-policed countryside, but also during mob skirmishes and massacres in the cities. Troops opened fire and killed ten students during one protest in 1954. Two years later, at a bullfight in Bogotá, government forces killed eight spectators and wounded a hundred others who had jeered at then-dictator Gustavo Rojas Pinilla. In 1957, the military killed another fifty protestors during the nationwide strikes that eventually drove Pinilla from office.

None of which deterred Thompson from heading into the fray, although it wasn't without anxiety. While he knew that Colombia had been a few years without a major urban massacre, this left open the possibility that the country was simply overdue.

"The cops are what give me the creeps," he wrote. "To look at them in the jackboots is bad enough, but to see photos of them firing wildly into mobs of students is a bit unreal. Running them into corners and piling up bodies three deep—this has happened often enough to make me feel nervous even standing near a demonstration."

The kids shooting paintball guns at the Catedral Primada are the direct ideological descendants of the student protestors outside Thompson's hotel. Both groups trace their lineage back to the undisputed patriarch of Colombian civil

disobedience, a fiery reformist politician named Jorge Gaitán. Gaitán was shot three times in broad daylight on a bustling Bogotá sidewalk in 1948, and his assassination birthed
Colombia's tradition of populist street protest—along with
La Violencia, the FARC, and arguably even the very specter
of Castroite communism that attracted Thompson to South
America.

The perky English-speaking guide at Bogotá's Gaitán
House Museum thinks that Jorge Gaitán was *amazing.* She
mentioned this three or four times as she walked me through
the former education and labor minister's historic home, an
unassuming white-stucco colonial in a university neighborhood. It was simply *amazing,* she said, how one man's oratory could bring together Colombia's peasants and urban
working classes to oppose the country's powerful oligarchy.
It was also *amazing* how a young lawyer could stand up to
big, international businesses after a *campesino* massacre on a
plantation owned by a US banana grower. She read me one of
Gaitán's most famous quotes, often deployed during his two
unsuccessful presidential campaigns: "The people are superior to their leaders." Wasn't that an *amazing* thing to say?

As the college-age docent guided me from room to
room, she cooed over various artifacts and extolled Gaitán's
contributions to Colombian people. As a national minister and mayor of Bogotá, he'd launched literacy initiatives
and school-lunch programs. He'd organized government
giveaways of shoes and clothing. And while he was known
as a champion of the common people, Gaitán was an educated man who'd studied in Europe. We strolled through
his library of more than 3,500 multilingual texts. He was
also a health nut, a jogger before there really were joggers, and when we walked into his former study, my young
guide proudly pointed to one of those old unexplainable

vibrating-belt exercise machines, tucked into a corner. So *amazing,* she sighed.

When Gaitán was shot by an unstable drifter during his second campaign for president, it touched off three days of rioting in Bogotá and violent clashes throughout the countryside. The urban unrest morphed into strikes and protests under the banner of *gaitanismo.* The rural violence didn't let up for fifteen years, and some might say it never has. Needless to say, Gaitán has since been pretty well lionized in the Colombian national consciousness. The ruling Conservative Party declared his home a national monument within weeks of the assassination (kind of a backhanded honor, actually, since it meant that his family had to move out). His name is attached to all kinds of infrastructure around Bogotá, and in 2001, he attained the ultimate form of national immortality: he made the currency.

"Do you have a thousand-peso bill?" my guide chirped as we stepped into the courtyard. I handed one over, thinking it was my admission fee, but she just held it out in front of me.

"So this," she said, pointing to the slick-haired, suited gentleman on the bill's front side, "is Jorge Gaitán, the hero of the people!" I squinted. He looked like a kindly young guy, his lips turned up in the slightest twinge of a smile, the kind of congeniality you don't much see on currency portraits. She flipped it over to show me the reverse—Gaitán again, this time pictured with one arm raised before a flag-toting crowd.

"This is a very famous image," she said.

Then, as an afterthought, she moved her finger to a tiny mustachioed face in the crowd, tucked squarely into Gaitán's right armpit.

"And that," she added, "is Fidel Castro."

Castro, it turns out, was a university student in Havana in 1948 who'd come to Bogotá with a coalition of lefty undergrads to protest an inter-American conference being held there. Candidate Gaitán was supposed to meet with him on the very afternoon of his assassination. During the riots that followed, Castro and his companions stole arms from an overrun police station and joined the raids on various government ministries and right-leaning newspapers. He eventually fled to his embassy and was flown back to Cuba, but Castro has since written that Gaitán's assassination provoked his transformation from a mere student rabble-rouser into a "true leftist radical."

Gaitán's legacy is an entrenched antagonism between the Colombian common man and the perceived elites, and it's this that keeps the strikers and protestors coming back to Plaza Bolívar year after year. It isn't a uniquely Colombian tension, of course. In fact, much of Latin America soon adopted Gaitán's pejorative use of the term *la oligarquía,* which once simply meant "the rule of the few," but which Gaitán helped imbue with its modern significance—a closed-off, self-perpetuating community of both wealth and political power. What's impressive about Colombia is both the intensity and staying power of this us-versus-them sentiment. To get a sense of Gaitán's legacy, think of the hue and cry that surrounded Occupy Wall Street. Then imagine that instead of lasting six months, it stretched on for sixty years.

Gaitán is buried in his own courtyard, and my peppy guide sobered up somewhat while showing me his tomb. Dirt from all corners of Colombia had been gathered to sow over the grave, then dampened with water from the Magdalena. The stone inscription read: JORGE ELIÉCER GAITÁN, 1903–∞.

III

I n an early letter from the Magdalena, Thompson men-tioned having made the social page of the newspaper in Barranquilla, where (not unlike Honda) a visit from a virtu-ally uncredentialed foreign journalist was apparently still a big enough deal in 1962 to warrant some coverage. The only archive I could find of Barranquilla's *El Heraldo* was at the National Library in Bogotá. The day I decided to go there turned out to be what the *bogotanos* call Dia Sin Carro.

Bogotá, of course, isn't all gloomy architecture and street violence. On the contrary, it's a fun city with great public parks, tasty street food, and what I would later come to ap-preciate as the only decent beer in all the Andes. It's also a town with a penchant for ambitious and offbeat social experiments. In the mid-1990s and early 2000s, a pair of progressive-minded mayors earned worldwide recognition for a handful of oddball initiatives that put mimes on the streets to shame bad drivers and banned men from appear-ing in public a few nights each year. To mitigate traffic, they grounded drivers on alternating days with a kind of license-plate lottery. If your plate ends in an 8, for example, you're not allowed to drive on Mondays or Thursdays in Bogotá. If it ends with a 6, then you're busing it on Mondays and Wednesdays. And if it happens to be the first Thursday of February, then all across Bogotá it's Dia Sin Carro (or Car-Free Day), and ain't nobody driving anywhere.

Or that's how it was pitched to me, anyway. So I rented a cheap ten-speed the day before my trip to the National Li-brary, and I was looking forward to cruising there in a Tour de France–style peloton. It turns out, however, that there are many exceptions to Dia Sin Carro. When I wheeled my bike out of the hostel the next morning, I was immediately confronted by the sights, sounds, and smells of the zillion or so taxis, buses, government vehicles, and *colectivo* micro-buses that all still managed to fill the streets.

OK, I thought, so only private cars are banned—surely this still relieves some of the traffic pressure. So I strapped on a rented helmet about as sturdy as a Tupperware bowl and pedaled out into the fray.

To say that Dia Sin Carro relieves some of the traffic pressure in Bogotá is like saying that Tylenol relieves some of the pain from a pencil jammed into your eye. It's a start. The cobblestone streets of the colonial Candelaria District weren't so bad, but the broad avenues of El Centro were a calliope of car horns and backfiring buses. I was the only bike on the road for ten blocks in any direction, hemmed in against the curb by a demonic fleet of taxis and more wildly swerving VWs than the parking lot after a Grateful Dead show. The painted lines indicating traffic lanes in Bogotá have as much authority as No Smoking signs on the moon, and the traffic laws are about as stringently enforced. It's the law of the jungle out there, and a guy on a rickety ten-speed is a hobbling wildebeest. By the time I pulled up to the library, I was white-knuckled and panting from my fifteen-block ride.

Colombia's national library is an imposing Art Deco building on the edge of the city's oldest park. Like every other public building in the country, it goes in big for armed security, and the strict visitor protocols seem more geared toward the protection of knowledge than the diffusion of it. This might be a sensible policy, given Bogotá's off-and-on history of wanton destruction, but navigating the library's byzantine security process can be challenging for a foreigner. At the registration desk, a brisk attendant issued me a photo ID, then ran me through some ground rules. I could bring in my laptop, but not its case. I could take a pen, but no notebooks. I would have to relinquish my English-Spanish dictionary, but my camera was OK. Except for its case. No cases of any kind. And after much thought, it was decided that I could bring in *some* papers from my folder, but only the ones I really, really needed.

Eventually, the attendant pointed me toward the periodicals room, where a librarian from the archives set me up with a hand-bound, two-foot-tall book—every edition of *El Heraldo* from the second quarter of 1962. The cover was disintegrating at the corners and opened stiffly. *"Todos originales,"* the librarian said. Microfiche apparently never caught on in Colombia. I turned the crisp beige pages with the utmost care.

There's something transportive about paging through an old newspaper, a tangible reminder that the events of history were once the events of the day. I inhaled deeply; the pinecone musk of newsprint only gets stronger with age. First, I leafed through a few articles about the student riots in Barranquilla ("the unfortunate events of last night . . ."), then a reprint of Kennedy's congratulatory message to Leon Valencia, Colombia's president-elect and Thompson's profile subject. I skimmed the entertainment pages. The season's biggest movie seems to have been a Raymond Burr romance called *Desire in the Dust,* renamed *Echoes of the Past* in Spanish. I scanned an article about some very early nuclear-disarmament talks in Geneva, then another about Kennedy sending his first major troop deployment to Southeast Asia. Echoes of the past indeed, I thought.

On the "De Sociedad" page of the May 26 issue—beneath a paragraph about a perfume-industry banquet and next to a photo of a froggy-looking but impeccably dressed toddler—I found a small column with the simple headline PERIODISTA NORTEAMERICANO. The text is straightforward:

Found in the city for a few days is the American
journalist, Hunter S. Thompson, a native of Louisville, Kentucky, who is touring South America. Mr.
Thompson writes for the newspaper company "Herald Tribune" and is touring several countries, about
which he has been writing a series of articles.

Thompson, who is also a photographer, visited La
Guajira. He arrived in Barranquilla and intends to
continue in the afternoon, bound for Bogotá, where
he will remain for several weeks and then continue
to Lima, Peru. We welcome señor Thompson, wishing him the best impressions during his visit to our
country.

Best impressions? In my head, I played back Thompson's
litany of complaints: the mosquitoes on the Magdalena, the
cold water at the Imperial, the strikes, the church bells, the
dysentery. By the time he was gearing up to leave Bogotá, I'm
not sure that "the best impressions" were among Thompson's
souvenirs. The blurb mentions the *New York Herald Tribune,*
for which he'd written a few stories from the Caribbean years
before. That the *National Observer* goes unmentioned is a
reminder that Thompson was only a freelancer—he had no
guarantee that *anyone at all* would be buying his articles. He
mentions selling two short items to the *New Orleans Times-
Picayune* for $20. It took the *Observer* weeks to pay up for
his first two pieces from Colombia, the Guajiran travelogue
and the Valencia profile, and until they did, Thompson had
virtually no money coming in. It occurred to me that one
reason for his bleak outlook on Bogotá might have been the
looming threat of utter destitution.

All the same, I smiled to read the *Heraldo* item. How
many other researchers had plumbed the Colombian archives

to dig up this piece of Thompsonalia? Not many, I thought. Maybe none. So I felt pretty good about myself as I wheeled my ten-speed back into the war zone of downtown traffic. For weeks, I'd been following a route parallel to Thompson's, but there in that fluorescent-lit reading room, my fingers smudged with fifty-year-old ink, I felt for the first time like our paths had crossed.

IV

"There is a hell of a problem here in Colombia with what they call the Rural Violence," Thompson wrote to an editor from Cali. "This means that out in the country-side, there are a good many people who pass the time of day whacking off their neighbor's [sic] heads with machetes. . . . I came over the mountains in a taxi from Bogota, right through the center of the bad area, and people here have yet to get over it."

The sun-soaked metro of Santiago de Cali is quite a taxi ride from Bogotá, three hundred miles west of the capital and across two of the three mountain "fingers" that Colombians (and geologists) call cordilleras. It's also a full mile lower than Bogotá, at the edge of a broad valley carved out by the Cauca River. Fertile and ringed with mountains, the Valle del Cauca is a longtime producer of industrial-scale cash crops like sugarcane, soy, and cotton. Then, in the 1970s, farmers there went all-in on the cashiest crop of them all: coca, the raw ingredient for cocaine. The subsequent rise and fall of the Cali Cartel brought money and glamour like caleños had never seen. It also brought horrific violence, which, as Thompson suggested, they'd already seen quite a bit of.

With regard to what motivated people to dismember their neighbors: Thompson happened to be passing through Colombia at a pivotal moment, just as the partisan chaos of La Violencia was coalescing into the orchestrated guerrilla campaigns that would plague the country for the next fifty years. Ever since Gaitán's assassination, rural bandits had been wreaking havoc on the countryside, taking advantage of the political freefall to settle old scores, seize land, and generally rule by brutal intimidation. Trying (unsuccessfully) to pitch a story to a men's magazine, Thompson described in gruesome detail the photos he'd seen of rural atrocities: dead pregnant women, their fetuses ripped out and replaced by cats; victims with their throats slashed and tongues pulled out through the wound, a maneuver known as the "Colombian necktie." Thompson called the photos "the goriest goddamn things I've ever seen."

The violence subsided a bit in 1958, when the Liberal and Conservative parties signed a power-sharing agreement after a decade at odds—a big reason why Thompson could write about Colombia's political stability four years later. But he also theorized in his pitch letter that the remaining bandits could represent "the nucleus for a guerrilla army," and in this he was proven all too correct. Rather than dispersing, some bandits decamped to semiautonomous mountain hideaways, many of them encircling the Valle del Cauca. These enclaves attracted political dissidents from the cities, and gradually the leftist ideology motivating urban strikers and students blended with the militancy of the rural outlaws. The FARC was born in 1964 when the Colombian military attacked one such outpost, near Cali. The rebels there, once a disorganized peasant mob, became radicalized, a socialist militia bent on government overthrow, and similar outfits emerged throughout the '60s and '70s.

These days, the FARC is the only real guerrilla bloc left in Colombia, and decades after insinuating itself into the narcotics trade, there isn't much ideology left, just a fanatical devotion to drug profits. The Valle del Cauca is one of the FARC's last strongholds, but even there, in post-Uribe Colombia, the group is pretty marginalized. On my own overnight ride into Cali, the biggest danger in the mountains was that my climate-controlled coach might lose its 3G wireless signal.

Cali today is no more dangerous than Bogotá, but it didn't take me long to realize that the two cities are profoundly different. For starters, Cali is hot. Never mind the 3,200-foot elevation—the city is just a few ticks north of the equator and every bit as sweltering as Barranquilla and the coast. With a year-round growing season, it's grassy and colorful where Bogotá is stony and muted. The day I arrived, I took a long walk through breezy palms lining the pedestrian trail downtown. The path led to Parque Jorge Isaacs, where flirty couples lounged beneath giant gothic banyan trees. Farther along was another small park with a few dozen colorful cat statues, any of which would have seemed out of place among the marble heroes and classical busts of Bogotá. There was still plenty of traffic, of course, but the café diners at their canopied tables seemed noticeably unhurried, sipping beer and not coffee in the early afternoon, and even among the steel towers of the business district, people walked languidly, stopping here and there to chat.

Sky was right about the women, too. They were indeed stunning, absurdly voluptuous and dressed to beat the heat— which is to say, minimally. Cali is famous for both its nightlife (it's the self-proclaimed salsa capital of the world) and its enthusiastic embrace of cosmetic surgery (with more plastic surgeons per capita than anywhere else in Colombia). So it's

maybe no surprise that Thompson found there the ambient
sexual energy he'd been missing in Bogotá. "Walking the
streets here can drive a man up the wall in ten minutes," he
wrote admiringly. Cali, he noted, was famous even then for
its beautiful women, although the city's obsession with sili-
cone probably owes much to the lifestyle of conspicuous consumption that prevailed during the heyday of the Cali Cartel.
Laundered money from that era also fueled (and is perhaps
still fueling) a building boom, so what Cali lacks in charming colonial architecture it makes up for with an impressive
skyline. Today's central Cali is a thick forest of luxury high-
rises, more than you'd expect in a city of 2.4 million, and
from anywhere on the streets of downtown I could crane my
neck to spot a half dozen rooftop oases, impossibly distant
and ringed with palms.

If high-mountain Bogotá is the love child of Denver and
DC, then Cali is Miami's less trashy, landlocked stepsister.
Thompson called it the "Valhalla of Colombia, which in
turn is the Valhalla of South America." He loved the city,
the encroaching rural violence notwithstanding. Whether it
was the sunshine, the women, or perhaps an *Observer* paycheck finally putting some pesos in his pocket, Cali seemed
to restore Thompson's enthusiasm for the trip. The *caleño*
poet Ricardo Nieto might have been speaking for him a few
decades earlier, when he wrote the memorable line "I would
rather have a hangover in Cali than a party in Bogotá."

One muggy afternoon in Cali, Thompson watched as a
wealthy British expatriate drove golf balls off the terrace
of his downtown penthouse apartment. Sipping a tall gin
and tonic, the tubby Brit chatted nonchalantly with Thompson and a dozen other guests, pausing every so often for a
swing, then relaxing his stance as the white orbs rose and

fell, landing somewhere among the sheet-metal roofs of the impoverished neighborhood below.

So begins "Why Anti-Gringo Winds Often Blow South of the Border," Thompson's *Observer* piece that arguably made the most waves. It's the only one of his stories that mentions Cali, written and published in the summer of 1963, after Thompson had returned to the United States. In about two thousand words, Thompson outlines a process of gradual disillusionment, cynicism, and finally hostile superiority that he saw playing out among many North American business-men, bureaucrats, and NGO types in South America. The story opens on the callous golfing "Britisher," then shifts its focus to a hypothetical American relief worker named John. How much either character is based on a real-world per-sonage is a mystery, but in Thompson's telling, John starts out sympathetic and ambitious, eager to make a difference in this part of the world. Soon, however, he finds himself a victim of petty crimes and hassles, perpetrated by the very people he's working to help. All the while, he hears dispar-aging remarks about the greedy capitalist gringos, and in a moment of frustration, he retorts with an insult of his own. His relationship with the community deteriorates thereafter, and as John imparts his increasingly caustic views to new recruits, it instigates a downward spiral of resentment and distrust between the locals and the formerly well-meaning Americans.

What's more, Thompson continues, the wealthy elite in much of Latin America in 1962 took a pretty dim view of empowering the poor. Too robust a democracy threatened to upset the apple cart for powerful upper-class families— those whom Gaitán would have called *la oligarquía*—many of whom didn't imagine they had much in common with the people in the streets. Meanwhile, since even a moderately paid American is wealthy by Latin American standards, a gringo abroad often ends up running with exactly this moneyed crowd. And in an effort to do as the Romans do, many an expatriate "not only tends to ape the wealthy, anti-democratic Latins," wrote Thompson, "but sometimes beats them at their own game." In other words, a decent middle-class guy from Montana suddenly finds himself living in a luxury loft, insulated from local hardships and screaming at the maid.

We have a phrase for this kind of behavior, one that was just coming into parlance in the early 1960s—acting the "ugly American." It's a term that derives from a 1958 novel by William Lederer and Eugene Burdick, a moral fable about arrogance, entitlement, and willful ineptitude among American diplomats and businessmen, and about how their actions were losing us the Cold War in a fictional Asian country called Sarkhan. The embassy crowd in Sarkhan is blithe and somewhat boorish. Most foreign service officers are indifferent to the culture, unable to speak the language, and more concerned with schmoozing the cocktail circuit than listening to the concerns of their host nation. Frater-nizing with the locals is discouraged, and the superiority of American ideas is sacrosanct. There's no telling whether Thompson read *The Ugly American* before coming to South America, but he could hardly have been unaware of it. The book was a phenomenon that spent seventy-eight weeks on the bestseller list and prompted a national conversation about the role of the US diplomatic corps. Senator John F. Kennedy had mailed a copy to all his legislative colleagues. Thompson would have made it home in 1963 just in time to catch the Marlon Brando adaptation in theaters.

What's more, *The Ugly American* itself came on the heels of Graham Greene's *The Quiet American,* another bestseller revolving around expatriate American antiheroes and the consequences of their hubris. Published in 1956, *The Quiet American* painted a different picture, this one of a true believer—"not one of those noisy bastards," as the book's British narrator explains, but an earnest young aid worker in Vietnam, so convinced of his essential rightness that it blinds him to collateral damage. (Thompson later praised the book, saying it "gave the Vietnam experience a whole new meaning.") The back-to-back success of these books was no accident. Both were published near the zenith of the Cold War containment era, when the battle for hearts and minds was raging fiercely and the question of how America represented itself abroad was a hot one. Sure, we'd been traipsing the globe for some two hundred years already, but only in the decade before Thompson's visit had it become a matter of policy that Americans *make a good impression* while we were out there. Television and the dawning jet age were just giving many Americans their first glimpse of what "out there" even looked like. At the same time, the Cold War was prompting a mass realization that American identity was shaped as much by our actions abroad as by our aspirations at home.

Of course, Cali wasn't the first place that Thompson had encountered the "ugly American" mentality. He'd seen his share of crass American profiteers two years earlier in Puerto Rico, and his unpublished manuscript for *The Rum Diary* actually borrowed themes from Greene. More recently, in Bogotá, he'd written off other American journalists and the embassy's "Alliance for Progress boys" as clueless hacks, in it only for show. "They are hauling the indians out of mud huts and putting them in huts made of concrete blocks," he wrote, "then hiring $100-a-day photographers to take pictures of the progress. . . . I think all the good Americans died in a riot somewhere."

But in the closing lines of "Anti-Gringo Winds," Thompson seems to acknowledge how easy it was to drift into this mind-set of cavalier self-importance. "Now, looking back on that man with the golf club," he wrote, "it is easy to see him as a fool and beast. But I recall quite well how normal it seemed at the time, and how surprised I would have been if any of the dozen people on the terrace had jumped up to protest."

What Americans were realizing about their national identity, Thompson was coming to realize about individuals—namely, that who we are away from home is a powerful indicator of who we are *really,* a window into our fundamental character. If I'm honest, my own suspicion of this was partly why I'd wanted to come to South America. I imagine the same was true for Thompson, coming up in the era of ugly and quiet Americans. As I sipped a beer in one of Cali's riverfront cafés, I could almost picture him sitting at the next table over, staring up thoughtfully at the high-rises and asking himself the same question running through my mind: *What kind of American am I going to be?*

Without any particular task to accomplish in Cali, I spent most of my time just walking around, eating chorizo from street carts and searching for a glimpse of the city as Thompson might have seen it. Fifty years ago, Cali was just a quarter of its current size, and I found old photos in bookstores that made it look manicured and idyllic, like one giant retirement community. I got a weird blast from the past as I walked by a small art fair, where portraits of John F. Kennedy seemed only slightly less popular than representations of Christ. One of the canvases showed the president seated with Jackie, staring nobly at something off and to the left, in the manner of a senior class photo. Kennedy was such a presence during Thompson's tour of South America—his policies shaping the continent even as Thompson traveled it—and I was tickled to encounter him here. When I asked the artist why JFK, she just smiled at me and shrugged.

"Era un buen hombre," she said, as if it were self-evident. *"Todos les gusta."* He was a good man. Everyone likes him. I didn't ask why there weren't any portraits of Eisenhower, Johnson, or Nixon.

I spent an afternoon trying to get up into one of the rooftop gardens crowning the many apartment towers. I was hoping I could soak up some of the colossus perspective and cold isolation that Thompson had attributed to the Britisher and his guests. If you're looking for a concrete manifestation of the distance between rich and poor, a high-rise penthouse is hard to beat—especially in an urban South American landscape, where movement and noise on the ground simply never cease. A penthouse in Colombia, I imagine, is equal parts castle, keep, and sensory deprivation chamber.

But every high-rise in Cali, it turns out, has large and intimidating guards, and none of them want to let a perspiring gringo with a backpack wander freely through their property. Under a brutal midday sun, I crisscrossed the downtown, cajoling to the extent that my crappy Spanish allowed, offering to pay a "fee" directly to the doorman, even playing the clueless tourist and trying to breeze right on through. No dice. After a few hours of fruitless inquiries, I was too sweaty for anyone to take me seriously, and I threw in the towel.

The one appointment I did make in Cali was for a short tour of the city's exquisite country club. Thompson had mentioned it while describing the violence encroaching on the city, telling an editor that things were getting "so bad . . . nobody goes to the big country club on the edge of town after dark." I thought I'd try to get a look at the place and maybe hear what it was like back when the *bandoleros* roamed the countryside.

My first move at the Club Campestre de Cali, though, was to embarrass myself with an inadvertent "ugly American" moment of my own. An assistant at the club had written to me earlier in the week, telling me to ask for Sr. Juan Manuel Gonzales, the club's head groundskeeper. But for weeks I'd had Colombian politics on the brain, and the current president of Colombia (Uribe's former defense minister and handpicked replacement) is the very similarly named Juan Manuel Santos. Like an idiot, that was the name I had scribbled into my notebook. I was a little edgy when I walked up to the gate, as I always am when I have to be professional in Spanish. So when I started talking to the buttoned-down matron in the booth, I simply read the name straight out of my notebook: Oh, hi there. I have an appointment at noon to see Juan Manuel Santos.

The attendant looked at me, puzzled, like I'd just requested a tee time with Che Guevara and Jesus Christ. She asked me to repeat myself several times, which only flustered me further. "I made the appointment by e-mail earlier this week," I stammered. "I'm just here to meet for a while with Juan Manuel Santos. I think he's in charge of golf."

I sounded not only like an idiot gringo, but probably a rube on top of it. Imagine your stereotypical small-town hayseed who storms up to a country club in Massachusetts and demands to see George W. Bush or Barack Obama—because this is where rich and powerful people hang out, right?

"The only Juan Manuel Santos I know, sir, is the president," she said to me very, very slowly. But it still wasn't clicking. I figured she meant the president *of the country club*. OK then, I thought. That was more of a higher-up than

I'd expected to give me a tour, but hey, that was the name in my notebook. So I doubled down on the stupidity and told her yes ma'am, that's the guy. I'm here to see the president.

Needless to say, the whole thing took a few minutes to sort out, and once I realized my mistake, I was so embarrassed that I lost control of my Spanish altogether. As the exasperated woman finally ushered me inside, it was all I could do to pathetically mutter, *Discúlpame, soy tonto.* I'm very sorry. I am an idiot.

A few minutes later, I climbed into a golf cart with Juan Manuel Gonzales himself, who laughed so hard at the story, he had to pull over. Gonzales turned out to be as gracious a host as I could have asked for. A slight guy with a mustache and an easygoing manner, he'd been working for the club for thirty-one years, and he sent two boys to college doing it. He was obviously proud of the place, and with good reason. It's stunning—spacious and impeccably landscaped, encircled by a blue-green stream and dotted with perfectly pruned bamboos and palms. Gonzales drove me around for over an hour, showing off bunkers and doglegs, state-of-the-art stables, and even a complex of tennis courts that was right then hosting a televised international tournament. He got particularly excited about the wildlife, urging me to snap pictures of herons and egrets, then scouring the fairways until we found an iguana and a pair of dog-sized tailless squirrels called *guatines.*

"So, what does it take to become a member here?" I asked, after we'd stopped at the ninth green for some lemonade.

"Not much," Gonzales said. "A form, a background check, and *plata*"—literally, "silver," a favorite slang term for money—*"mucha plata."*

"And what about gringos? Can they become members?"

"Oh, of course," he said with a nod. "We have a lot of gringos. Many, many gringos."

Two men, toting their own bags, walked onto the teeing ground of the neighboring eighth hole. We watched as they lined up their drives.

"And golf is the most popular sport here?"

"No, definitely not." Gonzales shook his head. "Well, maybe for the gringos. Otherwise it's *fútbol,* then tennis and *chaza.*" *Chaza,* he said, was a Colombian paddle game like tennis, but played without a net. "Golf, you know—that's only for the elite."

I smiled, embarrassed but not surprised to hear him so casually equate the gringos with the elite. We looked over at the eighth green to see one of the men teeing off. He had a good drive, releasing his swing with a graceful swish that sent the ball out low across the fairway.

Thompson's British golfer probably spent some time out here, I thought. Assuming he was real, anyway. In one of Thompson's biographies, I'd read a quote from his former editor at the *National Observer,* speculating that the lede to "Anti-Gringo Winds" had, in fact, been embellished. It seemed a bit too perfect, the editor said, the bourgeois Brit launching golf balls into the slums. It's not as if the paper could have done a lot of fact-checking, and Thompson did eventually acquire a reputation for blending fact with fiction. True or not, though, it is indeed a perfect image.

What is it about a golf swing, I wondered, that implies such casual conquest? Surely we have a whole host of cultural associations with the sport—it's the game of the elite, as Gonzales said, but there's more to it than that. While Gonzales and I watched the second golfer tee off, I thought about the way that golf delivers violence in such an elegant and controlled package. Supposing for a minute that

Thompson did make up the incident on the penthouse bal-
cony. He couldn't have used an American kid batting fly
balls or a tennis pro working on her backhand. The first is
equally "gringo," the second very aristocratic, but both actions are too overtly aggressive, too forceful and abrupt. The
best golfer can drive a ball three hundred yards with a motion as subtle and fluid as any tai chi maneuver. And Thompson needed that imagery to capture the sort of person who
could sow violence so nonchalantly—the detached oppressor
in his high-rise tower, dapper in a coat and tie.

What about the more manifest violence, I remembered
to ask Gonzales, the banditry toward the end of La Violencia? He was just a child then, but he seemed to have a handle
on the country club's eighty-year history, and the club, he
said, had never really been in danger.

"Most of that happened out in the country," he reminded
me. "Things in the city were very different. More *tranquilo*."

Sure, I said, but Cali was so much smaller back then.
Wasn't the country club sort of on the edge of the city? He
thought about that for a while.

"I suppose it was," he said, and then he paused again.
"Well, anyway, inside the club, I'm sure it was always quite
safe."

A few yards away, an iguana clambered up a nearby
palm. A scatter of polite applause drifted over from the
tennis courts. Gonzales and I finished our lemonade as we
watched the golfers make their approach.

The Normandie Exclusivo sits on a steep hill just north of
Cali's downtown, the slope of which is already crowded
with elegant and vaguely modernist apartment towers. Or
anyway, the Normandie Exclusivo *will* sit on it, once the

construction is completed. On the day that I showed up, the hilltop was a mess of sky-high scaffolding, construction equipment, dirt tracks, and one genuinely stunning model penthouse overlooking the sprawl below.

I saw a flyer for the Normandie Exclusivo the day after visiting the country club while wandering around again, trying to schmooze my way to the top of someone's apartment tower. It was stapled to a telephone pole in a neighborhood already crowded with new construction. *A Privileged View in Every Room,* it said, with an arrow pointing up the hill. *Model Now Open!*

I walked up the hill and into the Normandie Exclusivo's temporary office, where a steely associate named Maria greeted me with barely concealed skepticism. I can't blame her. I was wearing a T-shirt and jeans that hadn't been washed since Bogotá. I couldn't remember my last shave, and an afternoon of walking had me sweaty and disheveled. She offered me a glass of water. Maria was a pantsuited fifty-something who was more sharp than pretty, with deep facial lines that were actually rather flattering in a town full of creepily Botoxed brows. Right then her features were particularly creased, because she was staring at me dubiously, her hands on her hips. She looked, unfortunately for me, like a woman who did not lightly suffer fools.

But Maria's attitude brightened considerably when I explained that my retiree parents were considering relocating to Colombia, and that I was certain they would love to see photographs of a potential new condo.

"Mostly, they've been looking in Bogotá," I lied. "But you know how it is there. So dreary, and everyone's always wearing a coat and tie."

Maria agreed politely and grabbed some literature from

off her desk. Gesturing at a scale model beneath a glass case, she gave me a brief pitch about all the marvelous amenities the Normandie Exclusivo would include—swimming pools, rooftop terraces, ample parking. Then we walked over to the model penthouse for a room-by-room tour. And that was that. After two sweaty days of supplication, all it took to get access to a Cali penthouse was playing the rich gringo.

For the next half hour, Maria shadowed me around the gorgeous air-conditioned apartment, nodding patiently at my ridiculous observations, which were all the more inane on account of my grade-school Spanish: "These windows have much sun." "That lamp is very tall." It was an unquestionably nice place, with vivid white walls, clean angles, plenty of light, and some splashy modern furniture. Kind of like living in an art gallery between exhibits, I thought. When I pictured myself lounging in the living room with my rich and imaginary gringo parents, the grit and noise of downtown Cali felt very far away.

"Our owners are the best people in all of the city," Maria said. "Business leaders, politicians, even some celebrities."

"And gringos?" I asked.

"Oh yes," she assured me, "we have many gringos!"

We walked through some sliding glass doors onto an open-air terrace. It had a three-stool, stainless-steel bar and a wall-mounted wine rack. The view took in the green hills west of town, the largest of which is topped with an open-armed statue of Christ. For a moment, I sensed what the place might have felt like for Thompson, how a wide, elegant veranda like this must have seemed a world away from the shouting students in Bogotá, the coarse crewmen on the Magdalena, and, God knows, the tie-clad Wayuu slugging Scotch and *chirrinchi* back in Guajira. I could definitely see how, on a sunny day up here, with the right company and a drink in your hand, all the people below might just cease to exist.

Maria and I walked back into the living room, and I turned to face the outside, taking in the whole terrace. "Take a picture of it," she told me, and I did. Then I tried to envision the golfer, the upward arc of his swing and the long, level trajectory of a ball disappearing into the city.

CHAPTER FOUR

Gringolandia

The North American presence in South
America is one of the most emotional
political questions on the continent.

—*National Observer*, August 19, 1963

I

L ooking around at statues in South America, it's hard not to think that the United States is kind of dropping the ball on statues. In cities like Bogotá and Quito, seemingly every street corner showcases some kind of dramatic granite monument, soaring memorials to middling politicians and battles too obscure to warrant mention on Wikipedia. Neither is this phenomenon limited to the cities. Even your most podunk Andean hamlet has at least two Virgins and a Bolívar. By contrast, I could only think of three public statues back in Missoula, Montana, and two of those were of bears.

No one does complex iconography quite like a Latin American Catholic, and some of the continent's most beautiful monuments are also masterpieces of esoteric ornamentation. In the center of Quito's Plaza de la Independencia is a statue honoring the heroes of August 10, 1809, when the city first proclaimed its independence from Spain. Standing atop four pillars is an avenging angel, wielding an ax in one hand and a torch in the other. Halfway down, a perched condor clutches a length of chain. An anchor rests at the statue's base, partially covered by a drape of cloth, and next to that stands a wounded, roaring lion. The monument is a veritable potpourri of puzzling symbolism. Those bear statues back in Missoula, meanwhile, just represent bears.

I came into Quito on a Sunday morning after a series of three bus rides from Cali. When I walked to the plaza to check out the architecture, I was expecting a quiet afternoon. The Ecuadorian capital is a devoutly Catholic city, and businesses, vendors, and municipal services tend to shut down for the Sabbath. What's more, Thompson hadn't exactly prepped me for a lively town. In one *Observer* article, he griped about Quito's "tomb-like dullness." In a letter, he wrote it off with Bogotá as "a pure, dull hell." Elsewhere, he suggested that all of Ecuador be "dynamited into the sea." There's more, but suffice it to say the Ministry of Tourism won't be citing his assessment anytime soon.

So I was pleasantly surprised when I stumbled into what seemed like a giant, freewheeling street party. Quito's central plaza, like Bogotá's, is surrounded by showy cathedrals and grand colonial buildings, and while the streets surrounding it were indeed eerily quiet, the plaza itself was a ragtag carnival of musicians, vendors, dancers, and the occasional shouting evangelist. Families roamed around with ice cream and balloons, and hordes of cyclists whizzed by on a weekend bike route. Jugglers and street performers worked a long line for tours of the presidential palace. On one end of the plaza, a crowd of at least fifty people was dancing and head-bobbing to a white-suited band playing an Ecuadorian folk music called *pasillo*. The songs were catchy and melodic, horse-trot waltzes heavy on guitar and a mandolin-like string instrument called a charango. I joined the crowd and bobbed my head right along, beginning to suspect that Thompson was a hopeless grouch.

"Where are you from?" asked a grinning old man next to me, unabashedly. He was dressed for church in a pleated gray suit and fedora, and his wife beside him wore a floral-print dress. When I said that I was from the United States, they seemed delighted.

"Is this your first visit to Ecuador?" the man asked, leaning in to give me his good ear.

"It's my very first morning in Ecuador," I said, which delighted them even further. The woman beamed and clasped her hands to her chest, like I'd just told her I was expecting my firstborn. The husband draped a comradely arm across my shoulder. Where was I coming from? he wanted to know.

How long would I stay in Quito, and what did I most want to do there? I said I most wanted to see the churches and that I was interested in history. I told him I'd probably stay a few days before moving on to the coastal city of Guayaquil.

"Excellent, excellent!" he said, patting me on the back. Many foreign tourists in Quito, he added, only visit La Mariscal, a neighborhood to the north with shops and nightclubs, but the city had so much more. With his arm still around my shoulder, he swayed the two of us in time to the music, mentioning landmarks I might seek out, while his wife stood by and beamed. I wondered for a moment whether I was friendly enough toward apparent foreigners on the streets of major American cities.

The old man pointed me across the plaza to the Centro Cultural Metropolitano, a stately stone building where he said I might enjoy a historic photo exhibit. And sure enough, a sandwich board out front advertised a decade-by-decade retrospective of Quito. I ducked inside and headed for the gallery dedicated to the 1960s.

To tell the truth, things really *did* look a bit duller back then. Judging from the photos, *quiteños* seemed to do a lot of marching back in 1962—military marching, marching for suffrage, marching for the Holy Virgin. None of the images showed anything like the noisy fiesta going on outside. In fact, the streets of the old capital seemed entirely filled with sour-faced men wearing fedoras. I reminded myself of Paul Simon's adage that everything looks worse in black and white, but the exhibit did make midcentury Quito look pretty humdrum, so I figured I'd give Thompson the benefit of the doubt. Besides, by the time he got to Quito, the gastrointestinally addled journalist was "medically forbidden to touch so much as a single beer," and I imagine that kind of enforced sobriety could turn even a Bangkok into a Boise.

Back in 1978, Quito was the first city in the world to be designated a UNESCO World Heritage Site, largely on the strength of its churches, monuments, monasteries, and public buildings, most of which were erected during three hundred years of Spanish rule. The Old Town surrounding the Plaza Grande is Latin America's largest and best-preserved colonial district. It's an open-air museum of Spanish and Moorish architecture, along with a decorative style called Quito Baroque, which blends European embellishments and traditional indigenous imagery. The Old Town is a genuinely charming place to walk around, with block after cobblestone block of bright stucco homes and picturesque courtyards. Each street is characterized by a receding horizon of iron balconies, and some of the churches will knock your socks off, so intricately carved, painted, and tiled, you'd need a magnifying glass and about a hundred years to really appreciate all the details.

Like a lot of places in Latin America, though, Ecuador has kind of a love-hate relationship with its colonial past. On the one hand, Quito alone has spent hundreds of millions of dollars rehabbing its Old Town over the last couple of decades. The capital's colonial district now attracts some 300,000 annual tourists, and each one comes with pockets full of dollars (literally, since Ecuador uses the US dollar as its official currency). Some 70 percent of Ecuadorians trace at least part of their ancestry to the colonizing Spanish, and the country rightfully derives a lot of pride from its historic churches, rich tradition of European-style art, and various other legacies of cultural hegemony.

On the other hand, every brick in every building on the Plaza Grande is also the product of hundreds of years of systematic exploitation of indigenous Ecuadorians. The plaza itself is a testament to the absurdly top-heavy concentration of wealth in colonial Latin America. *Quiteños* are justifiably proud of having raised the New World's "first cry of independence" from Spain back in 1809, the same event commemorated by the omni-symbolic monument on the plaza, when a cabal of Quito's city fathers signed a declaration of independence and installed a provisional government (the Spanish Army quickly retook the city and imprisoned or executed the conspirators).

More recently, since leftist president Rafael Correa came to power in 2007, the very concept of colonialism has become a popular rhetorical punching bag. President Correa was a vocal admirer and a close ally of former Venezuelan president Hugo Chávez, and since Chávez's death, Correa is regularly held up as the new flag-bearer for leftist populism in the Andes. Like his windy socialist mentor, Correa governs on a platform of strident anti-imperialism, decrying Ecuador's victimization (past and perceived present) at the hands of the advanced industrialized world. In some ways, the term "colonialism" in contemporary Ecuador probably rings a bit like "terrorism" in the United States—it's something everyone knows they hate, even if they don't spend a lot of time thinking about it. And under Correa, the threat of "neo-colonialism" has been loudly invoked to justify everything from defaulting on loans to withdrawal from international commissions to the dramatic expulsion of a US ambassador.

The first time I heard Correa speak was in 2008, about a year into his presidency, in an interview on the American radio program *Democracy Now*. Tuning in to the unabashedly lefty news show, I was impressed by the US-educated economist and former Ecuadorian finance minister. He came off like a defender of the poor, an environmental advocate, and a thoughtful critic of globalization. I've since heard Correa described by more conservative sources as a bully, a provocateur, a consort to terrorists, and a squelcher of the free press. The trouble is, both sides make a pretty convincing case.

One of Correa's first moves as president was to push for a constitutional rewrite that, among other things, centralized power and loosened his presidential term limits. This is always an ominous sign. Hard drives seized from a FARC camp inside the Ecuadorian border noted substantial donations to his campaign. He's drawn serious fire from free-press advocates for bringing a parade of lawsuits against opposition media outlets, creating a government watchdog agency to police the news, and launching an empire of state-run TV, radio, and newspapers that mostly serves to disseminate political propaganda.

But even while silencing critics at home, Correa's government has made a show of assisting some high-profile freedom-of-information champions. Ecuador's London embassy granted asylum to WikiLeaks founder Julian Assange and later issued travel documents to stateless National Security Administration leaker Edward Snowden—both morally divisive figures in their own right. What's more, Correa has pushed through a new and innovative constitution that grants legal rights to the environment. He successfully refinanced piles of questionable foreign debt accumulated by previous administrations, a move that even his critics acknowledged as savvy. And on his watch, Ecuador has made undeniable strides against extreme poverty.

It's the sort of ambiguous record that almost makes you nostalgic for the superficial moral simplicity of the Cold War. Say what you will about the prickly echoes of McCarthyism whenever one of Thompson's letters mentions "the Reds"—at least back then, everybody knew who the bad guys were.

———

Which is not to imply that Thompson's *Observer* reportage sensationalized the communist threat. His stories are actually rather measured and thoughtful at a time when it would have been easy to phone it in by playing up the Red Scare. In most of the articles, Thompson is at least as critical of Kennedy's Alliance for Progress as of any South American leader or movement. Occasionally, he shows an ahead-of-his time sensitivity to the marginalization of indigenous people, and in his letters he's genuinely scornful of the kind of cultural imperialism that tends to irk leaders like Correa and Chávez.

"They have imported ping-pong and the Twist to combat the Red Menace," he once wrote of the Alliance-motivated diplomats in Bogotá. Many of his letters echo "Anti-Gringo Winds," exposing and discrediting the lingering colonial attitudes that allow, for example, a nonchalant gringo to peg poor people with golf balls.

But for all his evenhandedness, Thompson's articles do tend to focus on the US vision for South America and on the defenders of US interests abroad. "How Democracy Is Nudged Ahead in Ecuador," his only story from the country, which ran in September 1962, recounts a day in the life around the Guayaquil offices of the United States Information Service. The USIS was a public diplomacy organ that evolved following World War II. Its mission, according to a long-winded memo from President Kennedy, was to use "personal contact, radio broadcasting, libraries, book publication and distribution, press, motion pictures, television, exhibits, [and] English-language instruction" to "encourage constructive public support abroad . . . and counter hostile attempts to distort or frustrate the objectives and policies of the United States." So, in a word: propaganda.

"We don't like to use that term because of its unfortunate connotation," a USIS officer in Quito told Thompson. But Thompson uses it anyway, and his story takes a fairly unblinking look at even some of the more cloak-and-dagger aspects of the job. It opens with an angry-looking Ecuadorian storming out of the USIS office, passing Thompson in the hallway:

> "I think that man has troubles," [USIS chief Fred] Shaffer explained. "He owns a radio station that used to broadcast so much anti-American stuff that we nicknamed it the Voice of Moscow." He shook his head sadly. "Then he had some bad luck: suddenly all his advertisers quit him and now he's nearly bankrupt." He smiled faintly. "And he has the gall to come in here and try to blame it on me—can you imagine such a thing?"

Thompson goes on to describe the everyday successes and frustrations of the USIS officers charged with promoting America's image in Ecuador. They're scrambling to issue a statement about a shipment of powdered milk, donated by an American NGO and discovered on the black market. They're awaiting results from an election of the national student association, in which they've unofficially lent support to an anti-Castro candidate. Behind all this is the day-to-day work of disseminating pro-American news stories to the Ecuadorian media.

Thompson paints the chaos of the office vividly, with

some nice scene-setting lines to boot ("the cabs rolled back and forth like animals looking for meat"). It's a good article. It is also the kind of thing that would send a leader like Correa into spasms. Ecuador's president is famous for bleating about "the selling-out, the snobbery, even the neocolonialism" of the media, and Thompson's story not only covers Ecuadorian issues *solely* from the perspective of powerful, self-interested outsiders, but also glibly lionizes America's backroom efforts to silence the Ecuadorian free press.

Of course, Correa has proven to be a pretty world-class free-press silencer himself, but it's hard to read "How Democracy Is Nudged" and not feel a smidgen of empathy. After all, ever since the day that Pizarro landed on the continent in 1524, the story of South America has always been the story of *other people* in South America. Often as not, it's been told by other people too. And when you get right down to it, this is perhaps the most insidious legacy of colonialism—it takes your own story away from you. So if someone like Correa seems dangerously fixated on imperialism and tyrannical about controlling his own message, part of me has to wonder, can you really blame the guy?

II

On the topic of other people in South America, it should be noted that Thompson's year on the continent predates the phenomenon known today as the Gringo Trail. In its broadest definition, the Gringo Trail consists of any and all sites in Latin America regularly frequented by budget gringo travelers. It's anchored by classic attractions like Machu Picchu and Iguaçu Falls, and depending on whom you talk to, it may be a pejorative term, something like "the well-beaten path." Just when the phrase came into use isn't exactly clear. According to Jack Epstein of the *San Francisco Chronicle,* a former Peace Corps volunteer who helped popularize the expression with his 1977 guidebook *Along the Gringo Trail,* the label was probably first tossed around by Latin American backpackers in the late 1960s. A search with Google's Ngram tool, which diagrams the frequency of words over time as they appear in millions of digitized books, puts the phrase's print debut sometime in the early 1970s. My own highly unscientific canvassing of a few dozen baby-boomer backpackers tends to support this, and while the trail is amorphous and subject to change, there seems to be some consensus that the classic South American leg is bookended by Quito on one end and Rio de Janeiro on the other, with swings in between through the central Andes, Patagonia, and the Argentine Pampas.

Backpacking, as we know it today—the style of minimalist, dollars-a-day foreign travel appealing mainly to First World young adults—had yet to really catch on in 1962. There were historical precedents, of course, from the myriad variations on American hoboism to the upper-crust tradition of the European Grand Tour. Modern backpacking has its roots in post-WWII prosperity, which swelled the ranks of young middle-class Americans, Australians, and western Europeans with the means to indulge their wanderlust. Then, according to Israeli sociologist Erik Cohen, the emergence of leisure-friendly airfare in the late 1960s fueled an international backpacking explosion.

Distinguished sociologists have done more research on grungy hostel-hoppers than you might immediately suspect, and Cohen is the Margaret Mead of the discipline. In his 1973 paper "Nomads from Affluence: Notes on the Phenomenon of Drifter-Tourism," Cohen examines the motivations of the young travelers he calls "drifters," and he offers "a four-fold typology" of the kinds of folks you might meet on the road: the adventurer, the itinerant hippie, the establishment "mass drifter," and the day-tripping "fellow traveler." The same year that his "Nomads from Affluence" ran in the *International Journal of Comparative Sociology,* a twenty-seven-year-old expat Brit named Tony Wheeler was self-publishing what would turn out to be the first Lonely Planet guidebook, further fueling backpacking's momentum. He and his wife had just traveled across Asia, along a route well known to Cohen's "drifters" as the Hippie Trail. The Gringo Trail was simply the Western Hemisphere's burgeoning backpacker equivalent, and in the coming decades, guidebooks like Lonely Planet would ensure that it stayed hopping with plenty of "itinerant hippies," "fellow travelers," and all the rest.

Thompson, by contrast, was sort of a proto-backpacker, running with a crowd of what you might call "working drifters": other reporters, embassy folks, volunteers for President Kennedy's brand-new Peace Corps. He mentions hanging out with some Ivy League English teachers in Barranquilla and a Fulbright scholar in Bogotá. In a sense, Thompson and his peers were actually *blazing* the Gringo Trail, and Cohen credits these "young professionals, who seek to combine travel with work in their chosen profession" as one of his four main "antecedents to the modern drifter."

If nothing else, Thompson was certainly an antecedent to the poverty aspect of backpacking. Broke again in Quito, he wrote to his *Observer* editor, "I am traveling at least half on gall. But in the course of these travels I have discovered that gall is not always the best currency, and there are times when I would be far better off with the other kind." How many subsequent generations of rucksack-toting seekers would stumble across South America adhering to Thompson's Law of Travel Economics, "Full speed ahead and damn the cost; it will all come out in the wash"?

My own meager currency reserves were what attracted me to Quito's Secret Garden hostel, where a dorm bed costs $9.80 a night. Wherever the Gringo Trail begins and ends, I am pretty certain it runs smack-dab through the middle of the Secret Garden. A narrow building with serpentine staircases and five mazelike stories—each crowded with cheerful English-speaking twentysomethings—the Secret Garden is what I imagine a frat house would look like at a nice liberal arts university in Whoville. The morning I arrived, the place was filled with attractive German girls gushing to their moms on Skype. As I humped my backpack up five flights to the reception area, I passed no fewer than eight of them, sprawled on couches, leaning on balconies, and chatting away on their laptops. The reception desk was on a sunny rooftop patio, with a bright yellow wall covered in posters for Spanish lessons and bike tours. Two American volunteers checked me in, both in their early twenties. He was a student and a part-time glassblower, eventually headed to Bolivia to volunteer with a land conservancy; she was killing time en route to a yoga retreat in Cusco.

Bohemian travel motivations like these are in no short supply around places like the Secret Garden. Over the course of the next week, I found myself in many discussions about Amazonian weaving workshops and endangered sloth rescue centers. It had been a decade since my own short college stint abroad, the last time I'd mingled in a crowd of starry-eyed backpackers, and I'd forgotten just how ritualistically the conversations tend to unfold. The first line of questioning between any two hostel-mates is like a loosely choreographed dance, with steps that everyone knows and some room for improvisation:

BACKPACKER 1: So, where are you from?

BACKPACKER 2: San Francisco/Kansas. You?

B1: Norway/Sydney.

B2: Cool, I've always wanted to go to Norway/Sydney. I'd really like to see the fjords/opera house someday. Have you been?

B1: Yeah, they're/it's pretty amazing. I have a cousin in San Francisco/Kansas who's a Web designer/farmer. Is it really quite hilly/flat there?

B2: Yes, it's a beautiful city/soul-crushing landscape. How long have you been in Quito?

B1: Four days. Tomorrow we leave to tour the Galápagos Islands/volunteer on a free-range sheep farm/study the Bhagavad Gita in a tree house.

B2: Wow, I'm actually really into wildlife/animal husbandry/Sanskrit epics. I just got in yesterday from Colombia/Bolivia. Do you know where I can find an Internet café/vegetarian restaurant/bar where Ecuadorian girls will sleep with me?

B1: There's one on the corner. What did you think of Colombia/Bolivia? Is it really dangerous/cheap there?

B2: Not really/absolutely. The guy who ran my hostel also owned a restaurant/led jungle tours/sold cocaine, so I got to try some traditional foods/see a monkey/do a lot of blow.

B1: Wow, that sounds really awesome.

And so on. None of this is to say that the conversations are fake or insincere. Relationships among backpackers are simply the friendship equivalent of mutually agreed-upon one-night stands. Everybody is just passing through, so the odds of forming meaningful, long-lasting friendships are slim. But regular backpackers can likely recall whole weeks spent in the very pleasant company of people they knew only as "the Danish guy" or "that couple from South Africa."

I spent several nights just hanging out on the Secret Garden's rooftop—signing up for in-house dinners of curry and veggie lasagna, swilling beer around the fireplace afterward—because I so enjoyed the ease of these English conversations with a rotating cast of strangers. This, of course, is part of the siren's song of the Gringo Trail. In your nicer hostels, it is alarmingly easy to be lulled by the relative comfort and the companionship of your countrymen, and I got the feeling there were folks around the Secret Garden who hadn't left the premises for days. As Cohen writes about the "mass drifters" in his "four-fold typology":

> The mass drifter is not really motivated to seek adventure. . . . Rather, he often prefers to be left alone to "do his own thing," or focuses his attention on the counter-culture, represented by other drifters whom he encounters on his trip. His social contacts, hence, become progressively narrowed to the company of other drifters.

I'll leave the comprehensive typologies to the sociologists, but after a few days at the Secret Garden, a few different backpacker "strains" certainly seemed to emerge. For starters, you had your garden-variety vacationers: athletic Norwegian students hiking the Andes between semesters; a pair of British secretaries sightseeing on their two-week holiday. These folks tended to spend less time around the hostel, having shorter timeframes and itineraries to follow. Budget is the primary difference between this crowd and the workaday tourists at the hotel up the street.

Then you had your earnest world-changers: a bronzed and bearded Ohioan who'd spent his summer fighting developers in the coastal mangrove forests; intern after willowy intern promoting literacy, hand-washing, or sustainable gardening along Quito's vast and slummy urban edge. The world-changers were a distinctly Gen-Y crowd, and many seemed to be hopping from volunteer gig to volunteer gig without much of a long-term plan. Most of them seemed to be more passionate about the general *idea* of helping people than about the specifics of their jobs, and in no instance did I meet anyone at the Secret Garden who was being paid for his or her work.

Then there were the seekers, the vaguely New Age types for whom travel is an exercise in self-improvement: the elfin yoga instructor at the registration desk; an Australian who loudly shared the spiritual lessons she'd so far learned on her tour of holistic massage schools. I met at least half a dozen ayahuasca enthusiasts, fans of the psychoactive and allegedly sacred vine that's increasingly marketed to gringos by "shamanistic retreat centers" and other purveyors of higher consciousness. Over beers on the rooftop, many of them acknowledged that, yes, the scene around the holy drug was indeed becoming commercialized, but that *their* shaman had been the real thing, man, a 130-year-old woman who ate nothing but burs and turned into a jaguar at night. Strangely enough, it was these ascetic would-be medicine men who tended to get the most excited when I mentioned Hunter Thompson.

Finally, you had your hedonists: a squadron of young Israelis, just released from their compulsory military stint, partying their way across the continent; a hardworking chef to the royal family of Bahrain, boozing off stress in Quito simply because the airfare was cheap. I shared a room with an Australian playboy and hostel volunteer who was refreshingly candid about having come to South America primarily to get laid.

Whether they're tutoring the locals or humping them, nearly all of the Gringo Trail backpackers seemed to share certain rhetorical habits. I noticed, for example, that my Secret Garden hostel-mates rarely talked about "going" places, but instead about "doing" them. "We did Galápagos last week," one of the Norwegian students told me, "and now we're deciding whether to do Colombia or stay in Ecuador." "Have you done Machu Picchu yet?" asked a couple of the ayahuasca devotees. "You should totally do Baños before you leave Ecuador," said the cook from Bahrain. "The hot springs there are amazing!"

If you want to read into this that many backpackers tend to treat the places they visit like theme-park attractions rather than complex landscapes and communities, you would not be alone in doing so. This is a common criticism of the Gringo Trail, that it alienates travelers from their environment rather than engaging them in it, presumably by creating a bubble of veggie lasagna and Skype from which travelers need only peek when they think there's something worth seeing. You might then be tempted to ask whether there aren't some parallels between this "do Ecuador" mentality and the old imperialist attitudes of segregation, superiority, and antagonism. And there again, our friend Erik Cohen and others will have you beat. "The easy-going tourist of our era," the sociologist wrote in 1972, "might well complete the work of his predecessors, also travelers from the West—the conqueror and the colonialist."

III

This particular easygoing tourist had plenty of time to contemplate all this thanks to two unforeseen events. The first was an e-mail from the US consulate in Guayaquil. As I'd told the old man back in the plaza, I had initially planned to stay in Quito for only a few days before moving on to that coastal city. I had tried to set up an interview at the Public Affairs Section of the consulate, which is the modern-day equivalent of the US Information Service that Thompson had covered in 1962. Unfortunately, said the e-mail, the public affairs officer had been called out of the country unexpectedly. Could I make an appointment with the embassy in Quito instead?

"Embassy people are shits," Thompson wrote to a friend after leaving Ecuador. "Consulates are better—this is a rule."

But I had no alternative. Anyway, Thompson was proving to be crotchety and wrong more often than he was right. So I e-mailed the embassy, hoping for a last-minute appointment and apologizing for the short notice. I had just clicked Send when my licentious Australian roommate walked in and collapsed on his bunk.

"You coming out tonight?" he asked, stretching his arms lazily above his head. He was a lean guy with the perpetually tousled look of a surfer.

"Um ... maybe," I said, in a tone that I hoped implied "Actually, I just bought a copy of *The Ecuador Reader,* and I'm sort of looking forward to raging the 'Catholicism & Democracy' chapter tonight."

"Come on, mate," he urged good-naturedly. "What's the matter? Don't you like pussy?"

I weighed my response.

"No, pussy's . . . great," I said. "It's just that, honestly, I don't really go out that often."

"Fine," he said, "but this is different. This is Carnaval!"

I didn't need to double-check the date to realize he was right. Of course it was Carnaval. I had completely forgotten about the multiday pre-Lenten bacchanal, synonymous in South America with parties, parades, costumes, music . . . and the nearly continent-wide closure of all businesses and services, public or private. I checked the website and discovered that, yes, it would be another five days before anyone at the embassy would even be around to answer the phone. It seemed I would be spending the next week in Quito.

Like a lot of clueless non-Catholics, I associate Carnaval primarily with Brazil and, to a lesser extent, the Caribbean. Trinidad and St. Thomas, sure. Certainly Rio and Bahia. I had heard it was big in Barranquilla. But high-mountain Quito? In the dustiest corners of my mind, I knew that the festival was a worldwide phenomenon, celebrated virtually everywhere they have Catholicism, masks, and feathers, but if I'm on my default setting, then Carnaval to me is an inherently coastal Atlantic affair, the province of beach towns and sunny former plantation colonies.

In fact, Carnaval is a pretty sterling example of cultural appropriation, a practice rooted in medieval Europe that most of us now unfailingly associate with the New World. Just like all those knockout cathedrals, it was a colonial import, emblematic of the new, European traditions and beliefs that were supposed to supplant the old. But rather than Europeanizing the people, Carnaval was indigenized by the zillion or so ethnic groups of Latin America, who now more or less own the holiday. In addition to the biggies along the coast, there are also massive celebrations in places like

Oruro, Bolivia, where celebrants don the masks of horned Andean mountain gods, and Cajamarca, Peru, where the fest centers on the chopping of decorative trees. In Quito, it turns out, costumes and music take a backseat to messy pranks. Ecuadorian Carnaval embraces elements of a pre-Columbian festival from the central highlands, where natives once bedecked one another with flowers, perfumed extracts, and maize flour. Over time, that's evolved into playful battles in the streets, in which strangers (and a lot of kids) chuck water balloons and handfuls of flour at one another and unsuspecting passersby. More recently, the Ecuadorians have embraced squirt guns and a white spray foam called *carioca,* a cross between Silly String and shaving cream. Within a day of learning it was Carnaval, I noticed bottles of the stuff for sale on seemingly every street corner in Quito, accompanied by mighty-lunged vendors crying, *"Cariocas! Cariocaaas!"*

Carnaval lasts a four-day weekend, during which the city basically shuts down. Ironically enough, Thompson had run into similar troubles in Guayaquil fifty years earlier. "We just finished a five-day lull having to do with Ecuadorian history," he wrote to his editor. "These holidays are maddening: every time you turn around they are rolling down the store fronts and locking the offices." Ecuador's biggest Carnaval celebrations actually happen outside of the capital, in the surrounding mountain towns, but I opted to spend the next few days just playing tourist around Quito. I watched a parade in the Plaza Grande and visited a colonial history museum. I toured the Basílica del Voto Nacional, a Gothic masterpiece and the tallest church in Ecuador (built seventy years after independence, so no credit to the Spanish for that one). I even spent a day hanging out in the bookshops and cafés of La Mariscal, the tourist neighborhood that the old couple in the plaza had mentioned. It's a flashy district of hostels, nightclubs, and chichi outdoor apparel stores, and from the crew at the Secret Garden, I learned that it's colloquially known as Gringolandia. The nickname is no joke. I knew I'd found the right neighborhood when Spanish all but evaporated from the street chatter around me. Gringolandia had twice as many cops and three times as many coffee bars. I bought a book about roses (Ecuador grows hundreds of millions each year in factory-like greenhouses), and I drank two beers at an Irish-owned Vietnamese restaurant with American bartenders.

But the best day I spent in Quito was also by far the most prosaic, and with nary a gringo in sight. One afternoon, I rode the bus to a large green spot on the map called Parque La Carolina, in the middle of the city's business district. I'd read about a natural history museum there and had seen a flyer in Gringolandia for something called a vivarium, which I thought might be a giant musical instrument but turns out to be a kind of reptile zoo. When I got there, I found the museum closed, but the park itself grabbed my attention. Shady, green, and swarming with happy *quiteño* families, Parque La Carolina is the kind of omnipurpose recreational Eden that urban planners fantasize about. It isn't huge—at 166 acres, it's about the size of your average community college—but the place was basically a showroom for the vast infrastructure of fun. It was like one of those science experiments where biologists replicate all of the world's ecosystems under a glass dome—a *biosphere* of fun. It seemed to have everything, every apparatus and pleasuring ground on which I could have imagined playing, plus another handful I never would have thought of—all of them being used, all at once, all around me.

It was a beautiful sight to behold, probably the most innocently uplifting thing I'd seen since my last elementary

school play. The air in Parque La Carolina was practically
dewy with laughter. Not far from where I wandered in, children were pinging like free radicals off every manner of
playground equipment: swings, merry-go-rounds, a small
Ferris wheel, a spinning gyroscope, and several rather sculptural variations on the jungle gym. Everywhere I looked,
there was movement. Bicycle traffic flowing briskly. Joggers streaming by from every direction: joggers with strollers, joggers with dogs, joggers with absurdly small athletic
shorts. There were so many, it seemed impossible that they
weren't running into one another, each one focused on his or
her own thoughts, bouncing to a backbeat of a dozen drib-
bling basketballs on a dozen blacktop courts.

I walked the pedestrian paths like one of those Buddhist
mandalas, just grinning like an idiot and taking everything
in. There were families playing keep-away and families
having pull-up contests. There were people on roller skates
and people on Rollerblades and people with those sneakers
where the wheels just pop out somehow. Ecuadorians love
volleyball, a three-on-three version with a high net that they
call *ecuavolley,* and teams were fanned out everywhere,
serving over raggedy nets, monkey bars, and frayed ropes
tied between trees. Needless to say, there were no fewer than
fifty *fútbol* games, raging across every open patch of dirt,
concrete, and grass. Every so often, an errant ball would
come my way, and I would kick it back to some small fanfare.

Mothers lined up alongside playgrounds like columns of
sentries, watchfully observing. Dads pushed their kids on
training wheels and tended imaginary goals. I watched one
father help his toddler sight a miniature rifle with a dart in
the end of it, aiming for a bulletin board covered in candy
and prizes. The dart struck a fun-size Snickers with the
sound of a wet gavel, and I'd never seen such celebrating.

The barker, a shuffling *abuelita,* broke open the rifle in a single movement, then inserted a new dart and closed the action by jerking one arm, like a no-nonsense lawman in a TV western.

"Cariocas!" cried the vendors. *"Cariocaaas!"*

Popped-collar toughs walked by with shouldered boom boxes and cigarettes dangling, extras in their own '80s rap video. White-haired old men, dignified in gray slacks and golf hats, strolled past with their heads down and hands behind their backs. Occasionally, two or three teenage girls ran by, screaming and bathed in *carioca,* while packs of puppy-eyed boys tripped over one another to catch up. Older teens nestled against tree trunks, sucking face shamelessly in the way that only Latin American teenagers can. Impossibly small kids walked impossibly small dogs. I saw dogs in strollers and dogs cradled like infants in slings. I saw dogs in matching two-piece outfits. I saw dogs in leopard skin.

The sweet smell of fried plantains filled the air. Armies of vendors sold ice cream, chorizo, candy apples, ceviche, pastries. Smoke from the grills hung in fragrant little clouds over the vendors' stands, and from anywhere in the park you could hear sausages sizzling nearby, quietly but unmistakably. For $1.25 I ate a kabob with chorizo, potato, yuca, plantain, and a whole thigh of barbecued chicken. I washed it down with ice cream. And then a beer. For a moment, I even considered buying cotton candy from a costumed character whose head was a squirrel but who was clearly Winnie-the-Pooh from the neck down.

At one point, I turned a corner to find the rear of an inflatable castle shaking gelatinously. Elsewhere, I almost strolled right onto a dusty BMX track. The boys lined up there straddled every manner of bicycle, from fat-bottom cruisers to high-end mountain bikes two sizes too big. The bleachers next to the tennis courts were only half-full, but the crowd cheered wildly after every point, and I thought of the courts back at the Cali country club, with their televised tournament and polite applause. Next to the bleachers were two long concrete pitches of an indeterminate purpose—too long for horseshoes, too short to land a plane on.

"*Cariocaaas!*"

Kites, model airplanes, a handful of whirring remote-controlled machines—even the air was lively at Parque La Carolina. All throughout the park snaked a concrete channel filled with crazily listing paddleboats, their occupants screaming and spraying *carioca* from boat to boat. A little boy peed off a dock while his mom sat next to him, breast-feeding. Onshore, a single paddleboat leaned upside-down against a eucalyptus tree, looking like the fallout from some perplexing accident. Beneath it, a golden retriever in shorts and a blue tank top was snoozing peacefully.

The pièce de résistance was a full-sized jetliner, painted nose-to-tail with a graffiti mural and parked permanently over a patch of scuffed concrete. The plane was teeming with kids and teenagers, climbing onto the wings via a metal staircase, clinging to the rudder, dangling out the windows, strolling nonchalantly across the fuselage. Everyone was entering via a small tear in a surrounding chain-link fence, but from the stairs and the twisty slide coming out of the cockpit, the airplane seemed to be an official playground component. For several minutes I just stood at the fence, wishing like hell to be a ten-year-old again. Laughter ricocheted off the pavement, and a contingent of moms looked up from the ground, watching like helpless stewardesses during some bizarre passenger rebellion.

Some other day, I might have thought about how a

jaw-dropping park like this is a testament to the kind of lav-
ish civic spending that apparently marks Ecuador as a fearsome socialist dystopia. But I wasn't thinking about that. I
was lost in a reverie of dopey, wholesome camaraderie, too
busy kicking soccer balls and licking ice-cream cones to put
the scene in any kind of geopolitical context. This is something that travel does, I thought: It allows fun to smooth over
all the difficult questions about how to live and be governed
and who's oppressing whom. There are no social theorists
standing around a bouncy castle. So maybe all those liber-
tines back at the Secret Garden were on to something.

It occurred to me that Thompson didn't really *do* a lot of
this, this kind of wandering around through the pleasantly
pedestrian tableau that's behind the curtain in all but your
most chaotic cities—judging from his letters and articles,
anyway, which tend to dwell on the cocktail chatter of expats, the machinations of the political class, and the often
turbulent goings-on outside the windows of his downtown
hotels. Thompson might have pre-dated the Gringo Trail,
but even without a laptop or a hosteling card, he seems to
have had a hard time breaking out of his own cultural orbit.
Part of this was an occupational hazard, I suppose. You can't
cover the Cold War from a jungle gym in Parque La Carolina. Or maybe it was a conscious choice. Maybe Thompson
knew that you can only watch so many laughing toddlers
stumble by—conductor overalls covered in *carioca,* grinning
parents in hot pursuit—before it affects your ability to take
international relations seriously.

That night, I did go out with the hostel crowd, down to
a cobblestone pedestrian strip in the Old Town, where hundreds of people were hopping from bar to bar, spraying
thousands of bottles of *carioca.* Music floated out the open

café windows, and the street was a melee of locals and tourists alike, gringos and *quiteños* making zero distinction as they gleefully smothered one another in soft white foam.

IV

Forget Gringolandia and the Secret Garden—when it comes to gringo enclaves abroad, there's really no substitute for the US embassy. My cab pulled up outside the embassy's nine-foot walls just two days after Carnaval. From the outside, the complex looks like the world headquarters of some colossal association of narcoleptic insurance salesmen. It is massive, boxy, and extremely drab. If not for a small seal with a bored-looking eagle on it, you might walk right past the place and not recognize it. Except that you're not likely to be walking at all, because the campus is in a rather distant neighborhood on the north edge of town. It was inaugurated in 2008, the newest embassy building on the continent, and both the walls and the remote location are legacies of a State Department construction policy that, until recently, emphasized security over aesthetics, local accessibility, and, apparently, good taste.

Inside the walls, the buildings are a tiny bit sleeker—maybe less like a boring insurance company and more like a boring software company. Following a security shakedown that made the TSA line at La Guardia look like a nice visit to Grandma's, I found myself in a Spartan marble-and-brick reception area, admiring some landscape paintings and listening to two Spanish-speaking guards discuss how they liked their sushi. I set my water bottle on an American-flag coaster and thought how nice it was to be back on American soil. Only later did I learn that the externality of US embassies is actually a myth, and that I was, in fact, still quite solidly on Ecuadorian soil, albeit with some special rules.

I was met by Counselor for Public Affairs Wes Carrington, Public Diplomacy Officer Jennifer Lawson, and Cultural Affairs Officer Lisa Swenarski, three of the four heads of the Public Affairs Section of the US diplomatic mission in Quito. The USIS that Thompson profiled in 1962 had been formed by Dwight Eisenhower nine years earlier, a direct response to the Cold War. In 1999, it was broken up and its functions divided. A new, DC-based agency was put in charge of overseas broadcasting, while the State Department's Public Diplomacy and Public Affairs bureaus took over the promotion of American views and interests on the ground. All but the smallest American embassies have a Public Affairs Section today. Not surprisingly, the largest PAS is at the embassy in Kabul, with an American staff of twenty. That Carrington's staff in Quito is only a few positions smaller gives some idea of the challenge of public diplomacy in "anti-imperialist" Ecuador.

"How was Carnaval?" Carrington asked, shaking my hand. He was a clean-shaven guy on the cusp of his fifties, with a silver paisley tie that matched his salt-and-pepper hair. He spoke with the easygoing authority of somebody who talks to strangers for a living.

"I think I'm still cleaning the *carioca* out of my ears," I said. "It's quite a campus you've got here."

It was nice, they all agreed, not that any of them had been there all that long. Foreign Service officers rotate into new posts every two or three years, a strategy designed to prevent what diplomats refer to as "clientitis," or an increasing allegiance to one's host country rather than the United States. Of the three, Carrington was the elder statesman, coming up on the end of his term in Ecuador. He'd been with the State Department since 1989 and served abroad since 2002, with rotations in Brazil and Portugal. Lawson and Swenarski were newer to both Ecuador and the Foreign Service, but between them, they'd had postings in politically "hot" countries like Serbia, India, and Saudi Arabia.

The four of us headed to the cafeteria, where a few tables of power-suited staffers were watching CNN and quietly munching chicken and rice (Ecuadorian food, I noticed— not burgers and fries). I'd already forwarded Carrington a copy of "How Democracy Is Nudged," and as soon as we'd sat down with our trays, he apologized that the embassy lacked the romantic chaos of Thompson's USIS office.

"I'm afraid things are rarely that exciting around here," he said, lifting a forkful of rice.

"Well, except maybe when they PNGed the ambassador," Lawson said.

"Oh yeah," said Carrington between chews. "That was exciting, but that doesn't happen very often."

It really doesn't, which is why it was a big deal when President Correa expelled US ambassador Heather Hodges in 2011, declaring her persona non grata (or "PNGing" her, in diplomat-speak) in retaliation for a WikiLeaked cable in which she accused Correa of condoning police corruption. After announcing her expulsion, Correa declared indignantly, "Colonialism in Latin America is finished." Only six US ambassadors have been PNGed from their host countries in the last forty years, and three of those have been in the so-called Bolivarian states of the Andes. In Bolivia, the US ambassador was booted in 2008, accused by leftist-populist president Evo Morales of fomenting political unrest. Venezuela's Chávez PNGed his US ambassador the very next day. It's a symbolic gesture, but a serious one. The ambassador and his or her family have just seventy-two hours to leave the country, which accounted for a lot of the temporary excitement around the Quito embassy. Diplomatic relations continue in the ambassador's absence, with a chargé d'affaires filling his or her shoes, but relations are often strained. When I visited Quito, the embassy was still working without an ambassador. A new one was reinstated three months later, and negotiations are still ongoing to restore full ties with Venezuela and Bolivia.

In the wake of the expulsion, Carrington's team had a media circus on their hands, but ordinarily life around the PAS offices moves at about the same pace as your average small Manhattan PR firm—and with significantly less glamour. The international propaganda biz has changed somewhat since the fall of communism, and today's heirs to the USIS are as much administrators and event promoters as artful spin doctors. Sure, disseminating news from a US perspective is still part of the job. Public Affairs officers issue press releases to the Ecuadorian media just like any other organization, and the embassy distributes an in-house newsradio show, *Reportajes,* to some 120 stations across the country. I listened to a couple of episodes and found the stories "not so much slanted as selected," as Thompson described similar USIS efforts in 1962. There was a piece about Hugo Chávez returning to Cuba for further cancer treatment, a story that Venezuelan officials regularly played down. There was coverage of Drug War negotiations at the then-ongoing Summit of the Americas in Cartagena, Colombia—an event that only garnered coverage in the United States thanks to a titillating Secret Service prostitution scandal. Meanwhile, quite apart from the embassies, the DC-based, semi-independent Voice of America networks broadcast radio and TV programs in forty-three languages on a worldwide network of transmitting stations.

But to hear my hosts tell it around the lunch table, managing the news is less important to the mission of public diplomacy than it once was.

"We've had a big shift of emphasis over the years to language and exchange programs," explained Swenarski, the cultural affairs officer. These days, she said, a lot of the bureau's money and manpower goes into supporting public and private English-language learning centers, sending students and professionals to study in the United States, and hosting American speakers and performers in Ecuador. The USIS in Thompson's story brought a commie radio station to its knees. The PAS in Quito recently brought an alt-country band to the Amazon.

Without any Cold War antagonists to outfox, today's battle for hearts and minds seems less like an ideological contest and more like a slightly crunchy outreach campaign. The bulk of the PAS's efforts are actually built around the rather simple and charming notion that the more foreigners know about the United States, the more they will like us. So the agency sponsors a vast network of cultural centers and "American corners"—libraries and community spaces with English-language books and movies, occasional free lectures, and cultural displays. Come for the free Internet, stay for the exhibit on civil rights! Lawson mentioned working with administrators and student groups at local universities, trying to drum up support for American studies curricula. Swenarski described a few of the PAS's cultural programs, an impressive slate of tours, exhibits, and performances that pivot around annual themes. Last year's "Rural America" theme, for example, brought in bluegrass musicians and school presentations about the rodeo. The year before had a black culture motif, with New Orleans brass brands and step-dancing troupes. Programs like these, it seemed to me, still followed rather literally what had been the old tagline of the USIS: "Telling America's story to the world."

International exchanges, meanwhile, are arguably at the heart of the PAS's mission. Youth ambassador and leadership programs send Ecuadorian students to workshops and conferences in the United States. Similar programs for adults target leaders in business, government, education, and media. To fully grasp the potential payoff of these field trips, consider that four justices on the Ecuadorian equivalent of the Supreme Court are alums of such programs, as are some three hundred heads of state or cabinet-level ministers worldwide. It's a forward-looking strategy, one that banks on the notion that today's familiarity with American culture will translate into tomorrow's support for American policies.

"The generation that knows you and loves you won't always be around," Swenarski said. "I'd say fifteen to twenty-five is the target age that we're trying to reach."

Of course, even the kinder, gentler face of soft power still has its turf wars. Around the world, for instance, Confucius Institutes sponsored by the Chinese government are increasingly muscling in on cultural territory dominated by PAS-backed language programs and community centers. The first one in Ecuador opened at Quito's Universidad San Francisco in 2010, and seeing as how China has invested more than $8 billion in the country since 2009, a *quiteño* could be forgiven for wanting to pick up some Mandarin. That undermines the PAS mission, Swenarski explains, since every hour that an Ecuadorian spends learning tea ceremonies at a Confucius Institute is an hour she's not learning the similarly delightful traditions of the supposed Yankee imperialists.

Unlike the USIS and its America-bashing broadcaster, the PAS is not likely to torpedo the Universidad San

Francisco for hosting a Chinese public diplomacy arm. Very much like their predecessors, however, today's democracy-nudgers still pay close attention to how the United States is represented in local media. After lunch, the two junior diplomats excused themselves, and Carrington led me upstairs to a nondescript door at the edge of a cubicle complex.

"This is the monitoring room," he said, "probably the only place in the building that has a little bit of a secret-agent vibe."

Inside was a fluorescent-lit room with cheap office furniture, utility shelves, and a half dozen PCs. Nothing particularly glamorous about it. It reminded me of the ammonia-stink janitor's closet that my high school handed over to the AV club, except that my AV club never had a seventy-two-inch monitor on the wall with inlaid screens simultaneously airing every Ecuadorian TV network.

"Usually we've got a couple of guys in here," Carrington said, "monitoring for any mentions of the US or US policy. I guess they're at lunch."

I stared at the grid of talking heads and *telenovelas*. It was a bit hypnotic, like the flickering, towering displays at an appliance store. "I know a couple of news junkies who could really get into this," I said.

"Yeah, mostly we get former radio and TV guys. Of course, we watch the newspapers and the Web too. Did you know three different papers reprinted that *New York Times* editorial about Correa this morning?"

The week before, Ecuador's National Court of Justice had upheld a conviction in a libel suit brought by Correa against the directors and a former editor of *El Universo,* the country's largest paper. The journalists were fined $42 million and sentenced to three-year prison terms for publishing an editorial that called Correa a "dictator" and alleged he had put civilians in danger by ordering troops to open fire during a 2010 police rebellion. *"Ha brillado la verdad,"* Correa had announced from the steps of the courthouse. *The truth has shone through.* It was his biggest lawsuit against journalists, although not his first. The trial was full of abnormalities, and the *New York Times* echoed other media outlets and watchdog groups when it called the ruling "a staggering, shameful blow to the country's democracy." Under heavy pressure, Correa issued a pardon a couple of weeks later.

"So, what do you do with everything you find?" I asked Carrington.

"Sort it by topic and organize it into a daily dossier, available for other diplomats and policymakers. I can get you a copy." He motioned for me to follow him to his office.

We walked through a dense jungle of cubicles, quiet but for the hum of monitors, the clacking of keyboards, and the occasional muffled whiff of phone conversation. Framed pictures of national parks and other American landmarks hung on the walls at regular intervals. The whole place had a very corporate vibe. If this was telling America's story, I thought, then storytelling had become rather systematized.

Carrington's office was clean and simple—a few crowded bookshelves, pictures of his kids, a framed map of Chesapeake Bay. On a wall-mounted flat-screen, Secretary of State Hillary Clinton was giving a speech in London. For a moment, I thought maybe the State Department had an all-Hillary channel, à la *The Truman Show,* but it was just CNN.

"It's a particularly fat one today on account of the *El Universo* ruling," Carrington said, handing me a thick folder of photocopied news articles. We took a seat as I leafed through. It was divided into sections, with headings like "Coverage of Outreach Efforts," "Economic News and Opinion," "Counternarcotics," and "Freedom of the Press." Many of the headlines trumpeted Correa's refusal to stay the *Universo* sentences, as requested by the Inter-American Commission on Human Rights. Correa had countered that the commission was dominated by "certain hegemonic states," a not-so-subtle jab at supposed US meddling.

On the TV, Hillary was offering condolences on the deaths of two journalists, a reporter and a photographer who'd snuck into Syria, covering the uprising there in defiance of that country's government. Carrington and I had both turned to listen when a loud buzz from the PA drowned out the television. Suddenly, a man's recorded voice filled the room—calm, but with a no-bullshit tone of authority.

"Duck and cover," the voice announced, pronouncing the space between each word. "Get away from the windows and await instructions."

The buzzing echoed again, seemingly louder and across the entire floor. Instinctively, I glanced at the window next to me, then looked at Carrington.

"Bomb drill," he said calmly. "This happens sometimes. It'll probably be over in just a minute."

We waited another ten or fifteen seconds for the buzzing to stop. Then the man's voice came on once more.

"Duck and cover. Get away from the windows and await instructions."

The buzzing continued, and Carrington's brow began to furrow. I stupidly peered out the window, expecting to see— what? Masked guerrillas? Government troops? It occurred to me again that I wasn't clear who the bad guys were in Ecuador, or whether there even were any.

"All right, then," Carrington said, sounding more confused than alarmed. "I guess we should probably duck and cover."

He started lowering himself out of his chair, and I followed suit. I realized that, while I've heard the phrase a lot, I didn't really know what ducking and covering looked like. Absurdly, I wondered whether Thompson, a child of the 1950s, had ever had to crawl underneath his school desk, like in all those old Civil Defense PSAs. I was gauging whether there was enough space under Carrington's desk for the both of us when the voice abruptly came back over the PA.

"This has been a drill," it announced, and the buzzing ceased. A muffled wave of chatter broke out over the cubicles outside. On TV, Hillary had finished speaking and was shaking hands with men in suits. We both slid back into our seats, and Carrington grinned at me a little sheepishly.

"Well, that doesn't happen every day," he said, straightening his tie. "I guess you got to see something exciting after all."

Public Diplomacy Officer Jennifer Lawson didn't come to the Foreign Service via the usual channels. She and I were headed back to the Plaza Grande in a government SUV—jet-black with tinted windows, a beefy driver in a dark suit, the works. We were tagging along with PAS intern Liz Mayberry, a chipper Minnesotan who'd invited us to sit in on her weekly after-school English class at one of the embassy's "American corners." The resource hub was actually in a wing of the same cultural center where I'd seen the Quito photo exhibit a week before.

Lawson's first love was modern dance. She'd studied it at Mount Holyoke College in the late 1980s, and she'd toured abroad with various dance companies before founding her own troupe in the mid-1990s. Her sister was an enthusiastic Foreign Service officer, and after years of her urging, Lawson took the Foreign Service exam on something of a whim. At the time, the pass rate for candidates was between 25 percent and 30 percent, and when Lawson saw that she'd passed, she opted to trade in her ballet flats for a pair of sensible diplomat's heels.

"I'd been to these amazing arts festivals all over the world," she said, "and after a while it dawned on me: government can make these cool, life-changing events happen."

She was blond, in her early forties, and she still had a dancer's slight build. The enormous purse on her lap made her look even smaller as she slouched in the backseat of the SUV.

"That might be a more popular idea in Ecuador than it is in the US," I said. "Not a lot of people at home these days are crowing about the wonderful role that government can play in our lives."

"You know, this job actually gives you a new perspective on that whole US political party debate," she said. "People in the US look at our own governmental system and political parties and say, 'These two sides can't agree on anything.' But they agree we should keep the Constitution, and you can't say that about every country."

The SUV dropped us off in front of the Centro Cultural Metropolitano, and we walked upstairs to what looked like a middle-school study hall. Liz the intern had a whiteboard waiting for her there, along with some markers and photocopied worksheets. The bookshelves were a hodgepodge of picture books, teenage vampire chronicles, and paperback versions of children's classics: Jules Verne, *Robinson Crusoe, Treasure Island.* There was a rack of magazines with a few well-thumbed issues of *National Geographic,* plus some conspicuously dusty copies of *Time* and *Newsweek.* Back in the United States, it was Black History Month, and all around the center were educational posters with photos and bios of prominent African Americans: Martin Luther King, Frederick Douglass, Sojourner Truth, and, bizarrely, Tyra Banks.

"We try and give people what our social media team calls 'veggies and candy,'" Lawson said with a shrug. "You know, balance out some info about foreign policy with some info about the Grammys."

A few minutes later, twenty elementary-schoolers in blue jumpers came wandering in, and Lawson and I grabbed desks in the back of the room. The median age was about nine. The kids were surprisingly well behaved as they gathered around the table, reaching for markers and grinning when they responded, "Fine, thank you" to Liz's round-the-table survey of how they were doing. Adjectives were the topic of the day, and she launched right in with a series of flash cards that paired nouns with modifiers. "Tall girl," the class repeated. "Fast car. Brown dog."

Lawson and I squirmed to get comfortable in our tiny school desks. I understood, I told her, why it was important for these kids that they learn English—it expanded their horizons, gave them a competitive advantage, and so on. But why was it important to the embassy? Why was it important for America? I wasn't entirely clear on how a tutoring program advanced our national interests.

"It has to do with making ourselves understood around the world," she said. "Look, it's in our best interest for Americans to be able to communicate with as much of the world as possible, even for those people who don't travel or speak foreign languages."

Liz asked the students to turn to their worksheets, and the room got quiet as they grabbed pencils and put their heads down.

"The other thing," Lawson whispered, "is that we hope a

bunch of these kids will someday come to the US and take that experience home with them. If you want to prevent a skewed impression of the country, there's really no substitute for cultural exchange programs."

"Skewed because of what they read in the Ecuadorian media?" I asked. "Anti-imperialist rhetoric and all that?"

"Sure, that's part of it," she said, "but also American media. Say you watch a lot of *Law & Order*. You'd think that our country was swimming in homeless people standing around on street corners and witnessing murders. Or, depending on what kind of media you're consuming, you could also come off with a simplistic, Pollyana-ish view, where everybody's wealthy and we have no social problems."

This, Lawson explained, is what ultimately motivates a lot of the PAS's efforts, a drive to present the United States as a more nuanced place than it might come off via Hollywood movies, music videos, or celebrity magazines. To a lot of Ecuadorian nine-year-olds—hell, to a lot of *Ecuadorians*—the United States is basically one big Miami, from sea to shining sea. Or maybe it's New York, but either way it's a cartoon version, where everyone drives a big car and lives in a skyscraper. So the bluegrass bands and the step-shows are more than just circuses, imported to keep the locals entertained and thereby well disposed to the United States. They're part of a coordinated effort to beat back ultimately harmful stereotypes of America as a land of urban millionaires who spend their days sunbathing and murdering one another.

In a sense, I realized, the United States is kind of its own worst enemy. We're victims of our own cultural success. In Thompson's day, USIS officers were battling negative images of America promoted by Cuban news agencies and socialist agitators. But so much of the PAS's job today involves fending off the American culture machine itself, the more pervasive and not always flattering elements of our society that manage to promote themselves whether we like it or not. If colonialism is somebody else taking over your story, then what is it called when your story starts telling and retelling itself, all over the world, without your control or approval? I thought of all those folks on the Gringo Trail, trotting the globe while carrying all the baggage of American culture, and I wondered if maybe they had more to do with international relations than I'd thought. Maybe more than all the sputtering anti-imperialists in Latin America. We have met the enemy, as the saying goes, and he is us.

Of course, if we're the bad guys in that scenario, then we're still the good guys too, which was easy to remember as I watched Liz the intern help her students read aloud from their adjective worksheets. They were clearly fond of her. All the kids seemed excited to be there, and they were, without exception, ferociously cute. They took turns writing their best sentences on the whiteboard, and I tried not to read too much of the American Dream into their examples of adjectives-at-work. *I have a big house. My watch is expensive. My girlfriend is beautiful.*

When class was over, I walked back outside with Lawson and Liz. It was late afternoon, and the Plaza Grande was full of people on benches, talking and smoking and eating empanadas. Ten or fifteen picketers marched slowly in front of the presidential palace, protesting the ruling against *El Universo*. The building was once the seat of the Spanish Crown, and they looked very small in front of its fat Doric columns. When the black SUV pulled up, I thanked Lawson and Liz for their time. The sound of their car doors ricocheted off the buildings in the square, and I waved as they drove away. I had to imagine them waving back on the other side of the tinted windows.

CHAPTER FIVE

His Once-Great Empire

Everybody here is working terribly hard
on some Worthwhile Project, and for some
queer reason it is depressing.

—Personal correspondence, June 6, 1962

I

There is a velocity that a plane achieves on a runway just seconds before lift-off, known to pilots as "rotation speed" or V_R. It is reached at the precise moment when the nosewheel of the plane leaves the ground, but before the rest of the aircraft follows. From your cramped seat in coach, you'll know you've hit V_R during that split second when you can physically anticipate lift-off, if only because the speed at which you're traveling feels so deeply, intuitively unsustainable. This is the speed at which buses in the Andes travel all the time.

South America offers a dazzling array of intercity bus experiences. On one end of the spectrum, you have your classic chicken bus—a Frankensteinian assembly of repurposed auto parts, packed with people and livestock, adhering to no discernible schedule. Far on the other end is the luxury cruiser, with reclining seats, movies, meals, and, if you're lucky, even wireless. These are a bargain by American standards and make even your nicer Amtrak routes look like jostling covered wagons on the Oregon Trail. Speed, however, is always a factor, particularly in Ecuador. Unlike in neighboring Colombia, where the law kindly requires bus companies to post annual fatality counts at the ticket counter, choosing a bus company in Ecuador is always a roll of the dice. Just days before I left Quito, a speeding bus plunged off a cliff two hours north of the city, killing twenty-nine and injuring another thirty. This is a common enough occurrence as to not make the front-page news.

My night bus to Guayaquil hit V_R somewhere in the mountains south of town, and it maintained that speed uninterrupted for the next eight hours. As we hurtled through the Andes, I settled in with a tattered copy of *Travels with*

Charley, which I'd picked up from an English-language bookstore in Gringolandia. A famously contemplative travel text seemed like an appropriate choice for the long miles ahead. Lost on me until later was the fact that John Steinbeck's classic road-trip chronicle was actually published during the same week in 1962 that Thompson would have been in Guayaquil. Today, we know Steinbeck to be as much a fabulist about his roadside encounters as Thompson would later become (and maybe already was), but the fabricated dialogue has never been my favorite part of *Travels with Charley* anyway. I enjoy the book because of Steinbeck's wistful commentary on the open road, because of elegant lines that remind me, for example, why it's possible to doze off even while your chicken bus is approaching Mach 5.

"The unbroken speeds are hypnotic," Steinbeck explained, "and while the miles peel off, an imperceptible exhaustion sets in."

I spent just two nights in Guayaquil, a hot and gritty port city that doesn't have much to recommend it. Unlike Quito, Guayaquil lost most of its colonial character to a massive fire in 1896, and the blaze was just a punctuation mark at the end of an already dismal century for Ecuador's largest city. It was besieged by the Peruvian military twice. It was invaded by Quito, its own national capital, once. During an epic yellow-fever outbreak in 1842, Guayaquil's own provincial governor described the city as "an immense cemetery of dread and horror." Guayaquil, in fact, has its own page in the *Encyclopedia of Plague and Pestilence,* which ominously notes that the low, wet town is "an ideal breeding habitat for the mosquito."

It was so low and wet that Guayaquil's riverfront remained unsettled for centuries after its founding in 1538. Rock was too distant and expensive to import and use as fill.

The surrounding mangrove forests, however, were loaded with a seemingly inexhaustible supply of hard-shelled oysters. The tasty bivalves were so numerous that they became, in the words of one nineteenth-century British lieutenant, "the continued and never-failing food of the inhabitants." So city planners dictated that shells from Guayaquil's favorite snack be strategically discarded in order to fill the bogs and build infrastructure.

"For instance," wrote the lieutenant, "whilst I was there the authorities wished to construct a battery below the town . . . ; subsequently every morning a crowd of people were to be seen opening oysters and throwing shells in the appointed spot, the daily increase of the battery giving promise of being sooner completed than the generality of public works in Spanish America."

The people of Guayaquil have been building up their riverfront ever since. Today, that onetime pile of oyster shells is about the only nice place to kill an afternoon in the otherwise dumpy city. I spent two days strolling the boardwalk there, enjoying the watery views and the watery pilsner beer. I admired the historic monuments and ate my fill of a tuna-and-onion stew called *encebollado*. Then I skipped town on the first bus for the Peruvian border.

"Nowhere is my natural anarchism more aroused than at the national borders," Steinbeck wrote after he and his dog Charley were turned away from Canada for a lack of veterinary papers. "I have never smuggled anything in my life. Why, then, do I feel an uneasy sense of guilt on approaching a customs barrier?"

I'm with Steinbeck. The immigration checkpoint at the town of Aguas Verdes was in bad need of a paint job and worse need of a janitor. I waited with fifty or so of my co-passengers to get my passport stamped by an unsmiling officer who stood behind an iron gate. Coming into Ecuador had been no problem. All of my papers were in order. So I had no reason to be nervous, but there is always some tension at a border crossing—that cultivated air of Serious Business, exacerbated by the presence of men with large guns.

Stapled on the wall next to the immigration counter at Aguas Verdes were posters of Peru's *desaparecidos,* the "disappeared" victims of one or another of the Andes' many armed conflicts. Most of Peru's "disappeared" are victims of the country's twenty-year war against the Maoist Shining Path guerrillas, which raged across the country during the 1980s and 1990s. It was a brutal campaign that left as many as 70,000 Peruvians killed or unaccounted for, many of them victims of clandestine *campesino* massacres carried out by both sides. When it was my turn to approach the customs booth, I saw that the victim on the poster closest to me was standing alongside an older woman I presumed to be his mother. The two of them watched over my proceedings with the gruff Peruvian official, and their gazes cast a shadow over the already grim exchange.

Or so it seemed to me. The truth is, I was in a melancholy funk for the entire ride to Lima. What Steinbeck wrote about driving long distances also holds true for long bus rides: "A large area of the conscious mind is left free for thinking," and this is doubly true when the terrain is monotonous. Peru's coastal-desert landscape looked like the Nevada high country, all sandy flats and low ocher mountains, with rare glimpses of the ocean through the dunes. It was barren, and in the absence of scenery, my mind started to wander.

How were things going so far? Would I call this trip a success? I had wanted to figure out how travel in a foreign land could turn a moony misanthrope like Thompson into a shrewd cultural observer. Maybe I'd wanted some of that transformation for myself. After a year in South America, Thompson said he suddenly understood why the United States "will never be what it could have been," but all I had found so far was a series of ambiguous relationships: between South Americans and their environments, South Americans and their governments, South Americans and North Americans. If any of this shed light on what America was, wasn't, or "could have been," I wasn't seeing it. And if I had so far been transfigured by the experience, I wasn't feeling it.

It's not that I was discouraged. I had learned a lot already, and there was plenty of Thompson Trail still spooling out in front of me. It's just that I could feel my wheels spinning, and for all the friction, I didn't yet know where I was going.

II

When he got to Peru in late July of 1962, Thompson was in no higher spirits. In fact, he was growing surlier by the day. His longest published letter from South America is essentially a litany of complaints written from his hotel room in Lima, describing the myriad ways in which the continent was slowly destroying him—physically, psychologically, spiritually, and sexually. Lima was gray and overcast, he wrote, almost as bad as Bogotá. All of the food was poison. His bowels were inflamed and the doctors had forbidden him anything but bread and mineral water. Cigarettes were expensive, and he was broke. He hadn't had sex since Colombia (and he was broke). His Spanish still sucked, and no one in the Andes had any sense of humor. Peru was oligarchical in the extreme, dominated by a snobbish aristocracy known as the "forty families," and only days before he arrived, the military had overthrown the government after a populist reformer in the mold of Colombia's Jorge Gaitán had won the presidential election. Lima's poor, Thompson wrote, were "unbelievably primitive." The rich were insufferable. The only Americans in town were businessmen, and they were golf-balls-off-the-balcony types, every bit as bad as the corrupt Peruvian elites.

"I'm beginning to think that my coming here is like an Abolitionist going to the Old South," Thompson wrote. "And considering the relations between the Indians and the wealthy (there is no other group) I think the comparison is fairly apt."

Thompson wrote three separate stories from Peru, one on his first visit and two more when he returned the next spring. The first two cover the country's deteriorating political situation: the military takeover, the following year's proposed "do-over" election, and what Peruvians' nonchalant responses to the coup said about their attitude toward democracy. The first article ran with the headline DEMOCRACY DIES IN PERU, BUT FEW SEEM TO MOURN ITS PASSING. In its opening lines, Thompson sums up the scene that he walked into: Nobody took to the streets when the military annulled the election results, and Thompson compared the "death of democracy" in Peru to "the death of somebody's old uncle, whose name had been familiar in the household for years. But he died where he had always lived, in some far-off town the family never quite got around to visiting."

When my bus finally pulled into Lima, it had been nine months since Peru's last election, but the campaign detritus still littered most of the capital's major thoroughfares. Big elections transform a Latin American cityscape like they transform prime-time television at home—they clutter it up with all kinds of obnoxious crap. Good taste has never been a prerequisite to run for the Peruvian Congress, and on my way into town, I saw one sun-bleached cardboard cutout of a candidate hitchhiking, another of a candidate flexing his biceps in a muscle tee, and a few torn campaign posters for a candidate named "Doctor Marcos," who wore a full lab coat and stethoscope, in case the title didn't sell you on his medical credentials.

The marquee event during the last election, though, had been the presidency, and most of Lima's dumpier buildings— including many private homes—still bore a fairly fresh coat of paint with the name of the candidate whose team had first shown up there with a paintbrush and a bag of rice.

Presidential politics in Peru are fabulously sordid. Consider that the country's last president, Alan García, had already held the office once in the 1980s, a term that bankrupted the country, immediately after which he escaped to Europe to avoid embezzlement charges. His successor was Alberto Fujimori, a conservative authoritarian who was eventually deemed "morally unfit" by the Peruvian Congress. After fleeing to Japan and attempting to resign via fax, Fujimori was extradited and convicted of corruption, kidnapping, and mass murder. He is currently serving twenty-five years in a Peruvian jail for approving death squads in the war against the Shining Path guerrillas. The following election brought in Alejandro Toledo, who confessed in office to having a secret illegitimate daughter and was plagued by media accusations of soliciting prostitutes and using cocaine. Following his term, the country took a long second look at old Alan García, decided he wasn't so bad after all, and elected him again.

I was beginning to understand why half of Thompson's South America stories were about electoral politics. His literary idol, Faulkner, couldn't have written better anti-heroes, and there's a kind of fatalistic absurdity to Latin American politics that seems to jibe with Thompson's later gonzo persona. You can't invent storylines like this: Toledo bounced back from the hookers-and-blow accusations to place a respectable fourth in the most recent election. He was edged out for third by an ethnic German economist, an affable gringo whose wife is from Wisconsin and who frequently appeared on campaign stops with his official mascot of a giant dancing guinea pig. Meanwhile, the top two candidates on the ballot were Keiko Fujimori, the chirpy thirty-six-year-old daughter of the imprisoned former president, and Ollanta Humala, a former military commander who once led a failed coup against Keiko's dad. Nothing awkward about that.

Neither Keiko nor Humala picked up 50 percent of the vote in the first round, so under Peruvian law, the election went into a run-off contest, a second round between only the two of them. To the nearly half of Peruvians who had voted for somebody else in the first round, the election seemed like a classic lose-lose situation. Keiko was an arch-conservative whose main platform seemed to be pardoning her war-criminal father. Many Peruvians feared a return to the days of secret police, forced sterilizations, and constitutional rewrites that characterized Fujimori's government in the 1990s. Humala, meanwhile, was on the far left side of the spectrum, but also the son of a prominent ultra-nationalist. He had narrowly lost the previous election after declaring his admiration for then-alive-and-kicking Hugo Chávez and vowing to nationalize several industries.

Of course, this lesser-among-evils scenario isn't new for

Peruvian voters. Thompson captured the similarly ambivalent atmosphere of 1963 when he described the front-runner of the reboot election as "the best of a bad lot." The same sentiment was echoed last time around by Peru's Nobel Prize–winning author Mario Vargas Llosa (a onetime presidential candidate himself), who told the press that choosing between Keiko and Humala was like choosing between cancer and AIDS.

I crashed in Lima with Reid Wilson, an old friend teaching second grade at one of the capital's most exclusive American schools. Reid's a monkish vagabond of a guy, a vegetarian surfer and avid reader of New Age psychology who always looks a bit drowsy but was in fact one of the sharpest guys in my college graduating class. His students are the children of the Peruvian elite: government ministers, old-money families, and corporate and industrial titans— what Thompson called Peru's "all-powerful aristocracy." Both of the Peruvians on the *Forbes* list of world billionaires send their kids to Reid's school, and even as second-graders, his students are being groomed for their eventual application into American colleges. Reid's a hardworking teacher, popular with students, parents, and administrators alike, but he's also pretty clear-eyed about the insular and privileged world that his students occupy.

"There was a joke making the faculty rounds during the last election," he told me on the day I showed up. "Ollanta Humala is driving through the streets of La Molina"—the country-club residential district where Reid teaches—"when suddenly, all the neighborhood kids start crowding the sidewalks and cheering his name. *O-llan-ta! O-lla-nta!*

"So Humala thinks, This is great! I'm finally making

some headway with the upper class! And he pulls over the car to thank the kids for their support.

" 'Thank you for believing in the revolution!' he cries. 'It is so important to have the youth on our side!'

" 'Revolution?' says one of the kids. 'All I know is that my dad said if you win, we get to move to Miami!' "

Among the kind of people who volunteer for the PTA at Reid's school, the prospect of a socialist-leaning president was about as ominous as a return to Fujimori-style dictatorship. It would herald the declining influence of the rich and educated class, along with a possible windfall tax on corporate profits and maybe even a government takeover of mines and utilities. In Bolivia, leftist president Evo Morales had recently nationalized the country's oil and natural gas fields. In Venezuela, Chávez had gone so far as to expropriate golf courses, vacation homes, and private yachts in the name of state tourism. Thanks to a booming mineral industry and high commodities prices, money has been rapidly flowing into Lima's private sector since the early 2000s. But all of this could dry up under Humala, the gentry feared—or anyway, it could be redirected into government coffers and social programs for the rural poor.

In Reid's neighborhood, a beachside condo and tourism district called Miraflores, evidence of Peru's recent prosperity was hard to avoid. Reid himself was living a solidly upper-middle-class lifestyle, paying just under $1,100 a month for a sleek and spacious loft that most Manhattanites would drool over (Peru's minimum monthly wage, by contrast, is about $280). Outside his windows, palm trees speckled a long beachside park and paragliders drifted on coastal thermals like windswept pieces of confetti. On the streets, there was no escaping the sounds of construction. Miraflores and its neighboring districts were veritable jungles of cranes and steel scaffolding, with gleaming apartment towers going up anyplace they would fit. In recent years, some of the best restaurants in the world have opened up in these neighborhoods, along with a clutch of designer handbag stores and modern art galleries catering to tourists and the Peruvian 1 percent.

My first task in Lima, though, was to venture into a very different part of the city—not a poor one exactly, but a working-class, light-industrial neighborhood called Breña, right on the edge of downtown. When the guidebooks mention Breña, which is rarely, they tend to use the word "dodgy." In the heart of all that dodginess is a walled complex with a wrought-iron gate known as the Casa del Pueblo, or the People's House. It's the headquarters of Peru's oldest political party, called the American Popular Revolutionary Alliance, the historic champion of Peru's common man. And it was here in 1962 that the military took a stand for the Peruvian elite the last time that a candidate of the populist left threatened to upset the established order.

On the night of August 7, 1962, Thompson stood outside the Casa del Pueblo with a crowd of onlookers, watching as the military relinquished the building they'd invaded two weeks prior. APRA's candidate had placed first in the presidential election that summer, but neither the military nor the upper class nor most business interests particularly wanted a lefty champion of the poor running their country. So the military annulled the election, drove some tanks through the gates of the presidential palace, seized power, and ransacked the Casa del Pueblo. Even then, the complex was as much a community center as a political nerve center, and Thompson's catalog of the destruction gives a pretty good idea of the range of services that APRA provided:

There were bullet holes in the walls and ceiling;
doors and windows had been smashed and party
records destroyed; and the entire building—
nearly a city block of offices and facilities—was
littered with glass, broken furniture, and water-
soaked paper. Among the smashed or stolen items
were the only dentist drills, all medicine from the
clinic and drugs from the pharmacy, typewrit-
ers, a radio transmitter, all phonograph records,
sculpture in the art workshop, instruments for
the children's band, food and plates from the dining hall, and records from the credit union.

I walked up to the Casa del Pueblo on a characteristically muggy afternoon. My walk over had led through a
tangle of blighted residential streets along the city's hopelessly polluted Rio Rimac, and I'd heard a few "Hey,
gringo!" catcalls from darkened doorways. The street out
front was a six-lane boulevard, traffic-choked and deafening, with irritable *limeño* drivers leaning on their horns for
every conceivable reason and no reason at all. The building
itself was an anachronism, a powder-blue colonial manor
wedged between dingy office buildings and staring across
the busy road at one of the big-box stores that South Americans call *hipermercados*. Even the giant red star atop the
Casa del Pueblo—instantly recognizable to Peruvians as
the APRA logo—looked antiquated and tired.

That red star, and its inevitable associations with communism, probably made some American business and policy types very nervous around the time of Thompson's visit.
APRA did indeed have its roots in socialism. Its presidential

candidate, Víctor Raúl Haya de la Torre, had founded the party in 1924 on a platform of land reform, state ownership of industry, and integration of the country's indigenous majority. But the rallying cry of APRA was "Neither Washington Nor Moscow!" In a photo that Thompson took of several young Apristas (APRA supporters) cleaning up the wreckage at the Casa del Pueblo, a sign in the background reads, APRA SI, COMMUNISMO NO! Because of this anti-Soviet attitude, the Kennedy administration saw Haya de la Torre as an ally in the Alliance for Progress. But Peru's wealthy and urban criollos (Spanish-descended "whites") wanted to preserve the status quo, and as Thompson pointed out, they didn't much care whether the country's leadership was democratically elected.

"The people [in Peru] who need democracy don't even know what the word means," he wrote. "The people who know what it means don't need it, and they don't mind saying so."

I walked into the Casa del Pueblo to find dozens of photos and busts of Haya de la Torre, the preempted would-be president. He was a doughy and clean-shaven guy with the benevolent look of a sitcom granddad. Thompson made no secret of his admiration, calling Haya de la Torre "a brilliant orator and writer and one of the most determined reformers in the history of Latin America." No one bothered me as I wandered around the courtyard, picturing the buildings as Thompson might have seen them fifty years before. There was still a dentist's office and a "people's pharmacy," and the on-site high school had just let out. I walked past a computer lab filled with uniformed kids checking Facebook, and a few others loitered around the courtyard, coaxing horrible sounds out of trumpets and clarinets. They stared at me blankly as I walked by.

I didn't find any statues or plaques commemorating the military's sacking of the building in 1962, but I did see some shallow divots in the courtyard's stone walls that I convinced myself were the bullet holes Thompson had described. I ran my fingers around a few of them, trying to look inconspicuous. A bullet hole in brick feels jagged and raw, like a scabbed-over wound that won't heal. I wondered how many of the students around me could honestly imagine their own military just up and seizing control of the country overnight. The days of the military coup in South America are arguably over, but in Thompson's day, the prospect of the army simply booting a democratic government was commonplace enough that it didn't warrant much outcry. The same thing had just happened in Argentina five weeks earlier, and as Thompson noted, the takeover hardly affected day-to-day life in Peru, where most citizens saw the military government as "nothing more than a dress-uniform version of the same power bloc that has held the reins for centuries."

"Can I help you?"

The dress-shirted attendant had snuck up on me from behind. He was no more than twenty-five, wearing a red-star APRA pin and toting a clipboard under one arm. I explained that I was an American history student who had read about the coup in 1962 and wanted to see the Casa del Pueblo for myself. The young man smiled at me apologetically and pointed toward a bookstand next to the dentist's office, selling pamphlets about the party's history.

"That was a very long time ago." He shrugged. "Perhaps you should try a museum?"

A few weeks before the Keiko/Humala election, a Peruvian newspaper published the results of a poll across nineteen Latin American countries, asking respondents whether they'd be willing to trade democracy for a military government if their country were somehow in dire straits. If you stacked up those results next to a decade's worth of economic stats, you would notice a trend. In countries where economic growth has been steady—places like Panama, Uruguay, and Costa Rica—authoritarianism was exceedingly unpopular. Meanwhile, in countries struggling with poverty and stagnation, clear majorities said they would accept some form of military rule.

Peru was the conspicuous outlier in this comparison. Even after a decade of whirligig growth rates on par with India and China, 52 percent of the country answered that they would indeed support a military government. It was democracy's fourth-poorest showing, behind near-destitute Honduras, Paraguay, and Guatemala. To understand this apparent contradiction is to understand how the country wound up choosing between "cancer and AIDS."

Sure, the success of mining and other resource-extraction industries sent Peru's stock market soaring in the 2000s, but only a small segment of the population felt the effects of the boom. The great majority of these beneficiaries were in Lima, home to the country's investor and entrepreneurial classes. As many as two-thirds of all employable Peruvians, however, work in the "informal economy"—think street vendors, subsistence farmers, and unlicensed taxi drivers—which is a very long way down for the wealth to trickle, especially outside of the capital. Meanwhile, in the country's far-flung Amazonian reaches, locals have taken to protesting what they see as exploitation of their natural resources while all the money flows steadily toward Lima. Dozens have been killed in periodic violent protests in the Peruvian Amazon since 2009, when a series of strikes and occupations brought much of the country to a standstill.

Of course, this dramatically lopsided balance of wealth and power stretches back well before the current mining boom, even well before APRA. Peru was ground zero for the Spanish conquest of South America, which kicked off in 1535 when Pizarro founded the city of Lima. Class subjugation, for that matter, was already a hallmark of the Inca Empire more than a century before the conquistadors even set sail. Highly stratified societies have been the norm in Peru for longer than any other place in the New World, and in Thompson's mind, a lot of the country's modern troubles could be blamed on a deep-seated cultural acceptance of the oppression of the many by the few.

"From the beginning of their history," he wrote, "the Peruvian people have been conditioned to understand that there are only two kinds of human beings—the Ins and the Outs, with a vast gulf in between."

For centuries, that gulf has been the dominant force behind Peru's social and political development, and when the avowed leftist Ollanta Humala emerged from the last election three points ahead, the results were widely interpreted as a long-overdue victory of the Outs over the Ins.

III

"*Cuidado . . . cuidaaaado . . . CUIDADO!!!*"

The other passengers in my *combi* were screaming in unison as our driver started merging without checking his blind spot. It was morning rush hour on Lima's Carretera Central, and our jam-packed minivan was about to drift right into its identical twin in the neighboring lane. *Combis* are Lima's cheap, privately owned alternatives to the city's drastically overtaxed bus system. They follow established routes, but without a set schedule, so it's in their best interest to move as fast as humanly possible, both to maximize their trips and to beat the other *combis* to the next stop. Vans, trucks, and microbuses like these account for some 20 percent of Lima's mass transit fleet and more than half of the city's automobile accidents. I watched feebly out the window as we neared, then ricocheted harmlessly off, the neighboring *combi,* my face at one point within kissing distance of a similarly helpless rider in the next van over.

"*Animal! Idiota!*" my fellow passengers cried.

Seated next to me, Lara Devries didn't bat an eyelash. "Stuff like that happens all the time," she said with a sigh, watching as the other passengers stood up to reshuffle themselves, changing positions in preparation for the next stop. "And now we all play *combi* musical chairs."

Devries is the willowy twenty-six-year-old executive director of the Light and Leadership Initiative, a nonprofit she founded in 2008 to serve women and children in an east Lima shantytown called Huaycán. Two or three times a week, she makes the death-defying *combi* trip from her apartment in central Lima to the outskirts of the metro, a two-hour odyssey that's helped her cultivate both nerves of steel and an above-average tolerance for body odor.

"So anyway," she asked calmly, "what was I saying?"

What she'd been saying, I reminded her, was why a twenty-two-year-old blond-haired, blue-eyed gringa from suburban Chicago had chosen to move by herself to Peru after just one visit, then take up work in one of the roughest neighborhoods in the country.

"Right," she said, re-cuffing one of the legs of her jeans, then sitting up and shrugging modestly. "I don't really know what to tell you. I just saw that they needed the help."

This much is true. Huaycán is one of the poorest areas

in the massively sprawling Lima metro. It didn't exist at all until the mid-1980s, when the largely rural war against the Shining Path guerrillas prompted an influx of refugees into the cities. The radical Maoist insurgency had evolved in Peru's mountainous interior, and as they battled the Peruvian military, both groups systematically "cleansed" any villages they suspected of sympathizing with the enemy. By some estimates, a million people were displaced between 1980 and 2000, mostly ethnic indigenous or mestizo families from the highlands, and as many as 200,000 of those migrated into Lima. Communities like Huaycán sprang up seemingly overnight, as *campesino* families staked claims along the city's uninhabited urban edge. Basic services like water and electricity took decades to follow. And while Huaycán today is more integrated into the city—more like a very poor suburb than a refugee camp—large swaths of the district still lack sewage and drinking water, the education and employment levels are abysmal, and health issues like malnutrition and tuberculosis are fairly common.

Devries was a friend of a friend who had met me for coffee, then invited me to tag along on a visit to her project's headquarters. At six foot one and extremely fair-featured, she stands out on the streets of Lima like a robot at a Renaissance Fair. She has, I imagine, turned the heads of more than a few *bricheros*—Peruvian slang for local guys who play up their exotic Latino flair to land cute and/or deep-pocketed gringas and, hopefully, a "bridge" to the United States. At an age when many of her peers are still letting Mom and Dad pay the rent, Devries is like some kind of Aryan expat Energizer Bunny, teaching English around town and pursuing a master's degree in psychology when she isn't managing volunteers and finances at Light and Leadership.

"Huaycán will give you a different view of poverty," she'd

told me over coffee. "People think of it in this Third World way, all sparse landscapes and swollen bellies. But some of our kids have cell phones. They have a lot of the trappings, but they still have trouble meeting basic needs, and they have zero in the way of social mobility."

On our way to Light and Leadership, our roller-coaster *combi* passed through the wealthy district La Molina, within spitting distance of Reid's American school, and I thought how strange it was that on any given school day, his students and Devries's are all of twelve miles apart. It took our *combi* over an hour to navigate the gridlock of those twelve miles, which seemed like an appropriate measure of the socioeconomic distance, if not the geographic one.

As we crossed into Huaycán, the first thing I noticed was how the dense rows of cinder-block shanties crowding the hillsides resembled all those old pictures of tiered Inca ruins. All that was missing were the llamas. In every direction, the landscape was brown and brittle, dry and sun-baked in a way that suggested a place not intended for human habitation. The community is actually built within and up the slopes of an alluvial gorge, like a giant skateboarder's half-pipe. It's a steep, dry, and dusty bowl of about 200,000 souls, and the word *huaycán* derives from Quechua lingo for the mudslides that still claim lives whenever the desert coast has an uncharacteristically rainy season.

Devries and I hopped out at a busy commercial intersection, the usual chaotic mix of fruit vendors and appliance stores, unmuffled engines and earsplitting boom boxes. The sidewalks were as crowded as your average Manhattan lunch hour, with all manner of merchandise spilling out onto the pavement from beneath dingy and sun-faded awnings. In the road, the dirt bikes and moto-taxis outnumbered the cars, whining and weaving around one another in an insectoid

swarm. The crowd was noticeably browner than in Miraflores or Breña, not a criollo in sight, and as we waded into
the throng, it would have been hard to lose track of Devries,
a full head taller than most anyone around her and possibly
the only blonde for miles.

Painted ads for Keiko and Humala still covered the sides
of most buildings. Keiko won Huaycán's district, as she won
virtually every other district in Lima, but here by a much
slimmer margin than in the city's wealthier sectors. She had,
in fact, kicked off her campaign here some months before.
Huaycán is a pretty compulsory stump-circuit stopover for
any Peruvian politician. It's sort of Peru's equivalent of a
hard-luck Detroit auto factory—you're not a serious contender until you've had your photo-op here. And I could see
why. As Devries and I walked away from the main drag, the
streets turned to dirt. Every third or fourth building seemed
to be crumbling in some conspicuous fashion—top floors
boarded up, roofs caved in—and the barrenness of the surrounding hillsides was like a wraparound metaphor for the
lack of opportunity. If you're looking for a classic tableau of
urban poverty to stand sympathetically in front of, Huaycán
is prime real estate.

We walked to a gated three-story house a few blocks
from where the bus dropped us off, easily the most kept-
up in the neighborhood. Inside, Devries introduced me to
her current crop of volunteers: a British guy, a Finnish girl,
and four Americans, all under thirty and all looking a bit
ragged. Light and Leadership's volunteers spend their afternoons and evenings running an exhaustive slate of classes
for some 150 adults and school-aged kids. Basic English is a
fixture, as is arithmetic. Adult women show up for bimonthly
workshops on subjects like nutrition and computer literacy.
Huaycán is divided into a scatter of twenty alphabetical

zones, most of them accessible by *combi,* and L&L's classes are spread across several zones, so when volunteers aren't leading sessions or working on curricula, they spend a lot of time shuttling from one dusty ridge and clapboard schoolhouse to another. I caught them during their lunch hour and listened quietly as they gorged on pasta and briefed Devries on which *combis* weren't running and which students hadn't been showing up for class.

After lunch, I got a tour of the classroom facilities next door, a clean and bright couple of rooms filled with donated books, computers, and art supplies. Everything was locked up behind heavy iron gates, of course, but the space compared favorably to your average Boys & Girls Club back home. About half of L&L's programs were held there onsite, Devries explained, in the centrally located neighborhood known as Zone D. That afternoon, though, the British volunteer was teaching an English class in Zone R, high atop the half-pipe's eastern slope and one of the more far-flung parts of Huaycán. So Devries and I walked a few more dusty blocks to catch a microbus and join him.

Light and Leadership is a textbook example of the modern phenomenon known as "voluntourism." In addition to covering their own airfare and pocket money, all of Devries's volunteers pay a weekly fee for their food, housing, and basic utilities. They also cook and maintain the house when they're not teaching or performing administrative duties. A month of volunteering in Huaycán costs each participant a little over $600, which is money that would set you up pretty nicely at one of your more upscale Miraflores B&Bs. The fact that Devries rarely wants for volunteers just shows how many gringos would rather spend their vacation days sweating in a shantytown schoolhouse than freewheeling along the Gringo Trail.

"Of course," Devries said, "when I explain this to my friends from Lima, nobody understands. They just look at me confused, like, 'Why would anyone do that?'"

Our bus was grinding its gears up a steep and gravelly incline, leaving a plume behind it like a tail-spinning jet. As we climbed the walls of the gorge, the cinder-block buildings out the window gradually changed over to jumbled rows of plank houses.

"But do you get a few volunteers from Lima anyway?" I asked. "People just who pitch in for a day or two?"

"Almost none," she said, matter-of-factly. "And it isn't for lack of trying."

"Really?" I was surprised. "Why do you think that is?"

Devries sat quietly for a minute and pursed her lips. She reached back and did a twisty maneuver with her long ponytail, pulling it tighter against her head. Then she leaned over and pointed out the window next to me.

"Do you see how all those houses are the same color?" she asked. I looked out. Sure enough, all the clapboard shanties out the windows were an identical shade of baby blue. "The neighbors here pitch in to buy their paint in bulk, so as you work your way up the hillsides, all of the neighborhoods look like they've been color-coded."

Higher up the hill, I could see where the blue houses gave way to residential clusters of dusty salmon, harder to pick out against the totalizing beige of the mountainside. Devries and I rode awhile longer in silence before she took a stab at answering my question.

"Honestly," she said, "I don't think the middle and upper classes here understand what it means to be poor."

She said it with a note of resignation, as if admitting something she hadn't wanted to—maybe to me, maybe to herself.

"That's not so uncommon, really," I said. "Like they don't understand the extent of it? They don't really get how bad it is?"

"No," she said, "it's more than that. It's like they don't even understand who these people *are*. 'How did they all get here? Where did they all come from? What do they want?' I'm not sure they really know how to process it."

I thought that over for a second.

"Why?" I asked. "Because they're sheltered? Because they don't *see* enough of it?"

"Oh, they see plenty of it," Devries said. "Maybe not out here in Huaycán, but they see it in the city every day. It's more like there's just such a dramatic gulf."

Without knowing it, she was echoing Thompson. *The Ins and the Outs,* he had said, *with a vast gulf in between.* It occurred to me that Huaycán didn't even exist when Thompson was here, that the notion of 200,000 people scraping a living off these parched hillsides would probably have seemed absurd.

"Fine," I said, trying to understand, "but there's a gulf between rich and poor in the US, too. I don't get why it should be so different here."

Devries furrowed her brow. We were the only two people left on the bus now, which was rapidly running out of road as it approached a one-room plank-and-sheet-metal schoolhouse, standing alone near the top of the slope.

"I think there's just less empathy here," she said finally. "Maybe it's because there's no social mobility. There's no conception that you could have *been* one of those people, you know? Or that they might work hard and someday become you."

We climbed out of the *combi* and headed into the tiny stand-alone schoolhouse. The inside was dim and cool, with dirt floors. Ten or so elementary schoolkids were gathered around a table, watching the British guy point to a stick figure on a whiteboard, phonetically repeating English words for body parts. *Ee-ur. Stuh-meck. Ell-boh.* When Devries and I walked in, a handful of the kids got up and gathered excitedly around her legs. How was their day going, she asked them in Spanish. Most of the kids clearly recognized her as the chief gringa, although a few may just have been captivated by the foreign creature in their midst—this tall, pale woman who spoke their language and had to crouch when she stepped through the doorways.

I grabbed a seat on a rough wooden bench and helped a couple of boys in baseball caps fill out their anatomy worksheets. They had a knack for English, I told them, and they laughed and said I spoke good Spanish—the first and last time I have ever received that compliment. The next hour went by very quickly as we all sat around the table, repeating after each other and pointing one at a time to our hands, our heads, our hearts.

On one of my last days in Lima, I took a taxi to La Molina to join a faculty game of Ultimate Frisbee at Reid's school. The campus, needless to say, made both my high school and elementary school look like the cinder-block facilities in Huaycán. Reid's was just one in a line of spotless, exterior-entry classrooms, with a whole wall of windows and more high-end AV equipment than a Tokyo Apple Store. We played Frisbee on an immaculate lawn stretched between clusters of brick buildings and were serenaded during the game by a talent show under way inside the state-of-the-art theater.

In case you're wondering, neither the students nor their successful capitalist parents ever fled to Miami. Peru's stock market plummeted the day after Ollanta Humala's victory, but it has since bounced back and then some, as Presidente Humala has turned out to be a surprisingly centrist leader. During the run-off election, he scrapped his plans to nationalize the country's private pension system, and he swore on a Bible before a TV audience to uphold free-market principles and abide by term limits. Today, Humala keeps leftist neighbors like Correa at arm's length and instead publicly identifies with former Brazilian president Luiz Inácio "Lula" da Silva, whose combination of market capitalism and generous social spending made him one of the world's most popular leaders. Meanwhile, the moneyed class in Lima has happily continued, as Thompson put it, "maintaining itself in the style to which it has long been accustomed."

Reid and I got a ride back to Miraflores with one of his coworkers, a high school English teacher whose beat-up sedan had sprung a serious exhaust leak. As we idled our way through the city's debilitating traffic, the car gradually filled with noxious fumes. Amid the stench, our conversation turned to those aspects of life in Lima that the two of them didn't much care for. Traffic, they agreed, was hellish. Reid said he had lately been unable to ignore countless tiny instances of petty rudeness—adults cutting in lines, pedestrians butting shoulders, cars ignoring the crosswalks. Sometimes, he vented, it seemed as if Peruvians simply had an ingrained disregard for other people around them.

"You know what's getting to me?" the English teacher said. "Walls and gates." He braked to avoid hitting a moto-taxi that veered into his lane. "Everywhere I go, I'm surrounded by walls and gates." They really did seem pretty ubiquitous around Lima. From Miraflores to Huaycán, most public buildings and virtually every private home seemed to be surrounded by tall iron bars or brick walls topped with broken bottles. The two teachers described private beaches south of town where security guards monitored gates like bouncers holding velvet ropes. Even after my short time in Lima, I could see how this might come to seem oppressive.

"I think I'd get tired of that pretty quick," I said, my head partially craned out the window to avoid the exhaust smell, "always feeling like you're being kept out of someplace."

"Yeah, but do you know what's worse?" the English teacher asked. "What's worse are the people on the other side, the ones who just have no idea about anything because they've only ever been on the inside of the walls."

He might have said more, but then a *combi* swerved violently in front of us, narrowly missing a taxi, and a deafening crush of car horns cut the conversation short.

IV

"Day and night are one," Steinbeck wrote in *Travels with Charley*. "The setting sun is neither an invitation nor a command to stop, for the traffic rolls constantly."

Overnight buses are a fact of life for travelers in South America. It's a big continent, with substantial geographic obstacles and occasionally shoddy infrastructure, so a distance that might require a long day's drive in the United States instead becomes a twenty-four-hour odyssey of stale air and wildly fluctuating temperatures. Thompson made some of his early jaunts by plane, but with his typewriter and camera weighing him down and his finances ever dwindling, he realized in Peru that it was time to join the great unwashed masses. "It cost me $38 simply to get my gear from Guayaquil to Lima," he explained in a letter. "It goes without saying that I have taken my last plane in South America." From

Lima to Rio, the rest of Thompson's route would be carried out by bus and train—"a mad, headlong, poverty-stricken rush across the continent."

The overnight bus from Lima to Cusco departs in the evening and climbs 15,000 feet in the darkness. I stared out the window at the central Andean highlands until my eyes hurt, thinking about the mountains back in Montana and tracking the taillights of the buses ahead. Sometimes I'd spot them an hour or more up the road, ascending a switchback on the opposite side of a gorge, faint red dots bobbing and gliding through the night like lit cigarettes. I slept as best I could, and in the morning, the high-country sunrise burned slate-gray and pink.

The bus route led through roughshod mining towns clinging to the sides of mountains and through valleys filled with sugarcane plantations, where every stooped laborer wore the patterned alpaca poncho of the Quechua-speaking highlanders. This was the other Peru, the one that Thompson said was as different from Lima as Manhattan was from Appalachia. Geography is culture, of course, and Peru sits at a crossroads of three disparate South American ecosystems. The criollo cultural elites make up a majority in the coastal departments (*la costa*), but almost half of Peru's population is of pure Amerindian stock, and these indigenous descendants overwhelmingly occupy the Amazon regions (*la selva*) and the thin air of the Andes (*la sierra*). In these inland provinces, poverty rates are a few clicks higher and literacy rates substantially lower. Lima feels far away indeed, and antiestablishment messages tend to resonate here, which is one reason why Ollanta Humala won handily in thirteen of the fourteen Peruvian departments that lack an ocean view.

Back in Thompson's day, support for APRA was also heavy in *la sierra,* but with one key difference: literacy and

ID requirements kept between 65 percent and 80 percent of the largely Quechua population from voting. And this kind of indigenous marginalization was at the heart of Thompson's remaining article on Peru, entitled "The Inca of the Andes: He Haunts the Ruins of His Once-Great Empire." It's a piece that paints a pretty brutal picture of the indigenous experience in the Andes during the Alliance for Progress era. It opens on downtown Cusco, where Thompson says that a Quechua drifter on the street was "as sad and hopeless a specimen as ever walked in misery. Sick, dirty, barefoot, wrapped in rags, and chewing narcotic coca leaves to dull the pain of reality." In the article's opening lines, Thompson describes the waiters scurrying to close the blinds in the lounge of his comfortable Cusco hotel, so that the tourists inside won't be bothered by the "Indian beggars" staring in from the other side of the glass.

Reading through his articles and letters, it seems to me that Thompson was particularly put off by indigenous poverty in South America. As evenhandedly as he described the Wayuu back in Guajira, he seemed to write with genuine surprise and revulsion about their squalid living conditions, about the food that was "unfit for dogs." In his letters, he gripes that "the whole continent is covered in Indian shit" and regularly complains of having to "carry a truncheon to ward off the citizenry." "From Bogota south," he wrote in the *Observer,* "the Andean cities are overrun with Indian beggars who have no qualms about lying on a downtown sidewalk and grabbing at the legs of any passers-by who look prosperous."

What to make of Thompson's outsize discomfort? To put it in context, it helps to remember that in 1962, what we then called the Third World hadn't really come into Americans' living rooms yet. If John Q. Public had any idea of what life looked like for an Andean farmer or a child in sub-Saharan Africa, he sure didn't get it from Alan Sader or Sally Struthers. The global proliferation of nongovernmental organizations (NGOs) didn't kick off in earnest until the 1970s, and up until then, most of the hardest-luck corners of the world were still largely the domain of missionaries. If Thompson at first seemed shell-shocked or even derisive about the extent of Andean poverty, it could be because very little in his experience would have prepared him for so many abject faces staring in through the windows—or the callousness with which the blinds were pulled.

Thompson pitched "He Haunts the Ruins" not long after leaving Cusco, but he was back in the United States by the time he finished writing the story, in the early summer of 1963. By then, he'd had some distance from the Andes, and he'd also passed through Bolivia, where the Amerindian population had voting rights and an increasingly prominent place in civil society. With the benefit of hindsight, Thompson took a more nuanced view of the Quechuas' plight, explaining how the active disenfranchisement of the indigenous population worked to benefit those in power. "Once the Indian begins voting," he wrote, "he has little common cause with large landowning or industrial interests. Thus the best hope for the status quo is to keep the Indian ignorant, sick, poverty-stricken, and politically impotent." By the end of the article, Thompson comes off as a strong advocate for indigenous empowerment.

Whether the indigenous descendants of the Incas are any more empowered today is up to debate. Voting is compulsory now, so even the most isolated Quechua-speaking family is at least that much more involved in the democratic process. Native Andeans are also a lot more "serviced" than in 1962. Over the last few decades, Peru in general has become a nexus of the booming NGO and nonprofit industry, and *la sierra* is the sector's major focus. One British think tank published a report nicknaming Peru "The Kingdom of the NGO," and the country's International Cooperation Agency lists more than three thousand such organizations on the books. A couple hundred of these are based in the Department of Cusco, home to the Sacred Valley, the historic heart of the Incas' "once-great empire." Today, the only thing that attracts more foreigners to the Sacred Valley than the NGO sphere is that great consecrated citadel of international tourism itself, Machu Picchu.

I spent my first few days around Cusco just drifting through the NGO orbit. Needless to say, the city is a historic marvel, very worthy of its status as a UNESCO World Heritage Site. The buildings surrounding the central Plaza de Armas are stoic masterpieces of stone archways and red tile roofs, and a person strolling across it can look up to see no fewer than six picturesque church steeples punctuating the skyline. Although the Spanish razed most of the Incas' former capital and built their city over its foundations, there are still any number of dramatic stone ruins found within biking distance of the city limits. Cusco is also arguably the beating heart of the Gringo Trail, packed year-round with multinational tourists of every socioeconomic stripe, and the city center is lousy with the restaurants, hotels, and curio shops that cater to them. Hopelessly unavoidable around the plaza are the gregarious reps for Cusco's dueling parlors— pizza and massage—who seem to assault passersby with flyers every six or eight yards.

Around the corner from all this is the quiet second-floor office of Asociación ANDES, also known as the Quechua-Aymara Association for Sustainable Livelihoods. I was met

there one afternoon by the organization's director, Dr. Alejandro Argumedo, a Peruvian-born and Canadian-educated
agronomist who agreed to talk with me about the contemporary issues facing indigenous Peruvians.

"Sure, wherever you go around here, there's an NGO
working," Argumedo told me with a smile and a shrug.
He's a mop-topped ethnic Quechua in his forties, with wire-
rimmed glasses and the habit of talking with his hands that's
common among those who regularly switch among languages. Argumedo speaks English, Spanish, and Quechua
fluently, and he understands a little Aymara, the mother
tongue of Peru's minority mountain indigenous group, cous-
ins to the Quechua and one of the main conquered peoples
of the Incas.

"The problem," Argumedo said, "is that too many of
them have these ultra-specific mission statements, these
little feudal spaces where they only ever take on micro
projects." I thought of posters I'd seen during my first walk
around Cusco, seeking "voluntourists" for projects that re-
volved around alpaca textile-weaving, building passive-solar
greenhouses for mountain villagers, and teaching digital
photography to street children. "Then suddenly they leave,
and eventually, it's all gone."

Asociación ANDES tries to break out of that mold, he
explained. As far as Argumedo is concerned, the baseline
threat to indigenous Andeans today isn't simple exploitation
or illiteracy or political oppression, but the far more subtle
loss of biocultural resources that enable a way of life. Allevi-
ating poverty, promoting civic engagement, putting food on
the table, and preventing families from migrating into city
slums—all of these things hinge upon making an agrarian
lifestyle in the Andes as viable as possible. To that end, said
Argumedo, he and his colleagues work to defend indigenous

rights over seed patents, cushion the agricultural blows of climate change, and alter macroeconomic policies that reward the cultivation of export crops at the expense of subsistence farming. In particular, ANDES works closely with the surrounding mountain communities to facilitate the kind of communal land structures that allow for diverse agriculture in a landscape so breathtakingly vertical.

"Fruit grows at lower elevations," Argumedo explained, "grains in the middle, and tubers on top." He stacked his hands one above the other, like rungs on a ladder. "If you only own one plot at one elevation, then you're kind of out of luck. That's why this Andean environment has always necessitated cooperation."

Thompson actually made note of this collective agricultural model in a memo to his editor, accompanying some photos of Quechua farmers at work: "The farms around the village are run on the old Inca communal system (communist, some call it), wherein the families help each other work the land and share the profits." The parenthetical seems significant, especially when considered alongside a quote from a government agricultural adviser in "He Haunts the Ruins," a technocrat frustrated that "the Indian lives almost entirely outside the money economy." I asked Argumedo, Is there some element of nostalgia at work here? I mean, why work to maintain these traditional lifestyles rather than helping the Quechua assimilate into a modern consumer society?

"Look, this isn't about some romantic cultural heritage," he said, sipping from a mug of heavily sweetened coffee. "Food costs are soaring around the world, thanks to a number of factors—oil prices, changing weather patterns, increased demand." He ticked off the items on his fingers, one at a time. "In Peru, we already import forty-five percent of our grain. A lot of our potatoes are imported from Canada. I mean, Canada? We're the *homeland* of the potato!"

He gestured to a few posters on the wall, showing different potato varieties in Day-Glo shades of red, purple, and orange. They were weirdly beautiful, like crosses between seed-catalog centerfolds and Warhol canvases.

"We can't afford to do this forever," he said, "and as we get closer to peak oil, our food transport prices are going to skyrocket. So this isn't a cultural preservation issue. It's about how to sustain ourselves right now, and not just us, but the entire country."

There was an appealing irony, I thought—that Peru's future prosperity might rely upon the very pre-Columbian lifestyles that its ruling class had been trying to squelch, or at least marginalize, ever since Pizarro first drew a sword against the Incas.

"So do people in Lima see it this way?" I asked. "Policymakers, potential donors?"

Sometimes, he acknowledged. But there was also a kind of disconnect between the mountains and the coast, even a disdain for what had always been viewed as a backward way of life. I had noticed this, I said, and I compared Peru's social tensions to the culture war between "red states" and "blue states" back home.

"I've lived in Colombia and Ecuador, and I regularly work in Brazil and Argentina," he said, setting down his coffee mug to free up his hands, "but there is no question that Peru is the place where animosity and distrust for indigenous people are the strongest."

"Why is that?" I asked, and the agronomist leaned back in his chair and showed me his palms.

"I think people tend to project whatever it is they want to be," he said, "and then they try not to see anything else. For instance, you see these advertisements around Cusco with the blond woman drinking Inka Cola." I had indeed noticed the poster ads for Peru's popular homegrown soft drink. Argumedo laughed. "Man, there is nobody around here who looks like that! Maybe this is the same reason a lot of people voted for Kuczynski," he said, referring to the gringo economist with the dancing guinea pig and Wisconsinite wife. "People just ask themselves, 'What is it that I want to be?' Well, white-ish! Prosperous!

"The thing is, people who think that way don't always want to *see* indigenous people. But we're here, and we need to be seen."

I thought of the closing line from Thompson's story: "The Indians are still outside the windows, and . . . they are getting tired of having the blinds pulled on them."

Argumedo shrugged again, then slapped his hands on his knees, in a way that said he'd had this conversation many times before, and this was the only bottom line he'd come up with. "If this attitude seems very entrenched here," he said, "it is because we were at the epicenter of colonization. And everyone knows that the people who get hit hardest are always the ones at the epicenter."

V

My last stop in Peru was Machu Picchu, the Andes' most magnificent and overexposed pilgrimage destination. On the way to the big MP, however, I stopped over for a few days in a town called Ollantaytambo, about halfway up the Sacred Valley, where I wanted to visit yet another nonprofit that a friend back home had helped to found. Ollantaytambo is a village of about 2,000 at the confluence of two rivers—the Urubamba, which carves out the Sacred Valley to Machu Picchu, and the Patakancha, which descends from the mountains and flows through the town in a series of ingenious stone aqueducts. Whereas most of ancient Cusco was destroyed by the Spanish, the residents of quiet Ollantaytambo still walk the same narrow stone streets laid by their ancestors, and they've incorporated the old Inca walls and doorways into their small houses. On both mountainsides hemming in the village are dramatic ruins of stone temples, storehouses, and farming terraces. The largest complex is a ticketed attraction on par with Machu Picchu, but the others are open to anyone willing to do some hillside scrambling. I spent a couple of afternoons there, picking my way across the mountains from ruin to ruin, enjoying the lateral exploration of a vertical landscape. Wandering among the relics was a nice reminder that there's more to do on a mountain besides get to the top of it.

Ollantaytambo has the region's only high school, which enrolls students from a wide radius of mountain communities. And by and large, they are boys. Many of the villages are a full day's walk from town, so sending kids to school means boarding them in Ollantaytambo—an expensive proposition for families, both in terms of lost labor and room and board. So you send only your brightest prospects, and in a heavily patriarchal society, that means your sons, by default. For most Quechua girls around the Sacred Valley, sixth grade tends to be the end of formal education.

The nonprofit I stopped by was called the Sacred Valley Project, a small dorm in town that offers free housing, tutoring, and support for Quechua girls pursuing secondary education. The group has just two full-time staffers—a kindly Argentinean program director and a college-aged, live-in "dorm mother"—and at the time of my visit, they were also hosting a mother-daughter pair of volunteers from Connecticut. On the day that I dropped in, the dorm's residents were just arriving with their parents for a kick-off dinner to celebrate the new school year. They were a shy and well-behaved bunch of otherwise prototypical teens, dressed in denim and sweaters and giggling among themselves as they toured their new rooms. The fathers were brisk and polite, the mothers mostly silent. Many spoke only Quechua. They wore the traditional braids and bowler hats of Andean women, and on their backs, they carried their trademark woven blankets, brightly colored and deftly wrapped around large, mysterious bundles.

"There's a game we sometimes play," one of the Connecticut volunteers confided in me, indicating the bundles. "We call it 'Baby or Vegetables?'"

I spent part of the day helping the women shuck corn and wash dishes. Later, I tried some chicha with the men, the tangy fermented corn drink that Thompson called "the Andes' answer to home brew." After a dinner of chicken and corn, I listened while the parents delivered short speeches, impressing upon their daughters the importance of good behavior and the value of this opportunity. The girls go home on weekends (an eight-hour walk, in some cases), and the parents meet at the dorm periodically throughout the year to gauge the girls' progress and discuss any concerns. That evening, everybody signed a participation covenant with a number of conditions. The one that jumped out at me was the no-pregnancy clause, a stark reminder of what a fourteen-year-old Quechua girl's life might be like in the absence of education.

I tried chatting up the girls a little, but they were mostly shy and probably appalled at my Spanish. Dina, one of the more outgoing students, was from a village called Pallata, about five miles up the Rio Patakancha, and she walked to and from her home every Friday and Sunday. Her favorite subject was math, she said, and she hoped she could be a teacher someday. I asked whether she had read any of the books on the sparsely filled bookshelf in the study room. She smiled bashfully and said, "I tried that one," pointing to a Spanish copy of *In Cold Blood*. The girls were timid, but they seemed bright and driven. Thompson had gone up into hill towns just like Pallata to take photos of ragged-looking Quechua farmers behind their ox-drawn plows. I wondered what he would make of their great-granddaughters trying to plow through Truman Capote.

"Are you going to Machu Picchu?" Dina asked me. The girls had a trip planned later in the year, and they seemed excited. None of them had ever been. Some of them had never been to Cusco, just two hours away by bus.

"You can walk there, you know," said another of the girls, timidly. She had maybe overheard me telling the program director that I wasn't looking forward to riding the expensive and crowded tourist train. Her family was from a village not far from where the road ended, and of course, the girls and their families walked just about everywhere. I asked the program director about it, and she said that, yes, the local people regularly walked alongside the train tracks to get to the farms and *pueblitos* along the muddy Rio Urubamba. It was a seventeen-mile walk to reach Machu Picchu from the end of the auto road—a full day's hike with my backpack. Along the way were a few short railroad tunnels, and technically it was illegal, but I was taken with the idea. Looking around the dorms of the Sacred Valley Project that afternoon, seeing the sandaled moms who had walked eight hours to send their kids off to high school, it was hard to imagine sitting in a cushy Pullman, staring out the windows at the very same women making the journey on foot. In a weird way, a long day's slog through the Quechua's ancestral homeland suddenly seemed like the least I could do.

I'm not at all sure that Thompson even went to Machu Picchu. It seems ridiculous that he would have skipped it, but nowhere is it mentioned in his articles or published letters, and it doesn't appear in any of his published photographs. Maybe he just wanted to avoid the crowds, maybe he was in a hurry to press on to Bolivia. Or maybe he just felt like shit. On top of his existing maladies, Thompson wrote at the end of August that he had been stung in Cusco by some kind of poisonous insect and once again had to visit a doctor. His leg was paralyzed for three days, he wrote, which would have definitely made it hard to hump around the hills and stone pathways of the famed Inca sanctuary.

In all honesty, I was less excited about Machu Picchu than I was about the long walk to get there. By no means am I a travel snob. Among my favorite places in the world are some of the most visited destinations in global tourism—Old Faithful, Niagara Falls. But everything I'd heard about South America's most famous ruins made me picture a beautiful landscape crowded with arguing families, kids too old to be in strollers, people who pose in pictures as if they're holding up famous architecture, and other stock vacation characters that tend to bother me. Hiking the Inca Trail, the only (legal) non-train way to reach Machu Picchu, didn't strike me as a whole lot more appealing. The popular hiking route is a small segment of a vast network of footpaths that the Incas once maintained all throughout the Andes. At the civilization's peak around 1500, an Inca messenger or army could theoretically have traveled all the way from present-day Quito to what is now Santiago, Chile. What we call the classic

Inca Trail today was actually just a spur from Cusco to access Machu Picchu—a seasonal site that was one part church and one part vacation home for the Incan ruling class.

Don't get me wrong, the route itself sounds fantastic. It's a four-day trek that passes through or near a number of dramatic ruins, crosses Andean passes at almost 14,000 feet, and looks down into the wild and roadless Sacred Valley. But concerns about litter, overcrowding, and erosion forced the Peruvian government to place tight restrictions on the Inca Trail in 2000. No more than five hundred hikers a day can head out from the trailhead (although this still sounds like a lot), and they're obliged to travel with a government-approved guided tour group at a cost of around $500 a head. While I'm certain that the hiking is stellar, it's the expense and the forced group dynamic that puts me off. Plus, the only Peruvians you're likely to meet along the way are the guides and the porters hired cheaply to carry your supplies, which, frankly, makes me a little uncomfortable.

Inca Trail hiking groups start at kilometer marker 82 along the Cusco-to-Machu-Picchu railway, the same spot where the adjacent road ends and where a *colectivo* bus dropped me off at six one morning to begin my own hike through the Sacred Valley. At the end of the road is a checkpoint where the Inca Trail tour groups have to show their government-issued permit before climbing into the mountains. The checkpoint also exists to keep freeloading gringos like me from walking along the railroad tracks. But the girls and staff at the Sacred Valley Project had told me how to avoid detection and even provided me with a hand-drawn map. So I hopped out of the *colectivo* and made my way up an inconspicuous livestock path skirting the hillside. It was just after dawn, the sky still gray, and I was startled by roosters as I snuck past a couple of small farmsteads. After less than a mile, the dirt footpath dropped through some scrubby brush to meet the railroad tracks and the surging Rio Urubamba. And then there I was, on my own private Inca Trail, one that's still in use by the Incas' modern-day descendants.

The Urubamba was the color of chocolate milk and espresso foam, surging with a ferocity that maybe should have made me nervous. It was the tail end of the rainy season, and the river levels were as high as they normally get. In 2010, the river flooded after a particularly wet year, and water washed out the bridges and the banks, taking the railroad with it. Tourists at the base of Machu Picchu were stranded for days and had to be airlifted out by helicopter. I'd been assured by the girls in Ollantaytambo that the water levels were safe, but as I started following a faint footpath next to the tracks, the white noise of the rapids was loud enough to drown out the birdsong.

Within the first couple of miles, I was already pretty pleased with my decision making. The route was unquestionably beautiful. The Sacred Valley is a deep V that narrows periodically into a steep canyon, with walls as green and lush as Huaycán's had been brown and dry. Small waterfalls bounced their way down the mountainsides, and wavy stalks with yellow blossoms sprang up in clustered bouquets on either side of the tracks. Rarely did I have to walk on the railroad ties themselves, since a faint trail usually followed alongside, sometimes diverging from the track altogether to look down on the river from a rocky ledge.

I was five or six miles along the first time I heard a train whistle. It spooked me a little, and I scrambled into the brush to let it pass. Five or six deep blue cars clacked by, slowly enough for me to make eye contact and nod to the curious tourists inside. I just grinned at them a little nervously that first time, feeling guilty and exposed. I had never heard of a train pulling over to scold someone, but then I had never walked illegally on a railroad track in Peru before. Eventually, that first little train rounded a corner, and all I could hear was its increasingly distant whistle.

This scene played out twelve or fifteen times throughout the day. The ticket agent in Ollantaytambo had explained to me that a few different classes of trains all ran on this line. There was a dirt-cheap locals' train, on which *turistas* are forbidden, plus a couple of varieties of tourist train, on which the locals are priced out. The first-class train has cocktails and perfumed towels, while a slightly cheaper option caters to family travelers and backpackers. The cars on the locals' train, I imagined, were something like steerage. The tourist trains, meanwhile, were actually rather beautiful as they came and went, deep blue or bright red against a landscape where the only other primary colors were the sporadic yellow wildflowers.

After a couple of miles, I came to a small set of stone ruins. A sign leaning nearby identified the site as Qanabamba, and I wandered around the ancient walls and weathered granite foundations for a while, feeling lucky to be there. Passengers on the train could only glimpse the site while chugging past, while hikers on the Inca Trail would be looking down on it from a distant ridge on the other side of the river. I ran my hands along the smoothed walls of the roofless houses, feeling like the last man on Earth.

When I walked back to the tracks, though, I was startled to find two young girls with backpacks, strolling in the opposite direction.

"*Buenos dias,*" I said. "*Como van?*"

They were dressed in skirts and simple cardigans and reminded me instantly of the girls at the Sacred Valley Project.

They greeted me without smiling, and the older of the two, maybe twelve, put her hands on her hips.

"So what do you think of the ruins, then?" she asked in Spanish, a bit brassy. "They're pretty, no?"

I smiled. They were very pretty, I said. Then she set about quizzing me, each time taking a stab at answering her own question.

"Where are you going? Machu Picchu?"

"Where are you from? Argentina?"

"Who are you with? Alone?"

I answered her in my bad Spanish, asking where they were from and how pretty the scenery was farther down the trail. They lived nearby, the older girl said, and she told me the village where they were going, but the name meant nothing to me. The younger girl, all of eight, smiled bashfully for a few minutes before piping up in a tiny voice.

"Sir," she asked, "do you have any cookies?"

Her companion tried to shush her, but I laughed and said that I did. In fact, I told her, I was hungry too. So I took out a few granola bars and split them up among the three of us. They thanked me, and for another minute we just stood there, chewing silently, staring at the mad river and the stone remnants of their culture that they walk past every day.

Eventually I came to the first of several short tunnels and quickly jogged through, pausing first to listen for approaching whistles. Inside, it was cool and dark, with enough room that if a train did come, I could probably have pressed myself hard against the stone walls to avoid being hit—but I didn't want to test that theory. Between tunnels, I passed Quechua grandmothers toddling toward me on the tracks, toting their mystery bundles and smiling their gap-toothed *buenos dias*. Occasionally, I walked by a rocky pasture filled with pensive-looking sheep.

Around noon, I rounded a bend to find a five-man rail crew loitering fifty yards ahead, conspicuous in their bright blue jumpsuits.

Busted, I thought. I had walked around the corner obliviously, and there was no chance they hadn't seen me. There was nothing to do but walk right up to them. I tried to look nonchalant, prepping my oblivious gringo shrug for when they asked me what I was doing walking along the tracks. The crew was leaning with their pickaxes against a gas-powered cart just off the line, a kind of flatbed trolley with a railing, like something you'd see in a mine. As I approached, they all looked up at me. I held my breath, smiled, and nodded at the closest one.

"Hola, amigo!" he chirped brightly, waving an oily hand. Then he looked back down at the sandwich in his other hand. A couple of the others gave me halfhearted waves, and the remainder ignored me altogether. I walked right past without so much as a questioning glance.

Well, I thought, so much for the strict security measures at PeruRail.

In the early afternoon, at a spot where the tracks veered briefly away from the river, I came to a small depot, which wasn't something I'd expected to find. It was a squat cinder-block building with another uniformed PeruRail employee dozing on a bench outside. Beneath him, a couple of puppies were playing in the dirt. I'd have assumed that the shack was just some kind of utility building or switching station, but even as I walked up on it, I heard the teakettle fermata of the train whistle behind me. Just as I reached the station, a single red car rolled up, so slowly that for a moment I thought that it must be railroad bulls, finally coming to pinch me after hearing from the crew up the line. But the car hissed to a stop in front of the depot, and two bundled *abuelitas* stepped out gingerly, holding up the hems of their skirts.

This must be the locals' train, I realized, and as I walked past the stopped car, I snuck a quick glimpse inside, where a handful of other Quechua passengers sat on plain wooden benches, surrounded by sleepy-looking children and parcels of wrapped blankets. How appropriate, I thought, that the Machu Picchu rail system should be as hopelessly stratified as everything else in Peru.

Then, as the lonely car chugged back into motion, I suddenly wondered whether this simple recognition of profound income inequality might not account for a lot of Thompson's transformation in South America. After all, here was a Louisville kid from relative comfort, confronted with a form of class separation so intense as to seem totally alien. Sure, Thompson had been in slums in the United States and the barrios of the Caribbean, but even the tin-roofed villages of Puerto Rico, he wrote, were "like Harlem" compared to South America's Indian lands. In Peru, he discovered a social hierarchy so entrenched, so inscribed into the DNA of its people, that almost no one even bothered to question its legitimacy.

Back home, the best and brightest minds in the country were locked into this modernization theory—a sociological school that considered income inequality something a place like Peru could simply transcend with economic growth. Our whole foreign policy at the time was built around this idea, that any gulf between the haves and have-nots was just a stage countries go through on their way to something better, something more egalitarian. But from his vantage point on the ground, Thompson was beginning to have his doubts.

"If the Alliance for Progress requires democracy in Peru

to become a fact instead of just a pleasant word," he wrote, "then the Alliance is in for rough sledding."

Maybe, I thought, Thompson was beginning to see the triumph of the oligarchy as something other than a blip on the path to modernity. Maybe it was more than just a bleak but temporary phase for developing nations to overcome. What if it was something that could take hold anywhere, regardless of a country's level of development? What would that mean for the places he'd visited in the Andes?

What might it mean for the United States?

The last tunnel before reaching Machu Picchu was the longest by far. It was actually two stone tunnels back to back, as my hand-drawn map warned me, with a distance of just a few yards in between. As with the others, a sign outside warned me that pedestrians were forbidden from passing through, and had the water level not been so high, it might even have been possible to avoid the tunnels altogether by walking along the riverbank. As things were, however, I strapped on my headlamp and crouched next to the track, listening for the sound of oncoming trains. I had noticed that I could feel a little vibration in the steel whenever one was approaching, but when I laid my palm on the rail, I felt nothing. So I headed in.

Jogging on loose gravel is possible, but running is difficult, and the ground inside was of the soft-pack, pebbly variety that mountaineers call scree. Some of the previous tunnels had clearly been blasted, with jagged sides of exposed rock, but these were symmetrical arches with smooth granite walls. I hadn't changed my headlamp batteries since Colombia, so the bulb threw off a dim yellow beam that I followed through the darkness as I tried not to stumble over an errant brick or a railroad tie.

I was about to emerge from the first of the two tunnels when I heard it—a shrill, reverberating note that sent a chill through me. For a moment, I froze, trying to hear which direction the train was coming from, but the valley's confusing acoustics had made that impossible all day long. The distance in front of me was roughly the same as the distance behind, so I didn't stop to weigh my options. I grabbed the straps of my backpack, pulled it tight to my body, and ran. If I'd have been thinking, I might have just stayed between the two tunnels, where I probably could have pressed against the cliffside foliage tight enough to let the train pass by comfortably. But I wasn't thinking, and I charged impulsively into the darkness of the second tunnel, the weak beam from my headlamp swinging wildly in front of me.

The whistle blared again. It sounded closer this time and had a note of urgency to it, more like the tenor blast of a bus bearing down on you than the screech of an old-school steam engine. More like an air horn, really. My feet struggled for traction on the gravel; I felt like I was running through a pile of tiny marbles. For the first time all day, I was conscious of the sound of my breathing and the weight of my pack. It jostled behind me as I pumped my legs, and I felt the sweat soaking through the collar of my T-shirt.

Shit, shit, *shit,* I thought.

The horn sounded once more, earsplitting this time and definitely echoing through the tunnel itself. Just ahead of me, the brightly lit opening was the shape of a bread loaf, and I squinted and exhaled hard as I burst outside.

I steered immediately into the brush, putting a good six feet between me and the tracks. Then, still panting, I turned to see the mouth of the tunnel.

Nothing happened. No train, no noise. *What the fuck?* A few seconds ticked by. I held my breath and heard almost nothing, not the rumble of an engine or the scrape of metal wheels, just a middle-range whine, like the drone of a revving go-kart.

And then, rolling along at the speed of a brisk jog, the jump-suited PeruRail workers emerged from the tunnel, puttering by on their mattress-sized utility trolley. They were leaning on its metal railings, scratching their armpits, and yawning.

"Hola, amigo!" said the same guy as before, and he gave me a friendly little toot on his air horn for emphasis. I waved back limply. Then I stood in the bushes for several minutes and watched as the tiny clown cart rolled its way down the track.

It poured on me when I reached Machu Picchu. The rain started the minute that I arrived at the tourist village at the base of the mountain, and it didn't let up for the next two days. Machu Picchu itself met the best and the worst of my expectations. The ruins were breathtaking and vast, prompting that same kind of generalized reverence that non-religious people feel in great cathedrals. When the clouds parted long enough to see them, the surrounding monolith peaks were equally impressive. Pedestrian traffic was, at times, shoulder to shoulder, and baby boomers in inexplicable canvas hats did indeed block vista after vista while mugging for their camera phones. I spent a long day wandering the ruins and a short night eating alpaca tacos and drinking beer in the village. Then it was back to Cusco and another long ticket queue, another border crossing, another overnight bus through the mountains.

CHAPTER SIX

Notes from Underground

If Bolivia were half as bad as it looks on paper, the government would send a crew to all this country's points of entry to post signs saying, "Abandon all hope, ye who enter here."

—*National Observer*, April 15, 1962

I

From above, which is the only way you can approach it, the city of La Paz looks like a crack opened up in the earth and every building in the world just fell in. It's a senseless jumble of a metro, skirting the eastern edge of a wide Andean plateau called the Altiplano, filling in a canyon there like a bucket of LEGOs dumped into a shoebox. Arriving in La Paz by bus means descending 1,500 feet from the canyon's rim, winding downward in a sort of toilet-bowl swirl. Gaze out the window during your descent and the city seems to glisten, with a zillion metal rooftops reflecting the unfiltered sunlight of the high Andes.

At 12,000 feet (the surrounding Altiplano is well over 13,000), La Paz is often hailed as the highest capital in the world. Technically, though, it's only the seat of the Bolivian government, the constitutional capital being some 350 miles away in comparatively sleepy Sucre. No matter. Lonely and oxygen-deprived, La Paz is still South America's undisputed capital of weird. This is as true today as it was in April of 1963, when the *Observer* ran Thompson's account of life there under the headline A NEVER-NEVER LAND HIGH ABOVE THE SEA, devoting a hefty twenty-three column inches to the "excesses, exaggerations, quirks, contradictions, and every manner of oddity and abuse" that he found while wandering its sloping streets.

Bolivia is eccentric like an old hermit is eccentric, the result of long years of isolation. Sky-high and buttressed from colonial population centers by mountains and veldt-like grasslands, the country once known as "Upper Peru" was subordinated for centuries to Spanish viceroys in far-off Lima and Buenos Aires. On the plus side, the Altiplano is remote enough to have helped shield the country's indigenous population from some of the devastation wreaked by European diseases. More problematically, though, the modern nation of Bolivia has been landlocked for most of its history, having lost its only ocean corridor to Chile during a disastrous nineteenth-century war over bird poop (then a lucrative fertilizer). Bolivia is so geographically sequestered, even its rainfall doesn't make it to the sea, instead draining into inland lakes and salt flats, where it simply evaporates over time.

Some of the results of this isolation include chronic instability, a poor but powerful indigenous majority, and a fragile economy based almost entirely on the extraction of minerals and other natural resources. Bolivia is a part of the world that has never had it easy, and so Thompson's "Never-Never Land" piece reads a bit like comic relief. The story is a descriptive litany of what he calls "the small problems— the laughs, as it were—in a country where people with responsibility have very few things to laugh about." Rolling blackouts, for example—a consequence of the nation's training-wheels infrastructure that darkened dinner parties and routinely trapped elevators between floors. Thompson's cigarettes wouldn't stay lit in the thin Bolivian air, and his toothpaste, manufactured at sea level, exploded upon opening. All around town, flatlanders with altitude sickness had an annoying habit of passing out and having to be brought to consciousness by onlookers.

The streets of La Paz, moreover, were full of oddball would-be revolutionaries in 1962, including a few self-proclaimed and loudmouthed communists who nonetheless retained soft spots for American pop culture. Thompson wrote of a psychic mediator who pestered the embassy, claiming to commune with Kennedy and Khrushchev using brain waves. The sky-high city, he said, fostered a "manic atmosphere" of strikes and street protests, a paranoid circus where "the Americans fear the Communists, the Communists fear the Alliance for Progress, and most people don't care about any of this as long as the money and aid keeps flowing in."

The La Paz that I stepped into fifty years later seemed similarly charged and offbeat. From the bus station, I set out on foot in search of cheap digs, and one of the first sights I came upon was an orderly display of dried llama fetuses, lined up outside a row of small shops. The hollow-eyed camelids were stacked up in fruit crates, staring dolefully at passersby. That particular retail strip, I later learned, was called the Mercado de las Brujas, the witches' market, and the pungent cadavers were sold as offerings, meant to be buried in one's yard as a kind of good-luck ceremony honoring the Quechua and Aymara Earth mother.

The sidewalks of La Paz had a carnival feel, crowded with shoeshine boys wearing ski masks (to remain anonymous in their low-caste occupation) and grandmotherly vendors in their bowler hats (commonly known as *cholitas,* from a colonial epithet once considered derogatory and now used with some pride). At a busy intersection up the road from the witches' market, I came upon another oddity: pairs of costumed zebras that dance and cavort at traffic lights during rush hours, distracting drivers so pedestrians can cross. The city evidently employs about one hundred such plushies, and since their introduction in the early 2000s, they've helped alleviate the bottlenecks and road rage that often characterize urban streets in South America.

I watched a pair of them frolicking out the window when I stopped for breakfast at a small café, an otherwise normal luncheonette that played Michael Bolton's "How Am I Supposed to Live Without You" on repeat for over an hour. The diner was out of coffee, so the waiter talked me into a

Bolivian alternative, a bright-purple corn drink called *api*, which was sickeningly sweet and thoroughly awful.

Welcome to Never-Never Land, I thought, and I sipped my purple coffee while Michael Bolton crooned and the zebras formed a chorus line in the intersection.

When it comes to national holidays celebrating public drug use, Bolivia is light-years ahead of the United States. I had been wandering among the zebras in La Paz for a couple of days when I heard on the radio that President Evo Morales had declared a "National Day of Coca-Leaf Chewing." Morales is the former head of the country's coca growers union and South America's first fully indigenous president. He's also another Chávez acolyte who, like Correa, considers himself both a "Bolivarian" populist and an antagonist of the United States. That afternoon, he happened to be in Vienna, pushing for the removal of coca leaves from a United Nations schedule of dangerous drugs. Coca, of course, is the raw ingredient for cocaine, of which Bolivia is the world's number three producer, behind its neighbors Colombia and Peru. It is also popular in the Andes in its raw leaf form, which is chewed or boiled into a tea and appreciated for its mild stimulant effects—boosting energy, suppressing appetite, and relieving altitude sickness, among other things. The radio told me that a couple hundred people had gathered in La Paz to demonstrate in favor of the leafy drug, so I headed downtown to the government plaza to get a glimpse of the demonstrations.

La Paz's Plaza Murillo looked more or less like the central plazas of Bogotá, Quito, or Lima, except that in La Paz, the men in expensive-looking suits were actually conversing with the men in ponchos and fedoras rather than just stepping around them on the sidewalk. In front of the presidential palace was a whole weird medley of guards and soldiers, all standing at attention. Mountie-looking guys in bright red coats were stationed next to white-helmeted MPs dressed like '60s G.I. Joe action figures. Thrown in here and there were a few serious-looking commando types in full camouflage, like Latino extras out of *Apocalypse Now*. In front of the line of soldiers, a smallish mob had indeed gathered, carrying signs and spilling into the adjacent plaza.

I skirted the periphery of the crowd, trying to look inconspicuous, but I noticed right away that few if any of the protestors seemed to be chewing coca leaves. When I scanned the placards and listened for snippets of comprehensible Spanish, I realized that this was actually a protest over some kind of public-park cleanup in the slums. It had nothing to do with coca leaves. My face must have registered some confusion as this dawned on me, because one of the olive-uniformed MPs strolled up and asked me kindly whether I needed any help.

"Are you trying to get inside?" he asked, gesturing at the palace.

"No, thank you," I said. "Actually, I think I just showed up at the wrong protest."

"Ah yes," he said, and smiled grimly. *"Esto es possible aqui."* That can happen here.

It can happen in La Paz because Bolivians love to protest. Or maybe because they have a lot worth protesting about, but more likely it's a combination of the two. Like very few other countries, Bolivia has an entrenched history of popular rule. In 1962, Thompson called it "a government dependent on Indian support and very literally of, by, and for the people." What this means on paper is that established political parties are less important or influential than groundswell social movements and their charismatic leaders. Trade unions are a huge voting bloc, career politicians are a minority, and there's a healthy degree of hostility between "the people" and the wealthy urban elites.

What it means in practice is that Bolivians are not afraid to ask their government for what they want. Or to demand it with street protests that are loud, lively, and frequent. Or to erect blockades of major highways until they get it. Or to march on the capital and throw out the sitting president if things seem to be taking too long.

That Bolivia has undergone some thirty different changes of power in the fifty years since Thompson's visit might suggest flaws in this system. During that time, the country has occasionally been ruled by military juntas and conservative presidents who made no claims to be "men of the people," but right now, popular rule is enjoying a shining moment in Bolivia. Morales came to power in 2005, riding a wave of strikes and blockades that forced the last elected president out of office. And as an instigator of those strikes, he is keenly aware of what a few hundred angry people with placards can accomplish.

Of course, none of this is new. Peasant mobs have been raising hell in Bolivia for as long as there's been a power structure against which to raise hell. South America's last great indigenous uprising against the Spanish was in Bolivia in 1781, when an army of 40,000 Aymaras laid siege to La Paz for a full six months. Colonial troops converged from both coasts to quell the uprising, but the spirit of indigenous solidarity and class revolt has stuck with Bolivia through the centuries. The country's modern era of popular rule kicked off in 1952 with what Bolivians call the National Revolution, and it was the fallout from this event that Thompson was still covering a decade later.

As it turned out, the coca demonstration had actually been held in front of a building called the Museo de la Revolución, which is dedicated to the National Revolution of 1952. By the time I showed up there in the early evening, the protestors had already called it a day. The sun was sinking behind the canyon rim, and the brick-cobbled plaza was empty except for a lone Aymara woman, breaking down a foosball table that she had evidently set up for the event.

For such a pivotal moment in Bolivian history, the National Revolution is not celebrated with much of a museum. It anchors a hilltop park a couple of miles from downtown, a grim trapezoidal building that looks like nothing so much as the torso of an Imperial Walker from *Star Wars*. I paid an admission fee of a single boliviano, or about fourteen cents, and the one employee running the place seemed genuinely surprised to see me. He also seemed ill inclined to turn down his boom box, so while I studied the one-room museum's black-and-white photos of rifle-toting miners and hanged ex-presidents, I was accompanied by the sultry croon of George Michael singing "Freedom! '90."

In a nutshell, 1952 saw a coalition of miners, *campesinos,* and urban radicals overthrow a government that had long been running the show on behalf of powerful foreign-owned mining interests. Taxes on the country's tin barons made up the lion's share of Bolivia's national revenue, and the government periodically lent out its military to help suppress miners' strikes and otherwise keep the labor force in line. The miners turned the tables during the revolution, though, when their militias marched on La Paz, joining Bolivia's outnumbered National Police in a battle against the country's remaining loyal military forces. The uprising was brief and a lot less bloody than many Latin American revolutions.

Around six hundred people were killed in three days of fighting, with many soldiers on the military side simply defecting or refusing to fight.

With the revolution came the nationalization of Bolivia's three biggest mining operations, which together had controlled about 80 percent of the industry. The revolutionary government also decreed universal suffrage for women and indigenous Bolivians, and it instituted far-reaching land reforms, breaking up the massive haciendas of wealthy landowners and redistributing plots among peasant farmers. On the walls of the museum, a wraparound mural visually summarized the uprising's major themes, with fist-raising *indigenas* and burly industrial workers standing tall over slain conquistadors.

"Freedom! Freedom!" cried George Michael patriotically. "You've got to give for what you take!"

Bolivia's new revolutionary government was avowedly anti-Moscow, but such dramatic shifts to the left still made US officials very nervous. By the time Thompson showed up ten years later, the country was struggling economically, and Washington was, in his words, "concerned that Bolivia is one of the most receptive Latin American countries to Communist infiltration." Thompson, however, didn't share these concerns. Three months on the continent had made him increasingly skeptical of the motivations of the avowedly capitalist elites, and he was coming to suspect that the communist threat in the Andes was "more a convenient whipping boy than anything else."

In La Paz, he befriended a USIS labor attaché named Tom Martin, an eager and hard-charging Bronx native on his first assignment abroad. Martin was connected with labor leaders, diplomats, and other movers and shakers around La Paz, and Thompson spent several evenings in Martin's living room, swilling bourbon with rabble-rousing mining bosses and other supposed communist agitators.

One night, Thompson walked into Martin's looking like Castro himself: unshaven, wearing a green Army-surplus jacket and a worn pair of hiking boots. In an *Observer* article from 1963, Thompson recalled being accidentally introduced that evening to two self-proclaimed communists as a correspondent for the *Observer*'s sister publication, the *Wall Street Journal*. The mistaken identity left the socialists slack-jawed:

> The Bolivians couldn't understand how I could possibly wear such an outfit and still represent Wall Street. It took several hours before they understood that I was no more from Wall Street than they were from Moscow, and when the evening was over we all understood each other a lot better than we had in the beginning. We didn't necessarily agree, but at least we could talk like human beings instead of political animals.

Most professed Reds in Bolivia, Thompson said, were not ideological zealots, but simply "naïve nationalists" who wanted to see more resources devoted to social welfare. One allegedly fearsome and anti-American labor kingpin told Thompson over whiskey that he'd learned English by reading *Playboy*. Such were the supposed Marxist militants whose actions struck fear into the hearts of US bureaucrats and businessmen—a bunch of blue-collar joes who, yeah, wanted to empower the workers but who had no particular beef with the US way of life. In "Never-Never Land," Thompson dismissed the Red Menace as "more than anything else . . . an easy way to frighten the Americans."

"There are about as many Communists in Bolivia," he wrote, "as there are bedrock conservatives—which leaves a lot of middle ground."

All of which means that the La Paz of Thompson's reportage owed a lot of its madcap charm to a kind of Chicken Little hysteria over a threat that wasn't even really there. Two years before *Dr. Strangelove* threw open the doors to Cold War satire, Thompson was already coming to see the comic absurdity of a whole planet fueled by paranoia and antagonism. In fact, he writes about La Paz in "Never-Never Land" in much the same way that he would eventually write about the Kentucky Derby or Las Vegas. There's a kind of budding cynical glee to his descriptions of crazed and frothing protestors, to his retelling of how the altitude had recently struck dead a hyper-fit ex-Marine. You can sense in his prose the excitement of an author who's beginning to thrive, if only a little bit, on the sheer inanity of it all. In his later work, Thompson wrote himself into the chaos as a character, a sort of whirling dervish of journalistic mayhem. But even in his reporting from La Paz, there's no mistaking the author's sardonic presence, that sense of an embedded observer who's surveying the Cold War landscape and smirking.

Sure, Thompson seems to say, this city is home to "almost every kind of madness and affliction that can plague the human body and soul," but there's something kind of funny about that, right? It's the same brand of fatalistic humor that would later characterize Thompson's gonzo journalism, and frankly, it's instantly recognizable to anyone who's ever had their luggage fall out of a rickshaw in traffic or who's ever navigated some backwater bureaucracy in a language they don't speak. It is the amused, enlightened resignation of a traveler in his fourth fluky month abroad. It is the manic surrender of the waylaid.

I won't go so far as to say that Thompson's travel writing gave birth to the style he became known for, but the young writer's proto-gonzo take on La Paz resonates with the epiphany of a guy who's through bitching about the strikes and the bug bites and is instead finally ready to double down and embrace the absurdities of the road. The Red Scare was absurd, Thompson decided. Bolivia's mobocracy was absurd. It was utterly absurd to be using his tripod as a cane after being semi-paralyzed by insect venom in Cusco. Even the constant panic of hopeless poverty was starting to take on a liberating absurdity.

"The hotel won't take my check so I can't leave," Thompson wrote from La Paz. "I just sit in the room and ring the bell for more beer. Life has improved immeasurably since I have been forced to stop taking it seriously."

II

I stayed in La Paz just long enough to catch a few street protests, wander a couple of museums, and buy my first llama fetus. Then I headed 330 miles south to the town of Potosí. This had not been a part of my original itinerary, but on the day I showed up at the station, not a single bus was headed east.

"*Hay un bloqueo,*" a ticketing attendant told me. "There's a blockade. Some kind of local border dispute between here and Santa Cruz. We can't go there until they clear the road. Could be this evening. Could be days from now."

She was leaning against her counter and smoking, taking a short break from her usual routine of bellowing her company's destinations at passersby. Andean bus stations are noisy like a carnival midway, echoing with the cries of dozens of barrel-chested ticket vendors, all chant-shouting their itineraries at once.

"So there's really just one route to Santa Cruz?"

The ticket vendor snorted. "Of course not!" she said, sounding insulted. "There are two."

"OK then," I said. "In that case, I'll take the second one."

She shook her head angrily. "That one is blockaded also. A truckers' strike that's been going on for weeks. You haven't heard, *señor*? There is no hope of going that way."

The agent herself sounded frustrated about this fact, so I tried to be sympathetic. "I guess this is a difficult week for buses," I said. She exhaled a thick cloud of smoke.

"Bolivia is a difficult country for buses," she spat.

So I opted instead for a six-hundred-mile detour on a dirt-cheap chicken bus going south. Onboard, I was seated next to a very kind, very large Aymara *cholita,* so wrapped in layers of skirts and woolen *manta* blankets that I assumed she was padding herself as precaution against bus collisions. My seatmate had the troubling habit of coughing without covering her mouth, which she indulged in even while leaning over my lap to look out the window.

On the way out of town, we made an hour's worth of stops in what's called El Alto, a sprawling suburb on the rim of the canyon that now outpaces La Paz for population growth. El Alto was originally founded as a shantytown by Aymara urban migrants in the mid-twentieth century. In 1962, it was little more than a pop-up nuisance, and Thompson acknowledged it only in passing, mentioning "squatters who have built shacks around the runways at El Alto Airport." These

days, those squatters have evolved into a sprawling city of
one million, more than three-quarters indigenous and
overwhelmingly fueled by an "informal sector" of produce
stands, cell-phone kiosks, pedicabs, and other low-wage, off-
the-books enterprises. Our bus crawled slowly through the
gray streets of the improvised city, passing every imaginable
sort of sidewalk vendor. By the time we were on the highway,
I was the only non-Aymara passenger aboard.

Technically, Potosí is off the Thompson Trail, as the
young writer never made it there, but he did write an *Observer* piece focused on Bolivia's troubled mining industry,
and Potosí is the undisputed eye of the five-hundred-year-
old storm that is the country's history of mining. Simply put,
Bolivia's future has always been underground. The Spanish built a new civilization there out of silver, the postcolo-
nial ruling class emerged from tin, and even as Thompson
crossed the country, Bolivians were pinning their economic
future to petroleum and natural gas reserves in the east. All
of this started centuries before at Potosí, when the Quechua
servant of a Spanish captain discovered silver on the side of
a lonely mountain in 1545.

The peak would ultimately become known as Cerro
Rico, or "Rich Hill," and although the Spanish had already
been plundering the riches of the Andes for a few decades at
that time, it was Cerro Rico that single-handedly launched
both an industry and an empire. Within twenty-five years, an
estimated quarter of a billion dollars in silver was extracted
from Cerro Rico. Potosí sprang up seemingly overnight. An
account from 1573 puts the population of the brand-new
city at around 120,000—London, at the time, had around
180,000. By the late eighteenth century, well over a billion
dollars in silver had been extracted, and the wealth of Cerro
Rico was almost wholly responsible for an international

silver standard that dominated world trade for centuries. In seventeenth-century Europe, the very word "Potosí" became shorthand for unfathomable riches. Writing his masterpiece *Don Quixote* in the early 1600s, Miguel Cervantes had his hero dramatically declare that he would relinquish "the treasures of Venice and the mines of Potosí" to free his enchanted Dulcinea.

Cerro Rico stayed profitable during the tin boom of the early twentieth century, but things went south after it was seized by the government during the National Revolution. Thompson set the scene in 1962: "Near each tin mine in the arid, poverty-ridden nation of Bolivia," he wrote, ". . . stands a large, bleak, and fully visible graveyard. The graveyard is a symbol of the condition of the miner, who is responsible for 88 per cent of Bolivian exports and whose life expectancy is 29 years. It may become a symbol of the nation."

As Thompson explained in an *Observer* piece headlined OPERATION TRIANGULAR: BOLIVIA'S FATE RIDES WITH IT, Bolivia's new government had seized copious underground resources following the National Revolution, but virtually no equipment, most of which had been exported by the savvy tin barons in the months leading up to revolution. In the decade since, worldwide demand for tin had fizzled, and the mines' new owner, the Bolivian government, had refused to trim back a hugely swollen labor force, justifiably afraid of the powerful unions who'd been so key in overthrowing the last government. The miners' militias, Thompson pointed out, were still "strong enough to topple the government any day of the week."

So the industry was hemorrhaging money, and without any revenue coming in, the miners' living and working conditions were only slightly better than the pre-revolution arrangement that Thompson called "one of the purest forms of exploitation existing in South America." That was fifty years ago, and very little has changed at Cerro Rico since.

Modern Potosí is windswept and whisper-quiet. Its wealth has long since dried up, and the city today is one of Bolivia's poorest, which puts it high in the running for poorest worldwide. I stepped off the bus on a Friday during Lent, and as I walked past the twin-towered cathedral, the only sounds were the muted hymns from inside, drifting like ghosts across an otherwise empty plaza. Dwarfing the cathedral—dwarfing everything, in fact—was the eerily isosceles mound of Cerro Rico itself. Potosí is the highest city in the world, bone-dry and chilly at more than 13,000 feet. The mountain tops out at close to 16,000, and its scraped-clean slopes are visible from anyplace around town, tawny and crumbled, like a sawdust pile. Cerro Rico looks like a good, stiff breeze could scatter it across the plateau, and considering how porous it must be after five centuries of dynamite and drills, I suppose it's kind of a miracle that it hasn't yet.

Just off the square, I found an eighteenth-century mansion now converted into a dirt-cheap bunkhouse, and I asked right away about the possibility of a mine tour. Today's miners work in small cooperatives, pulling tin, copper, zinc, and some low-grade silver out of Cerro Rico, and the smarter co-ops have learned to supplement their meager profits with no-frills, at-your-own-risk crawling tours of the working caverns. Around Potosí, a number of former miners have hung out their shingles as tour guides, most of them with a little education and occasionally some English.

My innkeeper made a few calls, then asked me to meet a guide downstairs the next morning. Bring a pair of long pants, he told me, plus a bottle of water and some money to buy alcohol for the miners.

The main thing I learned the next day is that mining in modern Potosí involves a staggering amount of drinking. In the morning, I climbed into a van with a pair of Israelis, a German/Portuguese couple, and a Brit. All of them were passing through Potosí on their way to or from the world-famous Uyuni Salt Flats—a considerably more popular tourist attraction a few hours up the road. Our guide was a brusque former miner named David who spoke a hodge-podge of English and Spanish. In his mid-thirties, David was too young to be a "former" anything, really, but since it's not uncommon for miners to take up the pickax at age fourteen, he might have had a long and storied career before transitioning to tourism.

On our way to the mountain, David pulled the van over at an edge-of-town street and ushered us out onto the sidewalk.

"This is the only street in Potosí," he announced, "where it is legal to buy and sell dynamite."

We walked up to a folding card table beneath a plastic awning, and David nodded familiarly to the *cholita* vendor standing behind, who nodded back. Then, abruptly, he grabbed a stick of dynamite off the table and lobbed it at me.

"Catch!" he cried, and I did, clumsily. It was the first time I'd ever held dynamite in my hand, much less had it thrown at me. The cylinder had the heft of a piece of sidewalk chalk and seemed tightly wrapped in something like butcher paper.

"Don't worry," David said. "It can't ignite without this." He grabbed a Ziploc bag off the table and handed it to me. It was full of small pink pellets that looked like candy and smelled like gasoline. "Ammonia nitrate," he said. "Power-ful stuff."

Before going into the mines, David explained, it was a custom to buy gifts for the workers we would encounter down there, a sort of a currency with which to buy their attention. The preferred tender was coca leaves and beer. Because it was Saturday, David said, most of his compatriots would be taking the day off from their other favorite beverage, a straight cane alcohol sold in flimsy plastic bottles and weighing in at 96 percent ABV. He grabbed one off the table and poured a few capfuls to pass around. The liquor numbed my tongue and burned like bleach going down. I flashed back instantly to the unsought *chirrinchi* sesh back in the Guajiran desert.

"Sir, you should have another," David said to me, in the voice you use to dare a little sister, "since you caught that dynamite." So I did, and my brain reeled just a little. Then each of us bought five cans of beer for the miners, and I threw in a bag of coca for good measure.

We continued up the hill, winding our way past heavy machinery and abundant piles of trash before parking next to a row of brick buildings and a gaping hole in the mountain. Emerging from the mouth of the mine, three men pushed a steel cart loaded with ore along a decrepit railway track. Another dozen miners stood in a semicircle nearby, grubby in their jumpsuits and helmets, chewing coca and looking on placidly. Their cheeks bulged like cartoon ballplayers in the bullpen. It was ten o'clock in the morning, and most of them were drinking cans of beer. A couple of rotting wooden beams shored up the entrance to the mine, and above it a sign read: LA MONJA II—KORIMAYU LIMITADA. Our mine was called "The Nun," and apparently it was a sequel. Korimayu, meanwhile, was the name of the co-op, which David said came from a Quechua phrase meaning "river of gold."

Miner-owned cooperatives are the norm in Bolivia now,

following the collapse of the government-owned mining system. What Thompson had called "Operation Triangular" back in 1962 was an Alliance for Progress program designed to stave off that collapse. The Alliance bargain was that the United States and other nations would bail out and temporarily subsidize Bolivia's ailing industry, provided that Bolivia started diversifying its economy, laid off 20 percent of its workers, and shut down unprofitable mines. Predictably, this agreement led to an armed revolt by the workers, who clashed violently with the military in 1963. Tom Martin, Thompson's buddy in the USIS labor office, was kidnapped by protesting miners and held hostage for ten days that December. His capture prompted an op-ed from Thompson in the *Observer*, blasting the miners for stupidly abducting "a man who understood their aspirations" and "the best source of American bourbon that Bolivian labor leaders have ever been lucky enough to find."

"If Operation Triangular fails," he predicted, ". . . the prospects for Bolivia are not pretty." And here Thompson was right yet again. The bailout helped for a while, and Bolivia's mining industry limped through the 1970s on the strength of cheap credit and high tin prices. At the same time, though, a series of military governments tried hard to crush the miners' unions using arrests, torture, and violence. In 1980, as many as 900 miners protesting a recent military coup were killed or "disappeared" during a massacre by the Bolivian Army in a mountain town southeast of La Paz. The market for tin tanked again shortly thereafter, and by 1985 a pound of tin worth $2 cost Bolivia more than $6 to produce. The government mining company finally succeeded at laying off workers—about 30,000 of them in a single year— and by 1990 mine ownership was privatized and restructured. Poor urban areas like El Alto exploded as the huge layoffs abruptly swelled the ranks of Bolivia's ragtag informal sector.

Of course, the industry's legacy of violence and oppression has its roots in Potosí, and as we donned jumpsuits and helmets to go underground, David explained how Cerro Rico earned its nickname, "The Mountain That Eats Men."

"Eight million miners have died here," he said. "From explosions, falls, silicosis, gases. There are many, many ways to die inside this mountain." Historians back up the number. For centuries, indigenous and sometimes African slaves were simply fed into the mountain by Spanish viceroys, and for the free miners who came later, a meager paycheck and a union were little protection against frequent cave-ins and the ubiquitous black lung. Today, silicosis is by far the main cause of death. The average life expectancy of a Potosí miner is just over forty.

All around us, stoic-looking men were going about their business, hauling bags of minerals and smoking in small groups, obviously accustomed to clusters of gringos lurking on the periphery. Single-file, we walked into the mine. The damp central tunnel was warm like a locker room, and the beams from our battery-powered headlamps dissolved helplessly in the darkness. As my eyes adjusted, I made out corridors peeling off to the sides, plus the occasional gaping pit topped with winches that looked like they'd been fabricated in a high school shop class. It was quiet enough to hear the breathing of the German guy behind me. We plodded along the tracks behind David. Every so often, he yelled to warn us of an oncoming cart, and we pressed up against the cave's slick walls to avoid being flattened as it hurtled by. Sometimes the cart-pushers stopped to chat with David, speaking Quechua or a heavily accented Spanish—I wasn't sure which.

"Give him a beer," David ordered each time, and one of

us would reach into our canvas sack to retrieve a lukewarm can. The miners took it wordlessly or with a polite *gracias,* then drained it quickly and tossed aside the empty. An unending stream of water bottles and beer cans floated in puddles next to the track. Here and there, I kicked them out of the way, like pinecones along the trail. For every ounce of tin that comes out of this mountain, I thought, the miners must put a pound of plastic and aluminum back in.

When we were deep enough that the air had turned sour, David peeled into a side chamber and motioned for us to follow. The seven of us clustered into a tight and low-ceilinged room. The German/Portuguese couple, I noticed, were holding hands and looking a bit tense. David pointed into the corner, and we shined our headlamps there to see a crude man-sized sculpture of some kind of saturnalian demon, with horns and hooves and a huge phallus, seated on a ledge and decorated with colorful string confetti.

"This is Tío," David said reverently. "Every mine has its own Tío. Down here, Tío is God. He decides whether you find minerals. He decides whether you live or die."

I drew in closer to the wild-eyed statue. This particular Tío ("uncle" in Spanish) was grinning like a rogue. He was decorated with a rainbow of paper-thin streamers and looked like something out of an occult fetishist's vision of a sinister Mardi Gras parade. On his lap and shoulders, the miners had placed cigarettes, small vials of cane liquor, and green baggies of coca leaves.

"Offerings?" I asked David.

"Of course," he said. "It is important always to keep Tío happy. We give him these things, and in return, Tío gives us his protection."

We left Tío and descended deeper, peeling away from the tracks and following David down narrow chutes and twisting diagonal passageways. Every hundred yards or so, we handed out beer to the dusty miners who seemed to emerge from the walls of the cavern itself, crouched in corners and chipping away listlessly. David didn't do much talking. Sometimes we slithered on our bellies for twenty or thirty feet at a stretch, shimmying through horizontal fissures like sideways chimneys. I was damp with sweat, and the cavern's ambient grit crunched between my teeth.

In Montana, I'd been on walking tours of limestone caverns with guardrails and electric lights, with guides like chatty real estate agents who coaxed you through the occasional tight squeeze. The difference between that and this was the difference between an interpretive trail at Mount St. Helens and a backpacking trip through Mordor. I have no particular discomfort in small spaces and a great, irrational confidence that strangers won't lead me into life-threatening situations. All the same, it takes a little deep breathing to keep the panic at bay when you're leopard-crawling through a thirty-foot tunnel the approximate height and width of a sewer grate and when your janky twenty-year-old headlamp picks that moment to come disconnected from its battery pack. The others seemed to be holding it together well enough, despite an occasional whimper from the Portuguese girl. *It's only a tourist attraction,* I imagined everyone saying to themselves, not fundamentally different from a ranger-led waterfall hike or a docent's tour of the Catacombs in Paris—just with an uncomfortably sullen guide and twenty tons of earth pressing down on top of you. So yeah, there was nothing to worry about, not really, and besides, I'd left a handful of my coca leaves back in the devil-worship chamber with Tío.

After an hour or so, we stumbled into a high-clearance cavern where a corpulent miner sat on a boulder, working a vein of tin and muttering to himself. David introduced him as Pablo, and I handed over a beer without waiting to be asked. Pablo was one of the older miners we'd encountered, pushing forty anyway, and he held the can out to me in a mock toast before bringing it to his lips.

"I'm going to leave you guys here with Pablo for a while," David said abruptly. He wanted to know whether there were any detonations planned for the afternoon, and he asked us to sit tight for a few minutes while he wandered off to find the jefe.

He was gone for over an hour, during which time we crouched in the cavern and plied Pablo with questions and beer. The Israelis and the Portuguese girl knew Spanish, and Pablo spoke simply enough that I could follow along. He was a third-generation miner, he said, his dad having come to Potosí in the '60s from whichever mountain his grandfather had once mined, somewhere farther to the north. He told us that working conditions were worse back then, before most mines had even the rudimentary ventilation systems they have today. Gases were a big problem, and Pablo remembered being new on the job when four of his father's friends were asphyxiated one day in a remote chamber, unable to escape when their carbide lamps went out for lack of oxygen.

"Yes," he opined, cracking the top of a second beer can, "it's a hard life, but if you're going to live here in Potosí, there are no factories and no other jobs. So maybe we die young! But mining is what we know how to do, and a lot of people out there"—he gestured vaguely into the darkness—"don't have any jobs at all."

That was true enough. About 9,000 miners are still plumbing the depths of Cerro Rico, making maybe $4 per twelve-hour workday. Half of Potosí's 150,000 people depend directly on the mines for their income. Pablo himself is a father of ten, he told us proudly. The city is a microcosm of Bolivia in this way: no one is particularly thrilled about the desperate dependence on mining, still Bolivia's second-biggest industry after hydrocarbons like oil and natural gas. Take it away, however, and there's really nothing there to replace it. It's the same old problem that Thompson described back in 1962.

I watched Pablo pour some beer into his mineral sack for good luck. Were things better or worse now, I asked, compared to when the government ran the mines?

"Today, I think, it's better," Pablo said without much conviction, setting down his chisel and pulling from the can. "We have more flexibility to work when we want. We negotiate our own prices, and we don't have to pay a government tax for all of our equipment."

He passed the half-empty beer around for us to share, clearly warming to the conversation.

"Of course now, we pay a lot for our carts, our drills and lamps, things like that," he said contemplatively. He shrugged in the darkness. "After the coca and the alcohol, there isn't much left over."

I took out my bag of coca and handed it over. Pablo pinched a generous handful and gave it back with a grateful nod. Each leaf was a smallish green spear, a dead ringer for a bay leaf. As he talked, Pablo expertly stripped each blade with his front teeth, tossing aside the petiole and adding to an already prodigious cud in the corner of his mouth. I reached into the bag and tried to mimic his technique, letting the chewed-up leaves gather and moisten in a pocket below my gums. They tasted bitter and earthy, like mature arugula or raw green tea.

Pablo pointed to the lump bobbing in his jaw. "Thanks to this," he said, "I can work ten or twelve hours with just one meal." He didn't look like a guy who skipped a lot of meals, I thought, although maybe his girth came from all that beer. Pablo was already opening another fresh one.

"Do you worry about cave-ins?" asked the Portuguese girl, a bit nervously.

"You mean getting trapped? Like those Chileans?" Pablo laughed and gestured around him with his beer can. "This mountain is like Swiss cheese. Everywhere there are holes. If something collapses?" He shrugged and raised his beer can. "What can you do but sit and drink for a while? You smoke and tell a few jokes. Then eventually someone says, 'OK. Let's go this way.'"

I could already feel a pleasant, localized numbness spreading through my cheek. I spat when I saw Pablo spit, and it was too dark to tell, but I imagined my saliva to be green.

"No, I don't worry much about that," he said, shaking his head. "I worry about silicosis. I worry about Tío." He said both words with the same conviction, drawing no distinction between the seriousness of either threat. "When you are alone sometimes, Tío comes to visit you, and this is very dangerous."

The Israeli guys chuckled. With a smirk in his voice, one of them asked why.

"Because he looks just like one of your friends," Pablo said, unsmiling. "Or maybe he takes the form of the dead, except that he has golden teeth. But if you don't give him what he wants, he will try and kill you."

"And what does Tío want?" I asked.

"Alcohol, usually. Sometimes food or cigarettes."

Pablo nodded somberly. It was like the old biblical

parable, I thought, only backward. Feed and clothe your neighbor, Christ said, because you never know when it might really be God, and he'll reward you with eternal life. Give your neighbor booze and smokes, said Pablo, because he may actually be Tío, and he can blow you to bits with a badly timed stick of dynamite.

We chitchatted and waited for David. Yet another beer was cracked open and passed, then another and another after that. After five or so had gone around, Pablo held out a can in front of him and squinted, like he was examining a fine specimen from his mineral bag.

"Yes, alcohol is good," he said with a sigh, and he took a deep swig. "I don't usually drink beer, though. Too many chemicals."

I asked him what he preferred, and naturally he said the miner's cane spirits, which is chemically similar to antifreeze.

We were partway through our second six-pack when David suddenly came scuttling around the corner. "Turn off your lamps!" he ordered, an excited edge to his voice. "Everyone turn off your lamps!"

We all flipped the switches on the back of our helmets, and in an instant, the cave went utterly, hopelessly black. It was the sort of darkness that most human beings don't often get to experience, the kind that prompts entire phyla of insects to evolve without eyes. In front of my face, Tío himself might have been dancing a jig, waving his giant phallus around, and I would have had no idea.

"Now, put your fingers in your ears," David commanded.

I did so, lightly, and waited. When the explosion came it sounded like suction, like all the air being pulled out of the mine. *Whump!* came the noise, both deafening and dull, and the chamber shook noticeably. I felt a shower of dust settle on my face and neck. And then, silence. After a beat, we all exhaled and flipped our headlamps back on, grinning nervously at one another. A fine particulate mist hung in the air, like dust blown off a bookshelf, a gauzy mineral cloud that miners like Pablo breathe every day.

"That was dynamite," David said needlessly. Then he sat down on a boulder and clapped his hands together. "So! Who has a beer left for poor, thirsty Pablo?"

The serious drinking began a couple of hours later, at a cinder block–sorting facility in the shadow of the mountain. We drove there with David and Pablo together, after helping haul several thirty-pound sacks of tin ore back up to the rail line. We walked in to find a sparse courtyard festooned with empty bottles and three soggy-eyed miners blasting Foreigner's "I Want to Know What Love Is" from a boom box covered in rock dust. Jesus, I thought. For a people so dependent on heavy metal, Bolivians sure go in for the soft rock.

We spent the rest of the afternoon milling while the miners drank and laughed, drank and crushed tin in two aging electric mills. A smiling, staggering assistant passed out beers for the *turistas,* and he kept them coming while the crew weighed the day's haul on a small flatbed scale. Later on, when we'd walked back out to the van, the German gave voice to what everyone had been thinking.

"Well," he said, unzipping his jumpsuit, "I guess if I had their life, I'd probably drink that much too."

I made one more stop before leaving Potosí, hopping a taxi to the large cemetery on the edge of town. It's a place that the city's few tourists tend to avoid. Like many cemeteries in Latin America, Potosí's is a patchwork of funerary vaults called columbaria—large walls lined with recesses for the storage of cremated remains. In the Potosí cemetery, these walls are arranged in squares surrounding simple courtyards. On the inside, each wall is a grid of crematory niches containing the remains of the dead, and in lieu of a headstone, each niche has its own plaque, along with a small shelf for flowers and other tributes.

It was a sunny Sunday morning, and the cemetery was crowded with mourners. At least a hundred people were lined up loosely along a central pathway, getting ready for some kind of procession. It wasn't a festive scene, obviously, but neither did it seem particularly somber. The crowd of mostly women chatted casually among themselves or sat on stone benches arranging flowers. Children chased one another around the benches, crying out from time to time and diving into their mothers' prodigious skirts.

The first columbarium I came to was dedicated to one of the miners' cooperatives. On a sign outside, a line of flowy cursive read: *Here rest those who left their lungs in the mines.* I walked inside the courtyard and found myself alone. The countless niches in the surrounding walls looked more or less the same. Each one contained a picture of a miner dressed in his Sunday best, some flowers in various stages of wilt, and a few small plastic replicas of beer and liquor bottles.

III

My bus to Santa Cruz broke down on a high Andean pass sometime just after four a.m., about eighty miles away from the closest city, Cochabamba. I'd been sleeping more or less soundly and woke to find the bus motionless and about two-thirds empty. There was no announcement, of

course. To hear my seatmate tell it, there had been a notice-
able clattering for some time. Then, while we were passing a
small farm at the crest of a rock-strewn hill, the driver had
simply pulled over, stepped out of the bus, and never come
back in. A few passengers eventually got out and started
walking, and I could see about fifteen others out my window, sitting on their luggage on the opposite side of the road,
waiting for some alternative conveyance.

I wandered outside and found the driver reclining against
a suitcase in the luggage compartment, silently smoking. It
was just after dawn, and the first pink rays were struggling
to reach into the mountains. A few thatched-roof buildings clustered on the neighboring hillside, and a leafy patch
of coca plants extended clear up to the road. I cleared my
throat, and the driver looked at me like I'd just interrupted
his favorite TV show. With my limited vocabulary, I tried to
inquire what was going on.

"We are waiting here for a person to come and fix this?"
I asked.

The driver shrugged impassively.

"Maybe a mechanic, maybe another bus," he said. "I'm
not sure."

The back end of the bus was open, I could see, which is
where I've always presumed the engines of buses to be. I almost asked what was wrong with it, but even if the driver had
answered in crisp Oxford English, I wouldn't have known
what he was talking about.

"And them?" I asked, nodding toward the people across
the street.

"They want another ride, but no one will come."

"When do you think we'll be moving again?"

He picked at a luggage tag on somebody's duffel bag.

"Mediodia," he answered, which could mean noon but

could just as easily mean any vague time around the middle of the day. It was not yet six a.m. So I asked for my rucksack and sat down across the street with the rest of the mutineers.

The group of us waited there in silence, trying to wave down trailer trucks, which passed sporadically and all seemed to be hauling livestock. I debated whether I'd rather wait in the mountains all day or ride into Cochabamba ankle-deep in manure. The question was moot, though, as none of them stopped. It was cold out, and later I figured that we were probably stopped there at about 10,000 feet. The driver crouched pathetically in his luggage carriage, smoking and avoiding our eyes. In retrospect, I realized he probably wished he could join us.

Eventually another company's double-decker bus came tearing around the corner, and we all waved like castaways. The bus pulled over and we hurried inside, abandoning the sorry driver and a dozen or so optimists still seated in the broken-down coach. In the new bus, I grabbed an open seat in the first row of the top level, where I could watch out the wide front windows as we descended into the valley. It had only been about ninety minutes since I'd woken up. That could have been a lot worse, I thought.

Then, no more than twenty miles up the road, my new bus slowed dramatically. I peered out the big window and did a double-take. A bus coming from the other direction had somehow swerved into our lane and crashed through the meager guardrail. It was perched on the edge of the mountain and dangling in space, seemingly three-quarters of the way over, tilting drunkenly toward the steep slope below. It looked like the slightest kick might send it hurtling into the canyon. Inexplicably, though, all of the passengers seemed to have come out unscathed. They were milling around glumly on the opposite side of the road.

We didn't stop, presumably because my companions and I had just taken the last remaining seats. Maybe our bus driver encountered this sort of thing all the time. Farther along, we passed a fleet of fifteen yellow taxis speeding in the direction of the accident. Bolivia is a difficult country for buses.

I f the rest of modern Bolivia has been shaped by labor unions, popular uprisings, and socialist impulses, then Santa Cruz is the city that multinational capitalism built. On the sidewalk outside my motel, a woman selling black-and-white prints of historic Santa Cruz showed me a few images from the early 1960s that might have been from the 1860s. The city that Thompson saw in September of '62 was a straight-up backwater, with horses clopping along unpaved streets and not one building over three stories tall. Electric lights and potable water were fairly new. A paved road connecting the tropical, low-lying city to the Andean half of the country had been completed just six years earlier, and the railroad that Thompson would ride east into Brazil was itself just eight years old.

Thompson, however, wasn't the only American drifting around Bolivia's wild, wild east. A few years earlier, the Bolivian government had signed a contract for oil exploration with the US-based Gulf Oil Company, and as Thompson noted, the region had since filled up with transplanted Texas oilmen "drilling the hell out of the Bolivian jungle," searching for petroleum and natural gas. If Gulf came up short, it would deal a serious blow to Bolivia's efforts to scale back its mining dependency.

"Should Gulf come through, however," Thompson wrote, "Santa Cruz will be a hell of a boom town."

Gulf did indeed come through, and today Santa Cruz is Bolivia's largest city, a thoroughly modern metro built with oil profits over the span of just a few decades. The *fútbol* team, founded by oil workers, is named Oriente Petrolero. The affluent neighborhood is called Equipetrol, once home to Gulf's employees and likely where Thompson would have hobnobbed with its execs. On a continent where unchecked urban migration leads to spontaneous communities like El Alto or Huaycán, Santa Cruz is just the opposite—a masterpiece of rationality and urban planning. The city center is surrounded by nine concentric rings of traffic, with broad palm-lined boulevards extending through them like spokes in a wheel. What Thompson would have experienced as basically the entirety of Santa Cruz in 1962 now occupies only the smallest, innermost ring.

The success of Santa Cruz has put the city at odds with the culture of the Altiplano and the government of Evo Morales. The largely white *cruceños* tend to have a Western, pro-capitalist attitude that defies Morales's socialist and indigenous-centric vision. Santa Cruz prides itself on what Americans might call a kind of blue-state urbanity: It has a reputation for turning out models, five-star chefs, and swaggering *fútbol* titans. Many *cruceños* see Andean Bolivians, known as *collas,* as a backward people who are unfairly partaking in the wealth of the east. When Morales nationalized Bolivia's oil and gas reserves in 2006, he did so with tacit support from Santa Cruz, but the city has since seen protests and referendums demanding autonomy from La Paz and more control over the country's fossil fuel revenues.

Never mind the underlying sociopolitical tension, though—Santa Cruz just *feels* different. For starters, it is ungodly hot. In the weeks since I'd left Lima, I hadn't been any lower than 10,000 feet above sea level. Santa Cruz is at 1,400 feet, and the thick air of Bolivia's Amazon basin hung on me like a wet beach towel. Around town, the Spanish tradition of the siesta seemed well observed, with stores and restaurants closing during the most oppressively sweltering hours of the day. There's an ice-cream shop on seemingly every block in the city center, and *cruceños* don't think twice about helping themselves to a scoop at nine o'clock in the morning on a Tuesday.

One afternoon, I took a walk from my downtown motel to the prosperous Equipetrol neighborhood just to the north, hoping to find some kind of artifacts, statues, or other remnants of the days when the district had housed the American Gulf Oil contractors. On the way, I noticed that consumer culture around Santa Cruz seemed much more prevalent than in any South American city I'd been to so far. Sure, there was the usual glut of mom-and-pop storefronts, clothing stores and Internet cafés and auto-parts retailers, all grouped together in blocks of similar businesses, as is strangely common in Latin America. My motel, for instance, was around the corner from a printing and graphics district, where no fewer than twelve shops all advertised impression services for signs, posters, and business cards—all within two blocks of each other. Back in Quito, I had asked a cab driver about this tendency as we drove past a long block consisting of nothing but sporting-goods stores. Why did this seem to be such a popular arrangement? Why set up an identical business right next to four of your competitors? He had just shaken his head and admitted that he'd never really understood it himself.

But Santa Cruz also seemed to have a lot of higher-end specialty services and commercial trappings that I wasn't used to seeing—import car dealerships, for example, and conspicuous billboards for credit cards. In Equipetrol, I didn't find anything reminiscent of the 1960s except for the influence of American suburban architecture on the older homes. What I did find were copious health clubs, wine bars, cosmetic dermatologists, and obscure professional services. The whole place felt like an upscale Florida suburb, and the coca-and-dynamite market in Potosí seemed a million miles away.

From Santa Cruz, I set out on a wild Google chase. Looking at my laptop one morning, I noticed on Google Maps a spot just north of Santa Cruz that was marked with the word "Texas." On the satellite view, it looked less like a town and more like some patchy green fields, but the label was tantalizing. Gulf had brought many of its employees from Texas to Bolivia back in the day. Surely, I thought, this area must have some connection to that era. Back then, the spot marked "Texas" would have been pretty far out of the city, but I figured maybe it was an oil camp, several of which Thompson had toured on his way through eastern Bolivia. Further Web searching offered no more information, and when I asked at the Santa Cruz tourist office, neither of the puppy-eyed college girls there knew anything about the place. I approached a few drivers at the bus station whose routes seemed to take them nearby, but the only Texas anyone had heard of was the cowboy capital back in the United States. I asked a few taxi drivers, but it never rang any bells.

"I have a cousin in Houston," one of them suggested helpfully.

So I got up early one morning and rode a city bus as far as Santa Cruz's northern airport, just outside the city, from where I could hoof it the last few miles to the general area where Google's cartographers had placed Texas, Bolivia. Thankfully, it was an overcast day, so the heat was bearable. The road north of town was a four-lane highway like something out of rural Kansas, busy with semi-trucks and buses, cutting across an empty, scrubby flatland. Inexplicably, I kept walking past piles of rotting fruit—rank mounds of bananas and oranges piled up along the shoulder, covered in buzzing flies.

After a couple of miles I came to a tollgate and a military checkpoint, where a young soldier standing off to one side eyed me curiously as I walked up. Just cruising on by seemed awkward, so I stopped and asked him whether I should pay the toll.

"Where are you going?" he asked, one eyebrow arched. He was justifiably suspicious. The vehicles next to us were six deep in three lanes, and I was the only pedestrian in sight. Santa Cruz, for all its prosperity, is also a drug-trafficking hub, and I'm sure he could think of reasons why I might hop out of a truck and try to breeze through the checkpoint on foot.

"Not far," I said. "Another couple of miles, I think. I'm looking for someplace called Texas, or maybe *Tejas*."

"And why do you want to go there?"

One thing about not speaking a language well is that sometimes it's easier to lie than tell the truth. Back in Cali, I had fibbed about my rich retiree parents because any attempt to explain about Thompson and the British golfer would have only led to confusion. In this circumstance, though, I had no credible alternative motivation. So I launched into a complex answer about researching the history of oil exploration in Santa Cruz, and I took out my phone to show the Google map. When I'd finished clumsily explaining myself, the soldier stared at me for a moment, then broke into a broad grin.

"First of all, the place you are looking for is called Texas Arizona," he said, pronouncing the *x*. "But more importantly, it doesn't mean anything. It is just a barrio, my friend.

There's nothing there. No petroleum history, no American history. No history at all. The people who live there, they just picked some names off a map."

He was smiling at me, amused and a little condescending, but I still wasn't sure if he was going to let me pass. Surely they must have *something* there, I said. Maybe I could just get some lunch and come back?

"There is no lunch in Texas Arizona," he insisted, smiling wider. "There is nothing there at all."

"Well, a *refresca,* then," I said hopefully.

"No *refrescas,* sir. There is nothing."

Well, I asked, could I please just go check it out anyway? I'd come all this way. The soldier was bemused, but he waved me through with a gloved hand and told me where to turn off. It was only another mile, he said, and Google's map had actually put it on the wrong side of the highway.

So half an hour later, I was walking down a dirt road, out of earshot from the paved one, when I walked up on a sign reading URBANIZACION POLICIAL TEXAS ARIZONA. It was painted with stencils on a couple of old two-by-fours: Texas Arizona Housing Development. It seemed like the soldier was right. For the next hour or so, I walked the community's dusty streets, surrounded by a few dozen simple brick hovels. The grid of unpaved paths was surrounded by beige scrubland, relentlessly flat, with the towers of the airport and the city silhouetted against the far skyline. Everything was quiet except for the occasional dirt-bike traffic. Most every family in Texas Arizona seemed to keep a few chickens, and all of them had sizable gardens, coaxing who-knows-what out of the sandy hard-pack soil. In the ditches along the road, a chorus of frogs cried like space babies—a weird, high-pitched vibrato. But I found no crumbling derricks and no tumbleweed ranches of forgotten American oil barons. It was just a flat, hardscrabble little housing project with none too many people around, and in all likelihood I was its first-ever tourist.

So I tried striking up conversations with the handful of pedestrians, bricklayers, and porch-sitters I ran into, apologizing for approaching them out of the blue and asking whether anyone knew the history of the community's name. The soldier, as it happened, was wrong about the *refrescas*. One house had a shed fixed up into a tiny bodega out back, and as I bought a cold beer there, I quizzed the twelve-year-old girl behind the counter. Elsewhere, a couple of teenage boys looked up from a disassembled dirt bike to stare at me, and I walked over and asked them, too. I was met with everything from blank stares to thoughtfully furrowed brows to observations that Grandpa might know, if only he were still around. But no one had any idea. A few folks seemed surprised to learn that "Texas" and "Arizona" were geographical entities outside of their little corner of Bolivia. In truth, nobody seemed to feel much like talking.

By the late afternoon, I was tired and a bit frustrated. It occurred to me that what I was doing in Texas Arizona wasn't so different from what I was doing all along the Thompson Trail—just grasping around for links with history. I feel a bit compelled to travel this way, always sniffing around for the cultural-literary-historical significance of this or that. It would be easy to chalk this up to a simple excess of liberal-arts education, but there's more to it than that. In a sense, I feel like this is the only avenue of exploration left to me. Sure, I had consciously set out to follow in Thompson's footsteps, but the truth is, we are all following in someone's footsteps now. There is no more terra incognita, if there ever was any to start, one person's incognita being another person's backyard. There are no trails left untrod. In only the most isolated of circumstances will a human being on this planet ever again stumble into a corner of the world that hasn't been thoroughly mapped, explored, photographed, and otherwise documented—if not probed for oil and covered up with a housing project.

This may seem demoralizing at first, but the silver lining is a gradual unveiling of whole new dimensions of travel, unknown and unknowable to yesteryear's swashbucklers. History is a space through which we can travel now just as easily as through longitude, latitude, and altitude. Thanks to the steady accumulation and diffusion of human knowledge, the enticing blankness of terra incognita has been replaced with bottomless layers of story and meaning and causality that, know it or not, we are forever drifting through, like scuba divers among the eddies. And if I can't tease out the links and the logic among these layers, I sometimes feel like I'm failing as a traveler.

Another mile up the road from Texas Arizona was a slightly larger community called Satélite Norte, with shops and services and buses into the city. I walked there to rest and regroup. The strip in Satélite Norte was actually a surprisingly happening place. Moto-taxis zoomed up and down the paved main road, and several blocks were filled with folks drinking beer in open-fronted bars with blaring video-karaoke machines. The bars were lined up side by side, five in a row, all blasting terrible adult-contemporary tunes at top volume. It was the philosophy of setting up next to your competitor taken to its full, nonsensical zenith, as each karaoke bar battled valiantly to be heard over its neighbor. The result was an unlistenable cacophony of synthesizers and power chords.

I picked a karaoke bar at random. It was my kind of place—no kitchen, no pool table, no bar. Just six tables, forty glasses on a wall-mounted rack, one video karaoke machine, and a giant cooler full of beer. I ordered a bottle and tried to figure out just what the hell I was doing there. I'd found Bolivia's Texas easily enough, but I still had no idea what it meant. And wasn't that the point of all this? To find some meaning in the experience of these places? Thompson seemed to think so anyway.

"I came to South America to find out what it meant," he wrote in 1963, toward the end of his trip, "and I comfort myself in knowing that at least my failure has been on a grand scale."

I looked out toward the dirt road back to Texas Arizona, then at a man who was herding three goats past the video bars of Satélite Norte. My failure was playing out on a rather provincial scale, I thought. I drained my first beer and ordered a second. The bartender was wearing a faded Green Bay Packers T-shirt, and even though that's my favorite football team, I kept quiet. You only have to see two or three grown men wearing *Twilight* tees before you realize not to read too much into fashion in South America. The shirt didn't mean that the bartender was a fan of American football. It didn't mean anything. He set a fresh beer in front of me and opened the bottle wordlessly.

Back in Wisconsin, on the wall of my favorite college bar, there was a large framed poster of a *Mr. Natural* comic book from 1971. The white-bearded character drawn by cartoonist R. Crumb is probably best known for his thumbs-up, keep-on-truckin' pose, but this particular panel finds Mr. Natural cruising down the sidewalk on a scooter. As he scoots along, a bystander shouts, "Mr. Natural! What does it all mean??" To which Mr. Natural, not pausing from his ride, replies, "Don't mean sheeit. . . ."

I must have drunk a thousand beers in front of that poster.

Maybe, I thought, Mr. Natural was right. Maybe Thompson gave up on finding meaning down here around the same time he started embracing the fundamental absurdities of life in South America. In another letter, from December of 1962, Thompson wrote glumly that he had already found out "what I came down here to find out, and there is nothing else left for me to do but document it. Dostoyevsky was right." What did he mean by that? What had Thompson found that validated the troubled Russian existentialist, himself famously obsessed with meaning and absurdity? Dostoyevsky's heroes tend to embrace suffering and neglect their own best interests. Is that what Thompson saw happening around him in South America? In Bolivia's mines, for example?

I thought about it as a hundred decibels of Hall & Oates went head to head against a hundred decibels of Toto next door. Above all, Dostoyevsky's characters are rarely motivated by reason. So maybe I was wrong to expect a rational explanation for Texas Arizona, Bolivia. Maybe it just didn't mean sheeit.

All the same, I walked back to Texas Arizona when I'd finished my beers. From the girl at the shed bodega, I bought three more warm cans. It was getting late, and I'd have to get back to Santa Cruz before the buses stopped, but with the sun going down and people settling into their leisure hour, I hoped that maybe I could find and lubricate an old-timer, some strolling graybeard who'd loosen up with a can of suds. But the streets were still eerily quiet. I walked twenty minutes before I saw a man in the road a short distance ahead. He was helping a woman and two small children onto the back of a moto-taxi that barely looked big enough for two. She straddled the driver and held a child on each thigh. Somehow the bike sputtered away without tipping, and the man stood in the street, waving good-bye.

I caught up with him and begged his pardon before introducing myself. He wore a polo shirt and a baseball cap and was probably somewhere in his fifties. Juan Carlos was his name, he said, and he considered my question thoughtfully as I followed him back toward Satélite Norte.

"This place has been called Texas Arizona since before there were people here," he said, "since even before they built the houses."

"And when was that?" I asked.

"Maybe fifty years ago."

Now we were getting somewhere. That was about the same time that the Gulf Oil Company was hitting its stride in Bolivia. Did he think that the area might have been named by the oil companies? Might there have been oil camps here? Juan Carlos just shrugged. He had never heard such a thing. We walked quietly for a while, and I reached into my backpack to offer him a beer.

"No, thank you," said Juan Carlos politely. "I don't drink."

It was getting dark, and the weird frogs in the ditches were trilling even louder than before.

"I guess I'm a little disappointed," I said. "I really thought that someone around here could tell me the significance of this name."

"You wanted to hear a story," Juan Carlos said, shaking his head, "but this is difficult, because sometimes the people come, and then later, they forget all the stories."

The wall of sound from the karaoke bars echoed a good half mile from Satélite Norte. On a side street, Juan Carlos spotted some friends walking a different direction, and he wished me well before joining them. I took a quick look back at Texas Arizona, then opened a beer and walked to the bus stop alone.

CHAPTER SEVEN

Hope for the Mato Grosso

There are no brochures on the Mato Grosso . . . which is one of the reasons land there is selling for $4 an acre. I have no idea what it's like except that it's god-forsaken and full of jaguars.

—Personal correspondence, February 28, 1962

I

A traveler who has booked passage aboard what is widely known as the "Death Train" is entitled to certain expectations. Among these is the prospect that, yes, at some point during the trip, one's life will be imperiled. Gazing out the window at the flat, grassy lowlands of eastern Bolivia, it's difficult to imagine how this might occur. Needless to say, the region lacks the sheer cliffs and gaping chasms of the Andes. There is, in fact, next to nothing off which you could tragically plunge. The Death Train's route follows the comparatively dry outermost edge of the Amazon basin, so the few adjacent rivers run at a trickle, wholly incapable of submerging a railcar full of frantically clawing passengers. Meanwhile, the gradual clearing of eastern Bolivia's forests and savannas for farming and ranching has put pressure on the local jaguar population, so a passenger stretching his legs during a stopover is less likely to be mauled by a big cat than mooed at by a Holstein.

In short, I am sorry to report that a 420-mile trip aboard Bolivia's *tren de la muerte* is actually a rather comfortable and pleasant affair. There's no clear consensus on how the train acquired this nickname, reliably invoked by travel guidebooks, tourism and hospitality types, and the ticketing agents at the Santa Cruz train station. The owner of my hotel told me that hundreds of workers died while constructing the line across Bolivia's eastern backcountry in the 1940s and '50s. At the time, this was a landscape so perilous and remote that a British travel writer of the day nicknamed it "the green hell." A number of guidebooks and websites disagree with this, however, claiming that the name stems from the train's violent shuddering and tendency to jump its tracks. Still another theory holds that the route was used to transport bodies in the wake of a well-documented 1946 yellow fever outbreak. I'm personally sympathetic to the notion that the sobriquet stems from the deadly tedium. From Santa Cruz to the Brazilian border, it's a sixteen-hour trip (only mildly shaky) across a rather monotonous landscape of ranches and gentle green waves. The few stops along the route are at rural stations that range from concrete bunkers to sheet-metal gazebos. The most exotic wildlife I saw during the ride consisted of a few large sows nosing around in the brush. To liven things up, the railroad showed the 1979 Christian propaganda flick *Jesus,* alternately known for being one of the most widely watched and one of the dullest films of all time.

At the Brazilian border, the thrill ride that is the Death Train reached its anticlimactic end. Beyond that point, the line carries only cargo. Fifty years ago, however, passenger service kept going clear across Brazil, and Thompson took the same train from Santa Cruz all the way to São Paulo in 1962, arriving there in mid-September. Ironically, the train would have breezed rather quickly through the Brazilian state of Mato Grosso, which more than any other region had fascinated Thompson since before he left for South America. Not that I think Thompson would have minded the rush. After four months on the continent, he was desperate to reach Rio de Janeiro, where there was an election to cover, but which, moreover, he'd built up in his mind as a sort of antidote to the Andes: warm, civilized, relaxed, and gringo-friendly.

But months before, Brazil's wild interior had captured Thompson's imagination. Back in the States, he had written long letters to friends, bemoaning his poverty and his inability to sell *The Rum Diary* and fantasizing about escaping to "the unplumbed jungle of the Mato Grosso." As a burgeoning gun nut, he dreamed of hunting wild game there and even schemed about buying land, which he had heard was going for a song.

"It is a rumor, you know," he wrote excitedly to a friend, "like GOLD! or WHISKEY! In this case, it's CHEAP LAND!"

Thompson's pre-travel letters show a somewhat starry-eyed fascination with South America's wild and primal landscape—a far cry from the largely urban reporting on culture and policy that mostly became his focus. All throughout his correspondence, Thompson confessed a romantic longing for the "wild country." Later on, after arriving in Rio, he regretted allowing his election coverage to curtail his time in the bush. He wrote to a fellow hunter back in California, wistfully mentioning a tall and foxlike predator called the maned wolf, native to Brazil's western grasslands. "I recently swung through Maned Wolf territory," he wrote, ". . . [but] I missed the animals. I am so fucking involved in politics, etc. that I don't have much time for the oddball stuff that is really the most important."

I think Thompson shared a bias that's common among overseas travelers, a tendency to view cities as somehow less authentically "other" than what he called the "wild country." Among the gringo nomads I ran into along the Thompson Trail, I regularly heard the statement "It's a city" deployed as a kind of verbal shrug, a shorthand method of telling a fellow traveler that Bogotá or Lima or La Paz was less worthy of description than, say, Bolivia's mountain villages or Ecuador's sparsely trammeled beaches.

BACKPACKER 1: What did you think of northern Peru?
BACKPACKER 2: I loved it! There's a huge nature preserve where you can run with the Andean wolves, and the

coast is spotted with dozens of Moche ruins that hardly anyone visits.

B1: Sounds great. What's Trujillo like?

B2: Trujillo? Oh, you know. It's a city.

Thompson himself did this in a letter from Colombia, after his very first urban encounter on the continent. "Barranquilla was a city, of course," he wrote dismissively, "too much like San Juan for my taste, but now we are heading into the wild country again."

There's nothing new about this mind-set. In La Paz, I had grabbed a dusty hardcover off a hostel bookshelf, a reprint of a 1922 travelogue called *The Real South America,* written by a journalist from the Jazz Age London *Times.* Even back then, the author had sniffed, "As the real South America cannot now be entered without crossing the civilized littoral, we must first see what the cities have to show before plunging into the crude life of the interior." It's the same sentiment as when the backpackers mutter, "It's a city," implying that cities are basically the same worldwide, or perhaps that even the very concept of a city is somehow not "real South America" enough, cities lacking things like llama trains and gaucho cowboys and pre-Columbian ruins—which, in addition to not being true, suggests that the phenomenon of the city is perhaps an American or European invention, imposed here and there upon an otherwise pastoral Southern Hemisphere.

Forgetting for a minute that Peru's ruined city of Caral is roughly contemporaneous with the pyramids at Giza, it's worth pointing out that South America's urbanization rate has been more or less on par with North America's since the beginning of the nineteenth century. Gauged by the percentage of its population living in cities, it is currently the world's most urban continent, and by the same measure, Latin America was actually "flipping" from predominantly rural to predominantly urban just as Thompson was passing through, way back in 1962. North America hit its tipping point in the '50s, but the world as a whole didn't reach that milestone until 2008. So I don't much truck with the notion that the cities of South America are in any way less authentic than the outback. The truth is, cities are as much an ongoing Latin American invention as they are an American, Chinese, or Mesopotamian one.

All of that being said, I am every bit as guilty as Thompson of romanticizing the "wild country," and I was pretty psyched to be getting into it for a few days, leaving the urban landscape behind.

Thompson's enthusiasm for Brazil's Mato Grosso was not misplaced. The area that Portuguese explorers wrote off as "Thick Forest" has since been partitioned into two states (Mato Grosso and its southern neighbor Mato Grosso do Sul). Together they contain the great majority of the 60,000-square-mile Pantanal—the world's largest wetland and easily one of the most biodiverse spaces on the planet. More than just a big swamp, the Pantanal is a patchwork of tropical forests, grasslands, river systems, and the wet savanna that Brazilians call the *cerrado*. It isn't so different from the Everglades, really, if maybe the Everglades were stretched over an area larger than the entire state of Florida. When conquistadors first glimpsed the Pantanal at full flood, they mistook it for a giant inland lake and presumed (as they often did) that El Dorado lay just beyond. It is one of those "Here Be Dragons"–type places, remote enough that the cartographers of the era simply let their imaginations fill in the blanks. On several eighteenth-century maps, the mythical lake contained a large "Isle of Paradise" at its center, based on the accounts of one inventive explorer who claimed to have there discovered a golden Eden full of abundant springs, kindly natives, and fruit trees in perennial bloom.

My expectations weren't quite so high, but I was definitely looking forward to a quiet interlude someplace a bit less affected by humanity and its failings. Bolivia had brought me a little closer to understanding Thompson's metamorphosis, his evolving gonzo outlook, but I didn't feel the epiphanic glow that I was hoping for. The tumult and hardship of Bolivia had simply gotten me down. I was starting to internalize Thompson's cynical observation that "Dostoyevsky was right." I needed to clear my head, and the Pantanal seemed like the right place to do it, since even at the apex of his cynicism, Thompson went so far as to exempt the Brazilian frontier from his bleak prediction that South America had a bad decade in store.

"I retain hope for the Mato Grosso," he wrote, "and ultimately for Brazil, but I think the next ten years are going to be ugly." Not a robust statement of confidence, exactly, but it was the first marginally uplifting thing he'd had to say since Cali.

Stepping off the Death Train and leaving behind the green hell, I figured I should probably take my optimism where I could get it.

II

It must be acknowledged that altitude in South America is a great determinant of the regional flavor of life. Not so much the *pace* of it, which to a North American seems always a paradoxical mixture of frantic and languid—the crush of traffic and the din of vendors on the one hand, the unhurried meals and the loitering in plazas on the other— but the *tenor* of it, the palpable mood of the people as they go about their everywhere-crazy routines. At around 400 feet from sea level, the Brazilian river town of Corumbá lacks the loony, brassy urgency of the Andes. Sure, folks in Corumbá still drive like maniacs and cut in line at the ATM, but they're slower to answer one another and quicker to laugh. Everyone there keeps bankers' hours, and happy hour along the wide, slow river is as faithfully observed as any mealtime. If life in Quito or La Paz is a trombone-heavy Sousa march, then life in Corumbá seemed like the same melody, but played Kenny G–style on a smooth alto sax.

Corumbá is probably the least utilized of any of the Pantanal's several gateway towns. These days, eco-tourism has a significant foothold in the Mato Grosso, and to the east and northeast, the metropolitan capitals of Campo Grande and Cuiabá each harbor dozens of tour groups and outfitters. Elsewhere, entire villages have reoriented their economies around adventure tourism. But I wanted a respite from the slick commercialism of the cities and tourist hubs, and Corumbá struck me as a working town with some history and character. It's built up along the Rio Paraguay, a 1,629-mile waterway that drains the Pantanal and flows eventually to the Atlantic. This winding river corridor made Corumbá a rich and strategic inland port around the turn of the twentieth century. For most of Brazil's history, traveling up the Rio Paraguay was actually the easiest way to reach the Mato Grosso, since Brazil didn't get serious about building roads into its interior until the 1940s.

Corumbá today is still a trade hub for the region's ranching, mining, and fishing industries, although as with the Magdalena, its commercial traffic has dwindled. I spent my first afternoon there hanging out by the waterfront, where the cargo ships were outnumbered by the wading, shirtless fishermen. I sat down on the beach to observe their technique. They fished without rods, using line tied to a plastic soda bottle, swinging the line above their heads like David battling Goliath. Then, holding the soda bottle with two hands, they spooled the line back in like a kite string on a spindle, occasionally reaching underwater at the last moment to pull up a giant, carplike *boga* fish with a hook protruding from its lip.

To learn a little about the Pantanal, I met up in Corumbá with Márcia Rolon and Ray Knowles of the Instituto Homem Pantaneiro, a behemoth nonprofit organization dedicated to cultural and environmental programs in the southern Pantanal. Knowles is the group's resident English-speaking attaché, a transplanted Brit who first came to Brazil as a photographer in the late 1970s. Rolon is a pretty and self-assured former ballerina who founded the IHP in 2002 along with her husband, a former captain of the region's environmental police and now a local politico. Over beer and pizza, the two of them informed me that the river basins of the Pantanal were not as unspoiled by human influence as either Thompson or I had envisioned.

"I need this river," Rolon announced as we sat down at a café alongside the rolling Paraguay. "The people of this region, the *pantaneiros,* need it. If this river were to die, we would die as well."

At forty-two, Rolon still has the lithe build of a dancer, and as we spoke I noticed how gracefully she gestured at the river, taking in the whole of it with a wide, slow sweep of her arm. In her previous career, she'd performed at festivals in Europe and all across South America, but her upbringing wasn't nearly so cosmopolitan. Rolon was raised in the Pantanal, she explained, a product of the region's entrenched cattle-ranching culture. Subsistence ranching in the Mato Grosso dates back to the mid-1800s, and when Rolon was young, her grandfather ran a small store for cattlemen and boatmen, strategically located on a key tributary of the Paraguay called the Rio Taquari. Her granddad had watched the Pantanal grow increasingly crowded during his lifetime, with more and more cattle run on smaller and more subdivided parcels. Settlers had really begun flocking to the interior after 1960, when Brazil christened its new inland capital of Brasília—a whole city raised up from nothing some 600 miles from the coastal population centers. When Rolon's grandfather was a boy, fewer than a million cattle roamed the Pantanal. By the time of Rolon's own childhood in the 1970s, that number was up to 5 million.

Cowboy-style cattle grazing in a seasonally flooded landscape is a relatively low-impact affair, but in the long term, that kind of whirligig growth is unsustainable, even in someplace as vast as the Pantanal. So it seemed like a good thing when Rolon said that ranching pressure has eased up in the Pantanal in the last few decades. Today, true to South America's urbanizing trend, Corumbá's population is twice what it was during Thompson's visit, while the cattle numbers have actually dropped by a million or more since their post-Brasília peak. Hurray for urbanization, I thought, for taking some of the pressure off the "wild country."

Except that it isn't that simple, because some of the very same factors propelling South America's shift toward urban living turn out to have pretty severe down-the-chain ecological impacts of their own. While there are a lot of reasons that a country-dweller might move into the city—job availability, the lure of education, escaping rural violence—the prime motivator in Brazil is the rapid expansion of mechanized, export-oriented agriculture, which has a tendency to squeeze out small-scale and subsistence farmers, both spatially and economically. And it's that kind of agriculture that benefited the most from Brazil's westward expansion in the later twentieth century. Lured by the same promise of "CHEAP LAND!" that captured Thompson's imagination, big-time agribusiness has thrived in the last thirty years in western Brazil. This is less true in the Pantanal itself than in the surrounding Mato Grosso highlands, where immense cattle and soybean operations have come to dominate the landscape. These industrial-scale farms and ranches have basically been *the* South American economic success story of the twentieth century, and one reason that cattle numbers have dipped in the Pantanal is that traditional gaucho ranchers there just can't compete.

But while Mato Grosso's beef and soybean empires have helped launch Brazil as an economic superpower, they had to clear a whole lot of land to do it. The rivers of the Mato Grosso highlands drain into the Pantanal, so land cleared upriver in soybean country means big-time sedimentation and erosion issues downstream. Just as deforestation back in Colombia caused the catastrophic silting of the Rio Magdalena, so the Rio Taquari that Rolon remembers from her childhood is now just a sediment-clogged and hopelessly braided mess. It's shallower today and prone to devastating floods, just like the one that eventually wiped out her grandfather's business and sent her family packing for Corumbá. Meanwhile, Rolon said, many of the Paraguay's other tributaries are trending in the same direction, with serious consequences for both grazing land and wildlife habitat.

"If my grandfather were to come back and see the Pantanal without the Rio Taquari," Rolon said, crossing her long ballerina's legs, "I think he would just die again."

Her colleague, Knowles, reached over to fill my beer. Brazilian bars serve liters of grimacingly cold beer in insulated cooler sleeves, like giant cozies—yet another altitude adjustment from the Andes, where cold beer is sadly underappreciated. Knowles followed Brazilian custom, filling everyone else's glasses first, then clinking his own glass against the bottle as a kind of toast. As Rolon spoke, he helped translate the Portuguese that she mixed in liberally with her English.

"The other problem with export agriculture," he chimed in, "is the demand it places on infrastructure. Do you know about the Hidrovia?"

In the 1990s, Knowles and Rolon explained, the governments of Brazil, Bolivia, Argentina, Paraguay, and Uruguay all jointly negotiated a proposal to dredge, widen, and "straighten" the countless meanders of the Rio Paraguay, hoping to streamline the channel for seagoing cargo barges. The cattle, cotton, and soybean industries of the Mato Grosso lobbied hard on behalf of the plan, and the mining industry was another big supporter, since the hills surrounding the Pantanal are rich in manganese, iron, and other minerals, all of them expensive to transport overland. Straightening the river would have boosted shipping speeds and accommodated larger container ships, but it also would have drastically and permanently altered the Pantanal's drainage, turning the world's largest wetland into something like a desert. Smart dredging to counteract the effects of sedimentation is one thing, Knowles said. Dramatically increasing the volume and flow of one of the continent's biggest river is another. The ecological consequences would have been severe. Thankfully, the Hidrovia proposal was defeated in the early 2000s, but it remains a cautionary tale around the Pantanal, and similar proposals are still regularly floated.

Knowles picked up the bottle and split the last of the beer among our three glasses.

"You know how Brazilians are really fond of proverbs?" he asked.

As a matter of fact, I did. Thompson pointed out this cultural soft spot for aphorisms in a 1963 *Observer* article about the Brazilian economy. "One concerns the bumblebee," he wrote, "which, according to the laws of aerodynamics, cannot possibly fly." But bumblebees don't know about aerodynamics, the Brazilian saying goes, and so they fly all the same. Thompson compared Brazil at the time to a bumblebee, "defying most known laws of economics in a headlong rush to 'development.'"

Knowles shared another Brazilian proverb, this one derived from the traditional method of hunting jaguar in the Pantanal. Come at the jaguar with a conventional spear, he explained, and the cat will feint, dodge, and retreat. But leave some bushy branches at the end of your spear, and the foliage will rustle irritatingly in the animal's face. A perturbed jaguar will grab at the spear, pulling it closer and allowing you to strike. Use too short a spear, though, and you risk being pulled in along with it.

"So when Brazilians warn you about something dangerous," he said, "they talk about 'provoking a jaguar with a short stick.'" He swallowed the last of his beer and looked out at the pale river. "When we start messing around with rivers in the Pantanal, we are poking at jaguars with a very, very short stick."

III

A gringo with a backpack at the Corumbá bus station is like Christ among the lepers, beset on all sides by gregarious recruiters for Pantanal tours. The system behind guides and outfitters in the Pantanal is still rather obscure to me. Knowles told me that back in the 1980s, Pantanal tourism was kind of a free-for-all, where locals with jeeps gouged foreign tourists, camped where they pleased, and often ran roughshod over the land. These days, outfitters are regulated by Brazil's tourism ministry, and local guides work with licensed companies that maintain established *pousadas* (lodges) and campsites throughout the countryside. Best I can tell, these companies then employ hordes of free-agent recruiters in towns like Corumbá—slick salesmen who mercilessly berate any gringo in sight until he or she signs up for a tour. Just standing outside of my hostel one morning, I got the hard sell from two different recruiters; another smooth-talker sidled up to me one day in line for the ATM. What's especially ridiculous is that all of these recruiters work on commission for the exact same five or six outfitters, so regardless of which one of them ends up parting you from your money, you will likely end up in the exact same van en route to the exact same *pousada*.

I went into the Pantanal with a guide named Gabriel, a lifelong *pantaneiro* from a family of ranchers. He spoke good English and drove a pickup truck built in the days before mufflers and shocks. Gabriel came recommended by the owner of my hostel, in part because the company he works for keeps a no-frills hammock camp a few hours into the bush, which was much more appealing to me than a lodge. I had really hoped to avoid the tour circuit altogether, to find some chummy local with a truck and an excess of free time, then press on into the virgin corners of the countryside to sleep under the stars and run with the maned wolves. But when a few days of asking around in Corumbá turned up no such Natty Bumppo, I settled for the hammock camp. So I took a bus out of town heading east, to a spot where a lonely dirt road peels off the main highway. Gabriel was waiting there, a big man with a baby face and a camo vest, standing alongside his truck and two pretty German girls he'd picked up in Campo Grande.

The road we followed was built in the late 1800s by a Brazilian explorer and folk hero named Cândido Rondon, a sort of composite of Lewis and Clark, Davy Crockett, and Margaret Mead. Amid the wetlands, it's a jostling seventy-five-mile ribbon of solid ground, crossing countless half-flooded fazendas by way of rickety wooden bridges. In the bed of the truck, the German girls and I settled onto a couple of wooden benches. It was too loud to converse, so we just smiled at one another and pointed to the animals we saw browsing on either side of the road. We hadn't been off the pavement for more than a few minutes before we spotted several herds of capybaras nosing around in the brush. The world's largest rodents, capybaras are basically guinea pigs the size of Saint Bernards. I had eaten one at a BBQ joint back in Bogotá, but I'd never seen one in person. They were oblivious to the truck, grazing nonchalantly on swamp grasses, snorting and poking at the reeds with their weirdly rectangular snouts. At least one capybara gets eaten in every wildlife documentary ever produced about lowland South America. They are the ecosystem's quintessential prey species, the wildebeest of the Western Hemisphere and a hot lunch for jaguars, anacondas, pumas, ocelots, and caimans— all of which make their homes nearby.

Most of these big predators are still a rare sighting in

the Pantanal, but not caimans. During two weeks along the Magdalena, I hadn't managed to spot a single one of the continent's smallish alligators, but in the Pantanal they litter the swampy landscape like sidewalk earthworms after a good rain. I was stunned by the reptilian multitudes that the Germans and I managed to glimpse on a two-hour drive to camp. There were caimans sunning themselves on scrubby beaches, caimans swathed in blankets of mud, caimans dog-paddling through the shallows. In the Pantanal, caimans number in the tens of millions. There are so many that before the Brazilian government cracked down on poaching in the 1980s, armed leather hunters called *coureiros* killed as many as a million animals per year, and they didn't have to work particularly hard to do it.

Once we arrived at camp, I had a chance to get to know my fellow travelers, a pair of thirtyish chemical engineers from Aachen nearing the end of a two-week Brazilian holiday. Peggy was a doctoral student in mycology, nerdy about mushrooms and at home in the outdoors. Tara was a city girl putting on a brave face for three days of mosquitoes and pit latrines. Our camp consisted of a screened-in pavilion with a dozen hammocks tied to a central pole, plus a simple cooking cabin and a row of outhouses. A small brown stream flowed nearby, and after we'd dropped off our backpacks, Gabriel led us down to the water, where a dozen or so caimans were lounging next to a decrepit-looking rowboat.

"You can walk right up to them, if you want," he said, sauntering right up to one and crouching down beside it. "Just make sure you move slowly."

As a son of the reptile-light northwoods, I have a mild fascination for all things lizardlike. There is something enigmatic about the sleek taper of a crocodile's jaw, and I've always appreciated large predators for the reminder they

offer that my species and I are not always top dog. I watched
Gabriel with what I imagine was an expression of childlike
glee. The grandest caiman on the beach was probably eight
feet long. The rest were in the neighborhood of five or six. I
moved in closer.

"They don't want to eat you," Gabriel joked. "Mostly
they just stick to the piranhas. If you look closely, you can
see that the piranhas eat them, too." He pointed to the caiman closest to me, a graceful five-footer gazing tranquilly
over the water. Along the serrated ridge of its tail, I could see
where a few scales had been blunted. The piranha nibbles
looked like the filed-down teeth of a well-worked handsaw.

"Go ahead and touch them, if you want," he said. "You
just have to move slowly."

That was all the invitation I needed. I crouched down
and waddled a few steps closer, careful not to lose my balance and arouse the caiman's strike impulse. It looked back
at me with statuesque indifference, the mottle of its scales
like a soldier's desert camouflage. I reached out and, very
gently, ran a few fingers along the jagged crest of the caiman's tail. It felt like a worn brick, much harder than I expected. Wow, I thought, piranhas must live up to the hype.
I let my palm drape over the width of the tail. The caiman
didn't move a muscle.

Later on, back at the campsite, we had a campfire with
another guide and a couple of Israeli backpackers who were
passing through on their way back to Campo Grande. They
brought a bottle of Brazilian sugarcane rum called cachaça,
and we mixed it up with lime and sugar to make a pitcher of
caipirinha, Brazil's sweet and potent national cocktail. For
a while that night, we heard the ferocious growls of howler
monkeys in the trees. The sky was a nonsense map of unfamiliar stars. I joked that I'd probably ignored Knowles's

advice about jaguars and short sticks that afternoon by petting the caiman, and this touched off a conversation about regional aphorisms. Gabriel knew a good one, he said, about piranhas biting caimans on the belly, which he translated as "In a river full of piranhas, a smart caiman swims on his back." One of the backpackers raised his *caipirinha* and shared an Israeli saying about the three things a person never gets tired of looking at: campfires, waterfalls, and strummed guitars. Peggy the German, who had spent some time living in Rio, remembered a Brazilian proverb that, right then, struck me as the most appropriate.

"God is big," she recited, the campfire flicker playing off her face, "but the forest is bigger."

We spent the next few days hiking, trucking, and boating throughout the Pantanal. Gabriel was a man of few words, but a knowledgeable guide with a knack for animal calls. I couldn't get him talking much about life growing up in the Pantanal, but I did watch him call a whole pack of suspicious wild boar to within ten yards of us, using a series of snorts and grunts. I particularly liked Peggy, who got comically excited about any fungi she encountered and who vocally preempted my own concerns about whether we had enough beer in the truck for any given drive. On a long hike one afternoon, the four of us spotted howler monkeys, armadillos, countless herons, and a pair of the five-foot, black-hooded storks that the *pantaneiros* call *tuiuiú*. During another walk in the woods, I stumbled right up to a family of coatis, long-snouted raccoons that looked at me a bit startled, then quickly skittered up a fat tree trunk in front of me. The four of them grabbed seats on a low branch and chattered excitedly, staring down with bright and curious eyes.

The Pantanal itself was a study in green, a staggering reminder of just how many shades of any one color can appear
in nature. Was it the wilderness primeval that Thompson
had envisioned? Probably not. In some ways, it hasn't been
for centuries. Along the road, we drove past weathered cowboys in pickup trucks or on horseback, periodic reminders
that the Pantanal has been a working landscape for quite
some time. Today, many of the ranches we passed seem to
incorporate a light tourism component. Many fazendas had
signs out front advertising eco-tours or guest bunkhouses,
while others sold basic provisions (like beers for Peggy and
me) out of makeshift convenience stores.

In other ways, the Pantanal's wilderness character is still
being eroded by the land rush that Thompson anticipated.
One morning, we drove out to an old dock on the meander-
ing Rio Paraguay, where we climbed into a skiff for a couple hours of piranha fishing. Gabriel motored us upstream
to the mouth of a wide tributary that he said was the Rio
Taquari—the same river where Márcia Rolon's grandfather had once run his cattlemen's store. The confluence itself looked healthy enough. Sure, the water was muddy, but
there were other fishermen nearby, trolling in the reeds. I
got skunked, but the girls pulled in a few well-fed piranha.
Later, though, while Gabriel and I were cleaning the morning's catch, I asked whether the silting of the Rio Taquari
had affected the fishing there. Characteristically succinct, he
kept his gaze on the piranha he was scaling and grunted in a
way that suggested I didn't know the half of it.

"It is a very different river now from when I was younger,"
was all he said. A recent report by the Brazilian government
answered the question in more detail. According to researchers, fishermen in the Taquari caught somewhere between 300
and 620 tons of fish a year in the late 1970s and early '80s.

Since the mid-'90s, that annual catch has dwindled to less than 100 tons.

Toward the end of the weekend, Gabriel pulled the truck over as we crossed one of the stream-spanning wooden bridges. In the lagoon below, four caimans were floating belly-up in the lagoon, their stubby arms spread out in something that looked like surrender. All four of them had gaping red holes where their tails had been. Onshore, a posse of vultures was strutting back and forth, alighting occasionally to pick at the nearest corpse.

"That isn't right," Gabriel said flatly. A couple of miles back, we had passed a lean-to that housed a work crew doing maintenance on the bridges. They had probably done this, Gabriel guessed. The tails were the best part of a caiman for eating, he explained. "People fry it, have it with some beer. Then they just leave the rest." The white bellies of the dead animals gleamed in the bright sun, and they looked out of place, the only splotch of white against an otherwise verdant canvas.

The tail harvesting struck me as less barbaric than simply irresponsible. Maybe it would have been more jarring to me if we hadn't gone on to see another hundred or so caimans that day before sunset. For better or for worse, this is something the Pantanal does: it provides the illusion of inexhaustibility, a glimmer of what it must have felt like to be a New England colonist watching flocks of passenger pigeons blot out the sun, or a westward pioneer staring at bison herds on the Great Plains, or a Polynesian arriving on Easter Island to find an endless forest of palm trees. It's easy for us now to dismiss those folks as simply stupid or villainous, greedily ignoring the fallout from their actions, but it's a rare thing these days for an American to be afforded the illusion of limitlessness. The supply of caimans in the Pantanal really does seem boundless. The outspread canopy and the shallow, mirrored floodplains give every suggestion of the infinite. The sheer biomass of the place is unfathomable. And this, I think, is what truly defines the "wild country"—not the absence of humans but the tension between inexhaustible possibility and the foreknowledge of our capacity to subdue.

That's what a frontier is, after all—a physical manifestation of that tension. It's a space where humanity confronts its own consequences, where a person can look out and see both the beauty of a breathing marsh and the bloody cavity between the legs of a caiman. I think that Thompson understood this. He called South America "the last decent frontier," and I suspect that part of his growing cynicism about the United States stemmed from a realization that we were fast running out of these kinds of spaces. In another era, I could even see him as a swashbuckling essayist-naturalist in the mold of Charles Waterton or Ernest Thompson Seton. In the late-twentieth-century United States, however, our few remaining physical frontiers were giving way to a new cultural one, and it was in this wilderness of biker gangs, youth politics, and drug culture that Thompson eventually immersed himself.

We spent our last evening in the Pantanal trolling in the skiff, heading a few miles up each tributary in the hopes of spotting a jaguar or another of the big cats that emerge from their dens around dusk. No luck. And no maned wolves, either. But the water was glass, and the sunset frosted the horizon like a pale pink cupcake. Herons tiptoed through the reeds, and caimans drifted lazily past, just the tops of their heads poking above the waterline. I've heard the snout of a submerged caiman likened to a twig drifting against the current, but that comparison only holds at a distance, because twigs don't have eyes, and a caiman's eyes look at you like they know all of your secrets.

Campfires, waterfalls, and guitars, the Israeli backpacker had said—the three things that a person never gets tired of staring at. It's a good list, but I would add big, slow rivers like the Paraguay. As the German girls clicked their cameras at every rustling bush, I leaned back and tranced out on the rolling waters, giggling at the ripples whenever a fish made a pass at the dragonflies. It's possible that I'm just easily entertained, but if being enthralled by a long, lazy current makes me a simpleton, then I hope I never wake up a sophisticate.

When I came back to Corumbá the next day, I found a weekly waterfront street party in full swing. It seemed like everyone in town was gathered down by the docks, drinking frosty bottled beers and listening to a band play Morrissey covers in stilted, phonetic English. I grabbed a beer and bobbed my head through the end of the set. When the band finished, a dreadlocked MC came bounding onto the stage.

"Let's hear it for the band!" he yelled, and the crowd hooted appreciatively. Behind the stage, a tied-up tugboat sounded two quick blasts on its horn, and the crowd cheered even louder.

"Let's hear it for our river!" the MC shouted, gesturing behind him. The tugboat sounded again, and Morrissey himself never heard such an ovation.

CHAPTER EIGHT

An Unaffected American

I really suggest you join the Peace Corps.
I would if I weren't such a reprobate, but
then I can be twice as effective for the
same idea by writing as I could by joining.

—Personal correspondence, December 17, 1962

I

On Easter morning in Asunción, Paraguay, the sad transvestite prostitutes of the Hotel Sheik leaned like toppled statues against a parked taxi out front. It was a couple of hours before dawn, and their cigarette smoke seemed to coagulate in the light of the streetlamp. The only sound on the block was the rattle and hum of the ancient air conditioners upstairs, clinging perilously to the hotel's window frames. The drag queens tugged listlessly at their skirts. Church bells would be ringing soon, I thought.

It was four a.m., and I was expounding passionately on American tax policy in the lobby of a brothel on Calle Tacuary. The conversation had started in a drowsy expat bar a few hours before, just an innocent late-night drink with a British couple and a Danish guy who were staying at my hostel. When last call came around, we had yet to divine the meaning of Occupy Wall Street, but the Dane said not to worry—he knew a place where we could get a drink after hours. So twenty minutes later we were settling into the dingy couches downstairs at the Hotel Sheik, getting eyeballs from the working girls while a surprisingly gracious manager served us beers from a fridge behind his desk.

No one starts a night on the town discussing economic policy. Our conversation had drifted organically in that direction after I asked the Dane about the closure of a famous commune in Copenhagen, which I'd read about online. His answer incorporated some light criticism of the permissiveness of Scandinavian governments, noting, among other things, their generosity with welfare for new immigrants. From there, the Brits had taken over, talking about the recent waves of immigration in England and what they saw as the pitfalls of European Union membership. That led unavoidably to some good-natured complaining about the United Kingdom being the United States' lapdog in the War on Terror, at which I threw up my hands and relinquished responsibility. During our fourth or fifth round, I fielded a barrage of questions about the Obama administration's foreign policy, and by the time we settled into our transgender bordello, I was holding forth on the transgressions of the 1 percent and the myth of the progressive tax system.

It's funny how travel abroad turns every one of us, to one degree or another, into unwitting junior ambassadors. Even in a setting like the grimy lobby of the Hotel Sheik—about as far from a United Nations conference room as you can get—each of us becomes a kind of reluctant dignitary for the country we left behind. For example, a significant portion of what I now purport to know about Denmark, I picked up during a six-hour drinking binge with a single Danish guy in Asunción. If you're lucky, you'll never find yourself in the worst-case scenario: having to face down someone who holds you personally accountable for your country's perceived flaws. But if you spend enough time mingling in hostels, riding in taxis, or drinking in airport bars, you will sooner or later be called upon to explain, if not defend or condemn, some policy, tradition, or cultural idiosyncrasy of your homeland.

This is particularly true if you're American, since the United States is one of those countries about which everyone has an opinion, regardless of whether they have any strong ties to the place itself. You can't say the same thing, for example, about Estonia. No Estonian has ever introduced himself at a party, then had someone who's never been there casually remark, "Estonia, eh? Let me tell you what's wrong with Estonia. . . ." In my experience, Americans abroad tend to respond in such situations with a kind of nervous, apologetic resignation. It's a tough scenario for any traveler to navigate: owning up to the role of cultural emissary without letting your country's shortcomings hang around your neck like an albatross.

Millions of Paraguayan émigrés had to pull off just this balancing act for decades. In his *Observer* article from January of 1963, provocatively headlined IT'S A DICTATORSHIP, BUT FEW SEEM TO CARE ENOUGH TO STAY AND FIGHT, Thompson notes that almost one-third of all Paraguayan citizens in the early 1960s lived someplace other than Paraguay. The reasons for this are complex. For starters, the country has a long history of fighting devastatingly stupid wars. Paraguay lost almost two-thirds of its population in the War of the Triple Alliance, a violent and quixotic nineteenth-century bloodbath that makes the US invasions of Iraq and Afghanistan look like *West Side Story* dance-offs. In the 1930s, Paraguay's Chaco War against Bolivia was the bloodiest South American conflict of the century, resulting in more than 100,000 casualties. Waves of Paraguayans fled the country during and after both wars, and then yet again, following a brief civil war in 1947. By 1954, the country was in economic shambles, paving the way for conservative dictator Alfredo Stroessner to come to power via a military coup. General Stroessner launched a terror campaign of kidnapping and torture against dissenters, and by the time Thompson showed up ten years into his reign, some 500,000 out of 1.8 million Paraguayans were living in exile—some forced, many voluntary.

Stroessner held on to power for a whopping thirty-five years, during which as many as 1.5 million Paraguayans left their country for greener pastures in Argentina, Brazil, the United States, and elsewhere. It's hard to imagine the kind of relationship these exiles must have had with their homeland. To hear Thompson tell it, a good number of them may actually have preferred life in exile. Paraguay's voluntary émigrés were overwhelmingly from the wealthier, educated classes, and even without the threat of political oppression, the appeal of life in comparatively glitzy Rio or Buenos Aires may itself have been a big draw:

> Asuncion is as different from Buenos Aires as Bowling Green, Ky., is from Chicago. It would not take a dictator to drive a man out of this town, and most of Paraguay's "exiles" did not need a dictator to make them leave. A big major-ity are students, young people, and professional men, and they go to the cities for the same reason young people have always gone since cities were invented.

This was in 1963, still early into Stroessner's reign, when the extent of his administration's atrocities were little known and less discussed. So Thompson might be forgiven if he seems to give short shrift to the exiles' potentially graver mo-tivations. He was straightforward, of course, about the ways that Stroessner rigged the political system—banning opposi-tion and renewing a state of emergency every ninety days, a habit he continued for the next twenty-six years—but he wrote very little about violence or oppression in Paraguay, except to acknowledge ominously that the dictator "doesn't look kindly on people who agitate for change." In Thomp-son's view, the relative backwardness of life in Paraguay was as much to blame for the exodus as the dictatorship itself.

Thompson and I arrived in Asunción from two different directions. I left the Brazilian Pantanal and headed south to Paraguay, whereas Thompson's "jungle train" continued east, arriving in Rio in mid-September of 1962. It wasn't until November that he headed to Asunción, flying in on a five-week reporting jag through Paraguay, Uruguay, and briefly Argentina. By then, Thompson was feeling refreshed and rejuvenated after his physically and psychologically exhausting trek through the Andes. The sun, sand, and sophistication of Rio had agreed with him, and he hadn't been eager to leave his new coastal digs. In Paraguay, he suddenly found himself back in the Third World and, more depressingly, in yet another stodgy, sleepy city. Despite a population of 400,000 at the time, Asunción seemed to Thompson more like some backwater village in the Amazon.

"It is about as lively as Atlantis," he wrote, "and nearly as isolated."

Asunción may well have seemed sedate. Thompson's photos from the time show men dozing on park benches, a trolley sliding down an empty street, and vacant sidewalks with storefronts shuttered for the midday siesta. The city still lacked water and sewage systems back then. Cars were a rarity. Not until the 1980s did Asunción get its first traffic light, and still today, it's one of the smallest capitals in Latin America, with just over half a million people. It is a stiflingly hot place, and there is absolutely no sense in which it is *on the way* to anywhere.

Unlike Thompson, though, I found Asunción's quietude charming. It was Semana Santa when my bus pulled into town, the Catholic Holy Week that's overwhelmingly observed in the more rural corners of the continent. I caught the tail end of a downtown procession on Holy Thursday, complete with the Easter carolers whom Paraguayans call *estacioneros*, singing about the Stations of the Cross in Paraguay's widely spoken indigenous language of Guaraní. After that, though, the city seemed to empty out, as residents left to be with their families in the vast Paraguayan countryside, the rural 99.6 percent of the country that residents of Asunción simply refer to as *el campo*. Most of the storefronts were shuttered, and I spent the weekend strolling through shady parks and the historic government district along the Rio Paraguay, feeling like I had the city to myself.

By one measure, Asunción is the true birthplace of independence in South America. Patriots there declared Paraguay's freedom from Spain back in 1811, when other South American revolutionary governments were still ruling in the name of the deposed Spanish monarch Ferdinand VII. The people of Asunción don't let a visitor forget this fact. On the day before Easter, I visited the Casa de la Independencia, an unremarkable house downtown where the plan for emancipation was hatched. When I left, I walked a few blocks and found myself standing on the corner of one street called Independencia Nacional and another called El Paraguayo Independente. Fifty years ago, when the summer heat convinced Thompson that "the only safe place to see Asunción is from the inside of a dark, open-front cafe," he set up shop in a popular watering hole called Bar Independencia (sadly, since demolished and replaced with a bank).

During my visit, Paraguay was just coming off its bicentennial anniversary, and the city still hadn't taken down the posters of Paraguayan national heroes adorning the streetlamps downtown. Every block had three or four of them, black-and-white images of persons significant to the country's history. In the United States, you might expect such a roster to be long on politicians: founding fathers, beloved presidents, pioneering leaders of minority groups, and so on. In Asunción, though, the ranks seemed to consist mostly of journalists, poets, composers, and other humanities types. It occurred to me that Paraguay's history of

dictatorship kind of limits its bench of leaders worth honoring. In the first quarter of the nineteenth century, while
we cycled through mythic framers like Madison, Monroe,
Quincy Adams, and Jackson, Paraguay had just a single
founding father, the dictator José Francia, who clung to
power for twenty-seven years and liked to call himself "El
Supremo." During Stroessner's time in power, Americans
saw eight sitting presidents, all the way from Eisenhower to
George H. W. Bush. If you haven't had many leaders—and
those ones not particularly admirable—I guess you have to
cast a wider net for your heroes.

The parade of paper luminaries around Asunción was
actually kind of stirring. In the days that I spent walking
around the city, I never once spotted a banner honoring one
of Paraguay's dubious presidents, warmongering generals, or
junta leaders, but I did see several commemorating teachers, painters, and priests. I took it as a reminder that it's
perfectly all right to compartmentalize a nation's problems,
villains, and misdeeds while instead keying in on its heroes
and core values. This, after all, is exactly what the four of us
were doing in the brothel on Easter night, trying to speak up
for the best aspects of our homelands without making ourselves into scapegoats for the worst. And if that's a kind of
cop-out, then so be it, because it's this kind of sequestration
that makes cultural exchange possible.

Of course, beer helps too, and the Brits, the Dane, and I
cleaned out the brothel manager's mini fridge before calling
it a night. It was light outside when we finally slunk out of
the Hotel Sheik, and we paused outside to squint and get our
bearings. The buses were running, and the few pious families left in the sleepy city seemed to be making their way either to or from church. My fellow diplomats and I reached
a consensus—the first of the night—about the direction of

the hostel, and we wished the prostitutes out front a happy Easter.

"Same to you," said the tallest one, in a surprisingly deep voice. She stifled a yawn and adjusted her slouch against the hood of the taxi. "Going to be a slow day."

II

The Librería San Cayetano is the kind of bookstore where the thick dust is a mark of distinction and serious biblio-philes can lose themselves for days. The shelves are packed three-deep with old volumes, the piles on the floor are belly-button-high, and the collections are organized with all the care and precision of a teenager's sock drawer. Every dis-turbed stack unleashes a cloud of dust and a skitter of silver-fish. If you've been inside San Cayetano for an hour and you have yet to knock over a leaning tower of books, you're probably not browsing hard enough.

The store had exactly one shelf dedicated to English books, maybe forty ratty paperbacks in total, so I was straight-up dumbstruck when I reached in and pulled out ex-actly the book I'd been looking for—one well-thumbed copy of *The Ugly American,* which had been on my mind since Cali. This particular edition was from 1961, a fifth printing that included a then-timely blurb on its back cover, asking:

Is President Kennedy's "PEACE CORPS" the answer
to the problem raised by this book?

As it happens, I had been wondering that myself. When Thompson arrived in South America, the United States' first-ever crop of Peace Corps volunteers had been on the ground for less than a year—yet another example of Kennedy's long shadow across the continent. The president had inaugurated the volunteer service program in 1961, pitching it as a sister project to his Alliance for Progress. He was a big fan of *The Ugly American,* having mailed copies to all of his legislative colleagues as a senator, and many historians view the Peace Corps as a direct response to the book's call to replace the country's decadent and insulated diplomatic corps with a "small force of well-trained, well-chosen, hard-working, and dedicated professionals . . . willing to risk their comfort and—in some lands—their health."

In the novel, a Philippine government minister explains the advantages of such a force to a fictional American ambassador:

> Average Americans, in their natural state, if you will excuse the phrase, are the best ambassadors a country can have. . . . They are not suspicious, they are eager to share their skills, they are generous. But something happens to most Americans when they go abroad. . . . Many of them, against their own judgment, feel that they must live up to their commissaries and big cars and cocktail parties. But get an unaffected American, sir, and you have an asset.

Of course, Thompson echoed this idea—about Americans trying to "live up" to their privileged position—in his "Anti-Gringo Winds" piece about the golfer on the terrace. Nonetheless, he was skeptical of Kennedy's new program, which sent American volunteers, usually with a trade or a college education, to serve two-year stints abroad in fields like health, education, and agriculture, often in isolated and rural areas. The Peace Corps was launched with a three-part mandate: to improve Americans' understanding of other cultures, to help build capacity in developing nations, and to better the US image abroad. At the outset, Thompson was unconvinced that troupes of "unaffected" young Americans would be any more competent on these last two points than the shortsighted Alliance bureaucrats or the earnest NGO professionals ("who make a man feel like a degenerate if he can't avoid a feeling that they are all phonies").

But Thompson's encounters on the continent gradually won him over. In the Andes and Brazil, he rubbed shoulders with several Peace Corps volunteers, and he chatted over whiskey with at least one of them in Tom Martin's living room back in La Paz. A few were jackasses, he admitted, but more of them struck him as smart, hardworking types whose hands he'd been proud to shake. By the end of 1962, he was advising an old girlfriend back in the States that she consider joining.

"Don't think I've gone gung-ho," he wrote, "because I came down here thinking the PC was a bag of crap, but now I think it's the only serious and decent effort the US is making in Latin America or anywhere else."

I thought hard about joining the PC myself after I graduated from college, but that was in 2002, and I had reservations about becoming a foot soldier for a Bush-era foreign policy that I often disagreed with. On paper, of course, the PC is a politically neutral entity, but its directors are political appointees, and the State Department ultimately assigns or withholds volunteers from any given country. At the time, post-9/11 posturing was in vogue, and the pre-Iraq propaganda machine was just hitting its stride. The notion that the PC might be misused for geopolitical ends didn't seem all that farfetched to me. I also worried about becoming some kind of missionary for industrial capitalism, the promotion of which was (after all) one of the original goals of the agency. So I signed on instead for two years of national service with AmeriCorps, often referred to as the Peace Corps' domestic equivalent, and in the years since, I've come to think of the PC as a sort of ace in the hole—like, hey, when everything else goes to shit, I can always join the Peace Corps.

Thompson seemed to have shared my inclination, but he joked to the girlfriend that he was too much of a scoundrel to join up. Then he dropped a line that has stuck with me since the first time I read it in *The Proud Highway* more than a decade ago. "I can be twice as effective for the same idea by writing as I could by joining," Thompson said in his letter.

I have mixed feelings about this statement. On its face, it strikes me as disingenuous and self-aggrandizing to suggest that the scribblings of a footloose writer are in any way more valuable than the sweat of a latrine digger, a malaria educator, or a clinic builder. Journalism is a critically important trade, no doubt, but those first PC members were out there in the trenches, and their efforts were literally saving people's lives. Thompson, meanwhile, was back in his hotel room, bitching about the hot water. In fairness, I'm not entirely clear what the "same idea" is that Thompson's referring to here. If he understood the central mission of the Peace Corps to be a diplomatic one—championing the American way of life, promoting mutual understanding across cultures—then I suppose he has a point. An *Observer* story like "It's a Dictatorship" reached 200,000 readers, after all. It certainly offers some insight into the realities of Paraguayan life under Stroessner, and it does paint an unambiguous picture of democracy as the preferred alternative.

If, however, we suppose that the main goal of the Peace

Corps is to improve people's lives in the developing world, then Thompson at his typewriter had less impact on his best day than an Amazon volunteer distributing mosquito netting on her worst. There's a dialectical tension between these two objectives that I'm hardly the first person to point out. The debate has existed within the Peace Corps, in fact, ever since its inception: To what extent does the agency's mission resemble that of the Public Affairs Section of the embassy, like I saw back in Quito? To what extent is it more like, say, that of UNICEF or Doctors Without Borders? It's hard to parse Thompson's statement without knowing the answer to these questions. On paper, of course, it is easy enough just to check "All of the above"—the Peace Corps does all of these things. But in practice, there isn't necessarily much overlap between helping villagers access clean drinking water, for example, and furthering their understanding of American culture. At the very least, a person can wholly succeed at one of these things without even attempting the other.

One former volunteer, recruiter, and country director recently criticized the PC in *Foreign Policy* magazine for its "unwillingness to decide if it is a development organization or an organization with a mission to promote world peace and friendship." A 2013 congressional report also acknowledged the tension, noting that administrators' conflicting views on the roles of diplomacy and development tend to affect whether they feel the PC should recruit more specialists or generalists. For my part, understanding how to evaluate the PC's success was the key to interpreting that quote that had echoed in my mind for years, Thompson's seductive assertion that a writer could do just as much good as a volunteer.

Burdick and Lederer, the authors of *The Ugly American*, would undoubtedly say that Shakespeare himself could

write a few good articles on South America and still not accomplish as much as a cadre of committed people working
hand in hand with the locals. But of course, both those authors and Thompson were writing from a pretty entrenched
Cold War perspective, which assigned "the locals" a choice
between grudgingly tolerating the Americans and grudgingly tolerating the communists. In that context, the more
delicate questions about the PC's mission would have been
easy to ignore. Was the Peace Corps ultimately discouraging communism? Well, then it was working, and there wasn't
much reason to chase down further rabbit holes of evalua-
tion. With those days long gone, however, it wasn't clear to
me just what any of them would suppose that an "unaffected
American" should be doing with himself these days in a
country like Paraguay.

George Ritz is about as unaffected an American as they
come. A few days after Easter, I climbed into a muddy
Toyota pickup with the guy, packed for a weeklong trip out
of Asunción and into the green sweep of the Paraguayan
campo. George was an associate director of the PC in Paraguay from 1982 to 1987. These days he spends about a month
in the country every year, during which time he thinks very
little about diplomacy and quite a bit about improving people's lives.

Genial and fit at sixty-five, George is a slight guy
with wide-lensed glasses and the kind of square-edged,
mustache-less beard that inevitably calls to mind the Amish.
Until recently, he was a forester for his native state of Maine,
working long, lonely hours in the remote northern wood-
lands at the very tip of New England. He worked in for-
estry for the Peace Corps, too, first as a volunteer in Chile
in the late 1960s and then again during his directorship in

Paraguay (where he literally wrote the book on Paraguayan tree species, still used in the country's universities today). When he left Paraguay at the end of the 1980s, with his wife, Sylvia, and a young son and daughter in tow, George didn't imagine that he'd ever be back. Then, in 1995, his daughter, Andrea, died of sudden-onset diabetes. She was twelve years old. George and Sylvia established a memorial fund and funneled their grief into the construction of two small clinics in the remote Paraguayan countryside—places where the kind of highly qualified, rapid-response medical care that Andrea had received in the United States was hopelessly out of reach. These days, there are five Andrea Ritz Clinics operating in eastern Paraguay, supported in part by donations and staffed by the country's Ministry of Health. The Ritzes and their Paraguayan partners have helped build schools and pipe in water and electricity, and George makes annual trips to stock medicines, gauge communities' needs, and make "house calls" to even farther-flung villages on the edges of the clinics' reach.

"None of this was here twenty-five years ago," George said on the way out of Asunción, gesturing out the windows at what still felt like a pretty central part of town. "A lot of the road we'll be driving on today wasn't paved either. This country's made a lot of progress since Stroessner." He paused. "Well, in some ways. Less progress in others."

Also in the truck were Dr. Laurel Parker, a twenty-eight-year-old ER doc from Connecticut, and Cessar Fernandez, head nurse at the clinic in the village of Cerrito, which would be our home base for the next week. George had introduced Cessar as his "Paraguayan brother," a stylish guy of thirty-five with blond highlights and a silver chain around his neck. Cessar had greeted me warmly and tossed my backpack into the bed of the truck, next to two huge, tattered suitcases filled with prescription drugs and supplies. Meanwhile, Dr. Laurel—as the other two called her in front of patients—was a childhood friend of Andrea's. This was her second volunteer trip to Paraguay, her first since finishing her residency the year before. She and George had managed to get the drug-filled suitcases into the country without any customs hassles, which George assured me was an auspicious start in a country famous for its vast and often corrupt bureaucracy.

East of Asunción, the Paraguayan landscape took on the color and character of the Kentucky hill country. Low forested ridges and humplike buttes interrupted vast fields of sugarcane—row upon row of wild green tufts bursting from woody stalks. A few cattle wandered around in open pastures. Paraguay is an overwhelmingly flat country, with no great mountain ranges to speak of, but after a couple of hours, we came within sight of Cerro Peró, a wooded peak that's the country's highest point at just shy of 2,800 feet.

"In Guaraní," said George, "they call that mountain Yvytyrusu, which basically means 'big pile of dirt.'" He chuckled contentedly. George speaks fluent Guaraní, and he seemed happy just to have the strange words rolling around in his mouth. Every so often, he shouted a guttural phrase or two at Cessar, and they both laughed liked crazy.

We stopped for lunch at Cessar's sister's place in a city called Villarrica, a small agricultural hub about 100 miles east of Asunción. Fifty years ago, George told me, the town was the terminus of the paved highway east of the city, very literally the "end of the road," beyond which the country would have looked much like it had before the Jesuits showed up in the sixteenth century. Thompson had come here to attend a meeting of a banned opposition party in the lead-up to one of Stroessner's sham elections. He didn't have much to say about the town back then, only that the revolutionary assembly there didn't amount to much. The dissenters in Villarrica were "quite sincere," he wrote, but four out of five of them were teenagers, and many seemed just as eager to get out of Paraguay as they did to overthrow the dictator.

To hear George tell it, simply attending an anti-Stroessner meeting back then took some balls. His recollection of Stroessner's Paraguay is a world full of corruption and paranoia, where the government paid citizen-spies to report on their neighbors' political and personal "crimes." *Pyragües,* a Guaraní word meaning "hairy feet," was the nickname for such trolls. One acquaintance of George's worked in the Paraguayan Forest Service by day but moonlighted as a snitch, spotting and reporting homosexuals gathered in the city's main plaza. Then there was the old man who ostensibly hawked brittle, yellowing magazines from a newsstand in front of the Peace Corps offices.

"The guy never sold a single issue," George said with a laugh. "He just sat there watching who was coming and going."

Stroessner has been out of office since 1989, when he was finally overthrown by a military coup, but Paraguayans are still living every day with his legacy. George mentioned, for example, how "El Excelentisimo" prevented the import of iodized salt, part of a calculated effort to lower his nation's collective IQ and keep the population docile. As a result, George said, we were likely to see many patients with cretinism and goiters in the coming days—hyperthyroidism affects Paraguay more than any other nation in the New World. The country's bloated bureaucracy is itself a holdover from the days of the dictator, when political cronies were rewarded with cushy jobs in post offices that never actually sent or received mail. George also warned me to be subtle about taking notes, since many of the older folks might still panic to see a stranger standing in the corner with a notebook, listening and jotting things down.

We left the pavement at a town called San Juan Nepomuceno, named for the patron saint of silence and flooding—two pretty common phenomena in the sparsely populated and low-lying countryside. Thereafter, the road wasn't even dirt, just a red and soft-pack clay so sculpted with ruts and divots that the truck had to veer back and forth to make any forward progress. George worked the clutch like a cartoon witch stirring a cauldron. Eventually, the road itself became little more than a rut, a kind of surreal corridor hemmed in by palms and other shaggy matter. Hanging from the trees were what seemed to be wisps of white garland, and I asked jokingly whether somebody was putting up welcome decorations.

"It's cotton," George said. "Paraguay's first cash crop. Middlemen load it up in dump trucks to take it to market, and they always leave some behind when they graze the trees."

The branches stretched out over the dirt path, forming a shaded corridor with cotton dangling everywhere, like threads off a torn cloud. It was beautiful, really, and I said so.

"Well, you can call them welcome decorations if you want," said George. Just then, the truck careened through a particularly yawning trough, sending the front bumper bouncing, a cascade of mud over the hood, and the four of us slingshotting forward like crash-test dummies.

When the truck righted itself, George turned around and grinned. "Welcome to the *campo*," he said.

By late afternoon we weren't far from Cerrito, but before arriving at the clinic, we had a house call to make. Three years earlier, on her last visit to Paraguay, Dr. Laurel had seen a young patient with a congenital heart defect whom she's since taken to calling "the Blue Boy." Thanks to a lack of oxygen in his blood, the Blue Boy's skin was the color of cobalt. He was distinctly blue from head to toe, a condition called cyanosis that indicates severe valve and/or vessel damage. Without a risky and expensive heart surgery, his life was unquestionably in danger. Recently, though, Dr. Laurel had swapped e-mails with a surgeon working for a Paraguayan nonprofit, and the surgeon had agreed to operate on the Blue Boy for free. So our first task in the *campo* was to find the Blue Boy and have a talk with his family.

We stopped the truck in front of a cinder-block schoolhouse, where a few dozen wide-eyed kids ran to the fence to have a look at the gringos. George and Laurel's arrival was already the talk of the township, and most of the students had probably felt the chestpiece of Laurel's stethoscope during her last visit. The kids pointed eagerly up the road to where the Blue Boy lived, and within a few minutes, we were parking in front of a crooked clapboard house with a corrugated tin roof. Outside, bags of cotton were piled up next to a lime tree, waiting for the dump truck to haul them away. A tall teenager looked up from the moped he was fiddling with and stood up to greet us shyly. His parents weren't home, he apologized, but they'd be back soon. He asked for us to wait outside while he fetched his brother.

So the four of us stood quietly in the yard, surrounded by a menagerie of chickens, dogs, and one shockingly white kitten. When the Blue Boy stepped out of his house a few minutes later, he was wearing plastic flip-flops and the striped jersey of the Paraguayan Fútbol Association. He was unmistakably blue. Not solidly painted, like one of those performance artists, but tinged and vampiric, like a comic-book villain who might shoot ice out of his fingertips. His features were fine and angular, and his dark hair close-cut and spiky.

He looked to be in his very early teens, although I suppose his growth may have been stunted. The Blue Boy looked delicate, but not frail.

"Buenos tardes," he said to each of us with a shy smile and a handshake. When it was my turn, I half expected his hand to feel clammy, but of course it didn't. He seemed to recognize at least George and Cessar, and he talked quietly with them for a few minutes in a mixture of Spanish and Guaraní. How had he been feeling? Had he been going to school? The Blue Boy said he had a toothache recently and showed Dr. Laurel a small infected spot on his jaw. Nobody mentioned why we had come, and after a few minutes, the conversation hit a lull. The Blue Boy leaned quietly against the lime tree while George and the medics conferred in English. Everyone agreed that he looked slightly better than the last time they'd seen him. I took a short inventory of the detritus lying around the yard: a naked and armless baby doll, a pile of roofing shingles, a toy truck made from woodblocks and bottle caps.

When the Blue Boy's dad pulled up in a rusty pickup, he didn't seem surprised to see us. Cessar had been on and off his cell phone all day, speaking Guaraní, and I'm guessing that the father knew we were coming. He was exceedingly polite, shaking everyone's hands and asking his sons to bring some wooden chairs from inside. At a nod from his dad, the Blue Boy excused himself, and we all sat down.

For the next few minutes, George and the father did most of the talking, with the occasional word from Cessar. They spoke mostly Guaraní, but I picked out a few words of heavily accented Spanish, and George played the conversation back for me later. Your son's condition is very serious, George told the man, probably not for the first time, and he needs an operation or else he will die. The father looked

George in the eye, seriously and respectfully, while George told him about the surgeon in Asunción. George was calm and not the least bit pedantic. He sat with his knees splayed and used his hands for emphasis, his palms faceup in a way that said he was offering advice and not giving orders. We can find a way to get you into Asunción for a consultation, he told the man. We can do something to fix this.

The father wore a baseball cap and what had once been a white dress shirt, now faded to a dingy brown. He smiled very slightly as he spoke. The last time the medics had proposed something like this, he said, it was very expensive, a hardship on the family. In Spanish, I heard him use the phrase "heart machine." They had taken his son to the city to use the heart machine, and nothing had improved. He was describing an echocardiogram, George and Laurel later explained, a test to see the extent of the boy's valve damage—not a treatment, but that distinction had been lost on the family. No, the father continued, his son was a smart and capable boy. He had to stop and take a breath sometimes when he walked more than a few meters, but he was going to be OK. He didn't need any difficult or risky procedures.

George countered exactly once with another pitch, but the father held firm, politely repeating that his son was a smart boy, a good boy. He just got tired sometimes. That was all. The boy's dad stood and shook all of our hands again, thanking us sincerely for our time and concern. Just think about it a little more, George and Cessar insisted, and they gave him Cessar's phone number in case he changed his mind. We walked to the truck past the bobbing chickens and the splayed cotton sacks.

"He doesn't understand that it's a miracle the kid has lived this long," George said, handing Cessar the keys and climbing into the passenger seat. He was clearly frustrated.

It occurred to me that the Blue Boy probably wasn't much older than his daughter had been when she died. Cessar turned the ignition, and the truck started with a feline growl.

"What will happen to him?" I asked. "I mean, what's his prognosis without any surgery?"

George swiveled his head to look at Laurel.

"He'll develop congestive heart failure with a few years," she said, sadly but calmly. "Without surgery, there's really no other outcome."

"It's a death sentence," George said, and he sighed.

We pulled out onto the dirt track. As we drove off, I looked back just once to see the Blue Boy and his dad, waving to us from the doorway.

I slept on a gurney in the clinic that night while George and Laurel crashed at Cessar's house next door. The clinic in Cerrito is a single-story rectangle of brick and plaster, about 2,000 square feet on what passes for the farm community's main drag. The bricks were made on-site with local materials. The poles carrying the electric lines were hewn from nearby woods and pulled to the site with oxen. Local communities contribute about a third of the overall construction costs to get each Andrea Ritz Clinic off the ground, providing materials and/or labor. I settled into one of two bare-bones exam rooms before poking around. There was a small dental office, a few bookcases' worth of pill bottles, and a dozen or so public-health posters in Spanish and Guaraní, describing the symptoms of STDs, discouraging bare feet to prevent hookworm, and offering tips on how to avoid snakes (of which eastern Paraguay has some of the world's most venomous).

It rained so hard overnight that the roof leaked. I sank ankle-deep in the muddy roadway on my way to Cessar's the next morning, and the rest of the crew was just waking up when I arrived. There's no driving in the *campo* after a storm like that, so we settled in for a couple of hours, just waiting for the roads to dry out and killing time with chit-chat and *mate.*

Britons' devotion to tea, Scandinavians' love of coffee, Americans' fondness for milkshakes masquerading as espresso drinks—none of these compare to the fervor with which Paraguayans drink tea from the leaves of their native *yerba mate* plant. For most Paraguayans, consuming *mate* is both an elaborate ritual and an unconscious habit. In his tiny kitchen, Cessar prepared our morning drink, and I watched as he first filled a cup with dried, ground leaves, then inserted a long silver straw with a filtered tip, called a *bombilla.* The cup itself was a smooth wooden chalice, but more traditional drinkers use a hollowed-out gourd. Cessar poured hot water from a thermos onto the tea leaves, then sipped from the *bombilla* until the empty straw made a slurping sound. As he refilled the cup, George explained to me the social rules of *mate* drinking among friends: One person is in charge of refilling the water and passing the cup (usually the youngest in the circle). It is always given and received with the right hand. Counterintuitively, saying "thank you" is an indication that you've had enough and want to skip your turn. This last one gave me trouble in the days to come, not just with *mate,* but more vexingly, with beer, which also tends to be consumed in a social circle from a shared glass.

Mate has a floral, slightly bitter taste and a caffeine level somewhere south of coffee but north of black tea. I liked it very much, and on a continent where you can't find a decent cup of joe to save your life, it makes a better morning alternative than the ubiquitous instant Nescafé. In Paraguay, drinking *mate* with cold water is equally popular. In that case, the beverage is called *tereré,* and the vessel is typically a cup made from a bull's horn, called a *guampa.* Many Paraguayans wouldn't dream of leaving their house without their three-piece kit of a thermos, *guampa,* and *bombilla,* and to spot a bunch of guys standing around sipping *tereré* is the cultural equivalent of seeing cubicle-dwellers or construction workers loitering with their white paper cups on an extended coffee break.

Over *mate,* George and Cessar told me about Pombero, a mischievous Paraguayan gremlin who lurks around the countryside at night, making life difficult for the *campesinos.* That morning, the power was out at both Cessar's place and at the clinic, but while I chalked this up to the overnight storm, George and Cessar chided me that this was surely the work of Pombero. Physically, he sounds like a cross between a mini-sasquatch and Gollum from *Lord of the Rings*—short, hairy, implike. Pombero steals eggs, flattens tires, spooks pets, and generally gets the blame for any other inexplicable annoyance (including, I gather, the occasional unplanned pregnancy). When Cessar first moved into the *campo,* he told us, he had definitely worried about Pombero, and plenty of grown adults still take the myth quite seriously. The only way to keep him pacified, of course, is to leave tricky Pombero some booze and cigarettes, and I wondered if the Paraguayan demon might be a distant relative of old Tío back in the Bolivian mines.

By midmorning, the sun had shone long enough that we decided to risk the roads, so we headed next door to grab supplies for our first satellite clinic. Inside George and Laurel's two suitcases were chaotic piles of prescription bottles, vitamin jars, packaged antibiotics, and tubes of every imaginable cream, balm, and ointment. The luggage itself dated back to the founding of the first clinic, George said proudly, and he estimated it had made the trip about eighteen times. With a haphazard heap of medications spilling out, the worn pleather suitcases looked less like the equipment of a successful medical mission and more like the getaway bags from a drugstore robbery.

I stayed out of the way while the medics packed their travel kits. They debated which drugs to bring and which to leave behind, and overhearing snippets of their conversation was like listening to dialogue from an episode of *Star Trek*.

"Bring that, it's a very effective alpha blocker."

"Did I pack Cytomel 10 or 40?"

"Grab an extra blister pack of Diamox."

The swampy roads were treacherous but not impassable. We fishtailed here and there, and some of the hills required multiple attempts, but it was nothing the Toyota couldn't handle. By late morning, we were pulling up to an empty brick schoolhouse in a valley full of small farms. Across the pasture, a straw-bale church with a false steeple was the tallest building for miles. Skinny Brahma cows wandered aimlessly through the street, the mud sucking persistently at their hooves.

George and Laurel set up their makeshift exam space in a Spartan, fluorescent-lit classroom, and again I tried my best to help without being obtrusive. Cessar chatted outside with the school's principal, and we had barely gotten the medications spread out on the table when the two of them stepped inside to say we had our first house call.

"An old man with some kind of pulmonary symptoms," Cessar said. "Not far from here."

"He's pretty sick," added the principal. "He smokes and drinks a lot."

So we followed her directions up a nearby hillside to a

ramshackle homestead at the edge of a barren field. At the gate out front, George clapped his hands three times ("the Paraguayan doorbell," he said), and four ageless women toddled outside to welcome us. We were led to a small livestock shed out back, a brick building sized somewhere between a large chicken coop and a small barn. Inside, an old man lay prone across a foam mattress sitting atop two wooden pallets. As we stepped in, he squinted in the light from the doorway.

The old man looked bad. At first glance, his hands and feet were grotesquely swollen, like latex gloves used as water balloons. He was wearing only a tattered pair of canvas shorts, and his chest rattled as it rose and fell. Even in the darkness of the shed, he looked pallid. George greeted him warmly in Guaraní, and Dr. Laurel crouched with her stethoscope. The old man's Darth Vader breathing filled the room.

"Strong signs of pulmonary edema," Laurel said, listening to his chest and gingerly examining his hands and feet.

One of the women brought in a dusty X-ray slide, and Laurel held it up in the weak light of the window.

"Long-standing COPD," she said eventually, "either emphysema or chronic bronchitis. Let's give him a bronchodilator."

Cessar grabbed an inhaler from the travel kit, and he and George tried to explain in Guaraní how to use it. You just put it up to your mouth, Cessar told the old man. First you exhale, then squeeze the trigger while you inhale. The man looked at him like he'd been handed a fish. He held the inhaler a few inches from his mouth and squeezed, and the puff hit harmlessly on his lips and tongue.

"Close," George said, and he showed one of the women how to use the inhaler instead. She held it up to the old man's mouth and got him to put his lips around it, but when she pushed down the cartridge, he exhaled hard.

"No, inhala!" she insisted. *"Inhala!"* Everyone in the shed began making deep-chested inhaling motions, trying to show him, but the man just looked confused. Then George took the inhaler and pantomimed using it.

"Like a cigarette!" he said loudly in Spanish, and a light went on in the old man's eyes.

"Ah, como un cigarrillo!" he croaked, nodding.

Everyone chuckled at the irony, but that first patient in the shed illustrated for me just what George and the medics were up against. It wasn't just that these people had no access to medical care. Many of them hadn't the slightest notion of how even the most rudimentary elements of medical care worked. All the same, that sad old man in the shed seemed to trust George implicitly.

Back at the schoolhouse, the line outside was already a dozen families deep, and it tripled by noon. I pulled up a desk in the corner of the exam room, from which I could watch and listen as I helped split pills, filled little baggies with painkillers, and generally tried to make myself seem useful. Patients sat down one at a time in front of Dr. Laurel, describing their symptoms. George and Cessar translated Guaraní as she took temperatures, measured blood pressures, listened to chest cavities, depressed tongues, inspected rashes, felt ribs, admired ear canals, tested reflexes, examined mucus, and generally poked and prodded her way to exhaustion. Laurel consulted not only Cessar but also George, who's built up an impressive knowledge of medicine over the years, and both men kept busy testing urine samples, mixing salves, and filling prescriptions as the young doctor requested them.

I sat back and enjoyed the cadence of their banter. In the

absence of complex tests and medical equipment, making a diagnosis seemed like a very Socratic process, heavily reliant on Q&A, and I could almost picture the decision tree that Laurel must have followed in her mind. This was probably a lot like how medicine used to be practiced in the United States, I thought, a century ago or more. George had a bedside manner that many veteran MDs should envy, and he joked lightly with patients who came in looking tense.

"Forty-five years old! It can't be!" he'd exclaim, drawing blushes from *campesino* women.

"This one's a heartbreaker!" he would announce, disarming a nervous-looking teenage boy.

"One every ten months, eh?" he joked with a pregnant woman, who came in trailing five wide-eyed kids, all seemingly under seven years old.

Sometimes, it was clear what an advantage it conferred to speak a common language that your patients do not. Often enough, George and Laurel were able to consult frankly on a grim diagnosis that they might not have discussed candidly in front of an English-speaking patient. They reached slow consensus about prescriptions, taking time to ask questions that they might not have if their patient had been able to understand them. Should we give forty milligrams or would eighty be better? Are you sure about Thalitone? Why not Sectral? It also allowed them to take bets on how high a patient's blood pressure was going to be, then to exclaim (like true Mainers), "Holy shit, that would kill a moose!" when it surpassed even the upper end of their wagering.

Sometimes, though, I wondered if the patients could guess what we were talking about. One young pregnant woman sat down across from Laurel and told her she just wanted a checkup, to see how her baby was doing. A three-year-old boy in a blue sweatsuit clung nervously to her leg.

The woman wore a white cotton T-shirt and a blue pleated skirt, and her right eye was clouded with blood. Dr. Laurel felt the woman's abdomen and moved her stethoscope across her belly. Everything sounds great, she told her, but she wanted to take a look at that eye. While Laurel grabbed an ophthalmoscope and asked the woman to lean forward, Cessar excused himself quietly and stepped out of the classroom.

"That could be an infection," she said in English, shining her light around the woman's eye, "or sometimes the blood vessels pop during morning sickness. I should know if she's puking extra hard."

Cessar stuck his head in and asked George to come outside. George stepped into the waiting area as Dr. Laurel gently prodded the woman's eyelid, asking in Spanish whether it hurt. The fluorescent lights buzzed softly in the fixtures overhead. I smiled at the little boy, who grinned back at me shyly, and I dug around in my pocket for some of the candy I'd brought along.

Then Laurel grunted a small "uh-huh" sound.

"What do you think?" I asked.

"Well," she said matter-of-factly, putting down her scope, "I'm actually going to say that somebody hit her."

And before I could respond, George walked back into the room.

"Don't worry about that eye," he said, disappointment in his voice. "I had a chat with the husband, and it's not a complication of the pregnancy. That's from him beating her."

Laurel nodded and sighed. She handed over a baggie of vitamins and told the woman she could go. The pregnant woman and her son got up silently to leave. I handed the little boy a wrapped piece of candy on his way out, and he stared up at me with eyes that were big, dark, and clear.

The remainder of our days in the *campo* passed in a similar fashion. I spent my nights in the clinic and walked over to Cessar's each morning just after dawn, keeping my eyes peeled for the poisonous snakes that George said regularly slithered between the two buildings. We chatted for a while over *mate* and oatmeal, which George—still iron-stomached from his Peace Corps days—supplemented with stale bread soaked in hot sauce. More than once, I watched him chase his daily malaria pill with a swig of the previous night's warm beer.

Then it was back into the truck and off to another community where Cessar had scheduled a pop-up clinic. Dr. Laurel saw 100 patients on our first day in the schoolhouse, and on some days that number swelled to 150. We set up in schools, in fields beneath wide-canopied trees, and in the bedrooms of locals who were acquainted with George and Cessar. Most mornings, the line outside the exam room was fifty people deep by ten o'clock, and more often than not, the vibe was somewhat festive, since George's annual visits were an anticipated community event. On our busiest day, working out of a private home on a well-kept little farm, a vendor actually showed up selling ice cream out of an insulated cart.

The most common ailments were parasites like giardia, a mostly waterborne bug that causes chronic diarrhea and vomiting, spread by contact with human waste. These are easily treated with antibiotics, but the central problems of uncovered wells and poor hygiene require more long-term solutions. Here too, though, the Andrea Ritz Clinics represent some progress. A clean water system that George and his team built for the Cerrito clinic years ago today consists of almost ten miles of pipe, reaching dozens of nearby farms and families. High blood pressure and heart disease were frequent diagnoses, and more than once we made home visits to deliver insulin to housebound diabetics. Occasionally, we encountered more serious cases—a boy with a skin disorder so severe that his back looked like the hide of an elephant, a few men presenting with early-stage prostate cancer—and Dr. Laurel treated their symptoms while Cessar made appointments at the clinic for further exams and referrals.

"We see fewer infectious diseases and chronic problems than we used to," George told me at one point.

"That's because we're having an impact," Cessar said.

Of course, the medics also encountered the usual maddening comedy routines that I imagine all doctors put up with: rambling hypochondriacs, patients who refuse to give straight answers, parents who are certain that something is wrong with their kids but can't describe any symptoms. Some of the patients lumped together weird sets of unrelated details. "I get terrible headaches and my nose itches," complained one sixty-four-year-old *abuelita*. Others came in with oddly specific complaints. "It hurts when I eat watermelon," one man kept repeating. "Every time I eat watermelon, my mouth just hurts!"

Other times, it wasn't clear what role folk knowledge was playing in a patient's description of his or her symptoms. A graying old man complained of chest pains, but only "when the south wind blows." On the one hand, this sounds a little superstitious. On the other hand, it might be an allergy or some kind of atmospheric joint pain. I was impressed by how much composure all three medics showed, even to those who had obviously come only for the excitement of being seen. When I was assigned the task of distributing reading glasses,

I struggled to show the same patience with the grabby-handed and clearly not all near-sighted crowd that mobbed me once word of "free glasses" got out.

All the same, I was happy whenever I could make myself somewhat useful. Hanging out with heroic Third World doctors can get a man thinking about his relative usefulness in this world. More than once—often while executing my primary task of pouring the *tereré*—I found myself reflecting on Thompson's idea that a writer could be "twice as effective" as a Peace Corps volunteer in the field. Standing in the dim corner of a one-room schoolhouse, scribbling uselessly in my notebook while a team of medics treated kids with chronic asthma, I was about ready to call bullshit on Señor Thompson.

Of course, the more dramatic the poverty and hardship, the easier it was to feel ineffectual. The medics and I spent another afternoon in a village called Tacuaro, home to a band of Paraguay's indigenous Mbyá people. The Mbyá were the first inhabitants of the country's once great Atlantic forests, and they watched the great majority of their ancestral lands sold off wholesale during the dictatorship. Stroessner spent decades pursuing a kind of reverse land reform, during which he parceled out indigenous lands to commercial ranching, logging, and agriculture interests. Huge tracts were awarded to political cronies, many of whom sold their new plots to Brazilian speculators, absentee landlords who decimated the forests to make room for cattle, cotton, and sugarcane. Today, most of the Mbyá are landless or live on small reservations like the one at Tacuaro—sunburned plots that represent fractions of their former territory. The once wide-ranging hunters and subsistence farmers have struggled to adapt to sedentary lifestyles on these marginal lands, and most Mbyá live in considerable poverty.

Other areas we'd visited had been remote and disadvantaged, no doubt, but at least the people there scraped out a
functional agrarian living. A few even seemed to be doing
rather well. The Mbyá, by contrast, were destitute. It didn't
take an agronomist to see that the soil in Tacuaro was next to
worthless, a brownish clay with scrubby vegetation and none
of the tall palms I'd grown accustomed to seeing (though
George did say that the Mbyá had cut down and sold many
of their valuable trees). The small wooden schoolhouse that
George had helped build was being used as a chicken coop,
so the medics set up in the shade of the tallest tree we could
find, next to the clapboard house of the community's chief.

Most of the patients that afternoon were children, suffering from the usual infections and parasites but also from
malnutrition, and a few had the brittle and blond-streaked
hair that indicates nutrient and protein deficiency. As a rule,
the kids were playful and unspeakably cute. While the doctors saw patients and dispensed medication, I played with a
few of them awaiting their turn. One of them held a piece of
yarn with a coati on the end of it. I'd seen several of these
small snouted raccoons back in the Pantanal. Thompson
actually kept one as a pet during his stay in Rio, a house-
broken coati that he claimed to have rescued from an abu-
sive owner in Bolivia. This one skittered around comically
on the end of his yarn, scratching at the dirt with fishhook
claws. In the wild, a coati can shred a heavy log like a house-
cat tearing at newspaper. Here, I thought, was an animal
that could raise some hell if it ever got tired of its leash.

There are twenty-six families living in the Tacuaro band
of Mbyá, and judging from the line that day, they're aver-
aging a minimum of four kids per family. So it's likely that
the hardscrabble reservation at Tacuaro will sooner or later
have to support more than twice its current population, and

when that day comes, the available arable land may not be enough. Needless to say, three volunteer medics dispensing antibiotics beneath a lime tree will not be enough either.

We were in and out of the village within a couple of hours. After Dr. Laurel saw her last patient, we took some pictures, then climbed into the truck, heading out along the same red-clay roads we came in on. A troupe of the Mbyá kids chased after us, and I watched as they grew distant in the side-view mirror. Then we turned a corner, and I lost them behind a green wall of sugarcane.

Here and there, George told stories from his Peace Corps days. He was in Chile in 1970, at the end of his volunteer stint, when Salvador Allende became the continent's first democratically elected Marxist president. Initially, there had been some question as to whether the new leftist government would allow the *yanqui* volunteers to stick around. An Associated Press article at the time actually quoted a twenty-three-year-old George, who said something remarkably similar to what Thompson had said about the communists back in Tom Martin's living room.

"No matter where you are, you'll find people who want to get rid of the Americans," young George had told the reporter. "But in my work here, I've met Communists and Socialists who have nothing against Americans personally. If you do a good job for Chile, they're all for it."

In George's mind, today's Peace Corps goes a bit heavy on classroom instruction and "raising awareness," and a bit light on the kind of hands-on, direct service that characterized his days as a volunteer and director.

"There's just no substitute for that on-the-ground stuff," he said over *mate* one morning, gnawing on a hunk of Tabasco-soaked bread. "Environmental education is big now, but the Paraguayans don't necessarily learn well by being told. They are great copiers, however, and if they see somebody actually executing an idea that works, they'll want to try it."

I asked George which philosophical side of the PC he saw "winning out"—the service mission or the diplomatic one.

"Well, in theory," he said, "they're supposed to be integrated." Then he trailed off, hesitated, and threw up his hands. "Look, I don't know. I've been out of that game for a long time. You should probably talk about that with a few current volunteers."

As it turned out, I got a chance to do just that. Toward the end of the week, we took the mobile clinic to a village called Oculto, where a PC volunteer happened to be posted. At one time, George recalled, Peace Corps volunteers in the region used to be a lot more numerous (Cerrito itself had one until 2003), but the agency has followed the continent's changing demographics and shifted much of its focus to urban programs. Greater Oculto, meanwhile, is decidedly not urban. The village is just down the road from Cerrito, and as we drove through a green valley a few miles away, George casually remarked that the area "used to be known for its leprosy." He said this calmly and without alarm, like you might say, "This area used to be known for its farmers' market."

When we pulled up to yet another simple brick schoolhouse, a PC volunteer named Sean Conway was waiting for us. Sean was a year and four months into his two-year stint with the PC, a baby-faced agriculture volunteer who had studied printmaking at Colorado State University. He was a couple days shy of his twenty-fifth birthday and seemed glad to have visitors passing through his little corner of Paraguay. As we unloaded the truck, George asked him a few questions about Oculto. Were the wells covered? What were most families' latrines like? Sean answered without hesitation, showing a thorough knowledge of the town's drinking water and hygiene habits, which was maybe in part because he'd battled several months of truly vicious giardia when he'd first arrived.

As the patients started rolling in, Sean led me on a short tour of the village. I got a look at the bountiful garden plot he'd helped to start with some of the schoolkids, and he told me a little about his first few months in the village—how hard it was to adjust, how his relationship with his host family had gone south pretty quickly. Initially, Sean said, he'd been viewed as kind of a means to an end by the woman who'd headed the effort to request a PC volunteer for Oculto. A few years before, in a neighboring town, another volunteer had helped start a women's cooperative and later worked with its members on some grant-writing skills. One of their grants came through, and a few months later, some NGO or another had awarded the town a few dozen chickens and some free supplies to build coops.

"So what my contact took away from that," Sean said, "is that if you get a Peace Corps member, then you too will get free chickens."

The woman was upset when Sean explained that, actually, it wasn't this easy. Fine, she said, then *we'll* just start one of these women's cooperatives. That's a great idea, Sean had told her, but it can't just be for the purpose of getting free chickens. The women would have to meet for a few months to establish their long-term goals, and then eventually, they could start looking into opportunities and working on their grant-writing skills. None of this is what his contact wanted to hear.

"So did you ever get the free chickens?" I asked.

"Man, we didn't even get the women's group," he said. Like most PC volunteers, Sean now lived alone.

In general, Sean said, he had realized that folks around Oculto approached life with a fairly hand-to-mouth attitude. One of his main goals was to encourage some agroforestry in the many fallow fields and logged-over plots scattered around town. Planted today, valuable and useful hardwoods could have a big financial and utilitarian payoff twenty or thirty years down the road. But so far, he'd had little success getting the locals on board. Even when the farmers had plenty of unused land, he said, they just didn't seem disposed to plan for the long term. Sure, they realized planting and growing trees required comparatively little work, but most preferred to focus on their sugarcane and their cotton crops, they told him. Maybe they'd get around to the trees eventually, but these were simply more immediate concerns.

"And you know what?" Sean asked dryly. "So is drinking a lot of *tereré,* and so is sitting in the shade for a couple of hours when the heat gets bad in the afternoon. So the whole thing has been an uphill battle."

We passed a few groups walking toward the schoolhouse, and Sean stopped to chat in a mixture of Spanish and Guaraní. *Que guapo!* they said to one another, a weird piece of Paraguayan slang and a common greeting for someone you admire. In other Spanish-speaking countries, it would mean "How handsome!" but in Paraguay it implies "How hardworking!" Sean's grasp of Guaraní was impressive (he knew zero when he first arrived), and judging from those few interactions, he seemed well liked around the village.

As we doubled back toward the schoolhouse, I asked him his thoughts about the Peace Corps' balance between service and cultural exchange. It was clear that he'd already given the topic some thought.

"There's a difference of opinion about that among Peace Corps volunteers," he said, "but I've come to place more importance on the intangible stuff." A lot of volunteers, he explained, drive themselves crazy trying to launch project after project. They worry that if they can't point to something permanent at the end of two years, they'll feel like they've failed. So they commit themselves to grandiose undertakings that aren't always well planned out—that sometimes no one even wants—because they're motivated by a fear of failure rather than a community's needs and desires. As far as Sean was concerned, the relationships he'd made around Oculto were already their own best legacy. Everybody learned something, and at the very least nobody was harmed. So even in the worst-case scenario, he joked, it was all a net-zero, right?

"I look at it this way," Sean said. "If I sit around all day drinking *tereré* and talking to these guys about baseball, there's still a value there. But it's hard to show that to politicians back home who want to see results."

We stepped back onto the porch of the makeshift clinic. Oculto had been slow all morning, and there was nobody waiting in line. Inside, a little girl was throwing a full-on, five-alarm tantrum, and we looked in to see a haggard-looking Dr. Laurel trying to peek into her ear with an otoscope. Sean and I exchanged a sympathetic cringe. For the moment, anyway, I think both of us were pretty glad not to be doctors.

George, Cessar, and Laurel drove back into Asunción at the end of the week, to drop me off and retrieve another doc who was flying in that weekend. Sean had a PC event to attend in the capital, so he came along for the ride. On the way into the city, it poured so hard that it made the first night's storm seem like a produce mister at the supermarket. We tried to cover up our gear in the truck bed with a tarp, but by the time we reached Asunción, my backpack was a sopping-wet sponge. Cessar's trusty Toyota dropped Sean and me off at a corner near the PC headquarters. I told George and the medics that they were doing important work. I thanked them sincerely for putting up with me and warned them to steer clear of Pombero.

That night, I went to dinner with Sean and five other PC volunteers who were in town for the weekend. After seven days of sharing beers and eating nothing but oatmeal, chicken, and rice, I'd built up a great hunger and thirst. Needless to say, the PC crowd was equally voracious. After dinner, I splurged on a bottle of Malbec and quizzed the table about what kind of projects they were working on at their sites.

In fairness, it was late, and these guys didn't come to the city very often. Their towns and villages probably seemed a million miles away, and I imagine the last thing they wanted to talk about was their work. So each of them hemmed and hawed. They made a few self-deprecating jokes about not accomplishing much. One of them mentioned a beekeepers' union she'd helped get off the ground, and another was organizing a market for local handicrafts. All were in their twenties except for one middle-aged volunteer, a Southerner in her fifties who was relatively fresh off her PC training. Maybe she sensed I was a bit disappointed with their answers.

"I think if you asked many of us," the Southerner explained, "there aren't a whole lot of real specific service projects we're involved in." She took a slow sip from her water glass. Her drawl was Loretta-Lynn thick.

"It's more about planting seeds," she continued. "It's

about an awareness of other cultures that changes people's lives. You think of all of these people living in these far-off places. Well, we're able to come in there, and now for the first time"—she spoke this last part with the singsong lilt of a big reveal—"they can say that they have a friend who's from the US!"

I nodded slowly and attempted a smile. In my head, however, I thought, What a cop-out. What a stupid, shitty cop-out.

It had made sense to me when Sean explained it, but right then, it sounded worse than shallow. I felt flushed with disappointment and wine, even a little angry. What good is having a friend from the United States, I thought, if you're still living with hyperthyroidism and no clean water? How useful are your new American pals when your bowels are raw with giardia and your road floods every time it rains and you have no decent land to grow anything on because the rich people in your country took everything and left you with nothing? How thrilled are you to have rubbed shoulders with an American, I wanted to ask, when your blue fucking kid is going to die of a broken heart because you're too stubborn and poor and uneducated even to take advantage of free health care when it's offered to you?

What about all that? I felt like shouting. Are you planting some seeds to take care of all that?

I wanted to ask these things, but I didn't. I didn't because it was late, and all of them were very nice, and I was suddenly very tired. So instead I just topped off our glasses with the dregs of the Malbec, and I raised my glass to them in a long, silent toast.

CHAPTER NINE

One for the Road

Thus the haze of optimism that hung on the land early this year is slowly being burned away by the hot glare of reality.

—*National Observer*, March 11, 1963

I

The only thing I did in Argentina was stop for dinner, and the only thing I ordered there was beer. The café was a roadside trucker joint in the big-sky province of Corrientes, the heart of a region so wide, flat, and fertile that the Argentines call it Mesopotamia. The waitress there didn't care what currency I paid in—Argentinean, Paraguayan, Brazilian, Uruguayan. "Right now, you are everywhere and nowhere," she told me.

Thompson passed through Argentina briefly in November of 1962, but he didn't publish any stories about it, so I only zoomed through on a bus bound for Uruguay. As it happens, he didn't write much about that country either, only a single and somewhat bland story about the country's upcoming election, less interesting for its political insight than for the sharp distinctions it drew between the rest of South America and the safe, modern, socially advanced, and comparatively wealthy little nation of Uruguay.

The Danish guy back in Asunción had spent some time in Uruguay's coastal capital of Montevideo, and when I'd asked him what he thought of the place, he had furrowed his brow and declared, "Montevideo is nice, but it is like a meal without salt." Now I could see what he meant. Montevideo reminded me of a pleasant, smallish European city, more like Milan or Brussels than Lima or La Paz. Its streets were clean, and the light traffic flowed briskly past joggers and dog-walkers. The requisite historic district was handsome enough, but the skyline consisted mostly of gleaming condos and office towers. To Thompson, who'd been growing increasingly preoccupied by the extent of South American poverty, what stood out about Montevideo was that it had "none of the vast, sprawling slums that disfigure other South

American capitals, and its streets are almost free of beggars." Fifty years later, the city does have its poor neighborhoods, but nothing on the level of its Andean counterparts.
Thompson also called attention to the country's social programs, which were, in 1962, "among the most advanced in
the world." Back then, Uruguay offered an eight-hour work-
day, a generous minimum wage, workman's comp, and pension for retirees. More recently, it's become the first country
in South America to allow same-sex civil unions and the
first in the world to issue laptops to every schoolkid.

Nearby Buenos Aires tends to siphon off most of Montevideo's more urbane young people and creative types, and
the city didn't strike me as particularly edgy or exciting.
It was nice, though, in the Minnesota sense of the word—
subdued, wholesome, nonthreatening. Nice was a welcome
change of pace. Ever since Bolivia, the general dysfunction
of life in South America had been getting me down. In my
head, it was all starting to ball up and press down on me a
little—the salt harvesters and the hopeless miners, the dying
rivers, the day-tripping backpackers and the ineffectual
Peace Corps workers, the street kids of Huaycán and the
starving ones on the Mbyá reservation. I felt like I was on
the cusp of a realization about what it was that most dramatically altered Thompson's thinking down here, but a small
voice was telling me that I wasn't going to like it.

I wanted to put it all out of my head for a few days, and
Montevideo provided the opportunity. It's a good city for
biking, loitering on the beach, and hanging around in waterfront cafés, so I rented a fixie from my hostel, and for
the next few days that's all that I did. I followed a well-kept
bike trail fifteen miles along the Atlantic coastline, heading
east of the city on a long, lazy ride. It was late April in the
Southern Hemisphere, too cold for swimming and sunning

(Montevideo is about the same distance from the equator as Virginia Beach), so the dozen or so picturesque beaches I passed were empty except for the gulls. It's important to stay hydrated while biking, so I stopped periodically for beer at a series of beachside patio cafés. The waitresses there draped heavy woolen blankets over my shoulders and gave me binoculars, the better to see the fortress-like trawlers pressing up against the horizon.

I spent a few hours one day hanging out near the container port downtown, watching the cranes stack up shipping crates like giant LEGO blocks. I walked out to the end of the seawall and made small talk with the fishermen, perched stoically against the spray. They all used spinner reels and handsome carbon-fiber rods, and I thought back to Julio and the net-fishermen beneath the bridge in Barranquilla, then to the wading old men with their soda-bottle reels in Corumbá. I stared out at the ocean, standing at the very tip of the concrete barrier, so the rolling sea filled my entire vision. What had the Pacific looked like out the window of Reid's high-rise back in Lima? Hadn't it looked the same? What about the Caribbean rolling up on that lonely beach outside Bernie's place in Guajira? Take the land out of the picture, I thought, and all of the world's oceans look alike to me. They don't change much over time, either. The churning spectacle in front of me would have looked just the same if Thompson had stopped to stare at it fifty years ago. Hell, it would have looked the same fifty *million* years ago, back when the Andes were just beginning to rise up out of the crust. The mountains project permanence, disguising a history of change. The flux of the ocean, meanwhile, just distracts us from its constancy.

I mooned around Montevideo for a few days, thinking thoughts like these and whiling away the hours in parks and cafés. Then one morning it all suddenly felt very dull, and I grabbed an early bus for the sleek, modernist airport on the edge of town. I hopped the first available plane there for Rio de Janeiro, where fifty years earlier, the Hunter S. Thompson Trail had come to its abrupt end.

II

R io is where Thompson penned the lines that had been bouncing around my head since before setting foot in Colombia. "I came to South America to find out what it meant," he wrote in April of 1963, "and I comfort myself in knowing that at least my failure has been on a grand scale. After a year of roaming around down here, the main thing I've learned is that I now understand the United States and why it will never be what it could have been, or at least tried to be."

It's a gloomy sentiment, but when Thompson arrived in Rio de Janeiro in September of 1962, he was actually feeling rather upbeat. One look at Rio and it's easy to understand why. The city delivers instantly on its sexy reputation: toned bodies, hypnotic sambas, miles of perfect beaches. There's a sensuality to the place that grabs you on your first seaside stroll. Part of it derives from the sticky heat and the seemingly constant pulse of music. Part of it stems from the fact that the beach is Rio's living room. At all hours of the day, the city's waterfront is packed with half-clothed residents (known as Cariocas, just like the spray foam that's named for the Carnaval-loving city). They're playing beach volleyball, beach bocce, and beach soccer. They're tying up beach slack lines and holding impromptu beach footraces. You get the feeling these people would play beach Battleship if the sand didn't clog up the little holes. It's hard to reconcile a place like Rio with the fact that Brazil itself is an emerging superpower, seeing as how no one in the country's former capital seems to put in a full day's work. The banks are only open from ten to three, the bars never close, and every time you look around, half the city seems to be barefoot and intensely focused on a game of Frisbee.

Thompson told his editor at the *Observer* that he planned to make Rio his home base for a while. "It is about time I lived like a human being for a change," he wrote. Rio was cheap compared to the Andes. Thompson had friends and contacts in town, including Bob Bone, a journalist and photographer whom he'd met years before during a brief stint at a small-town newspaper in New York. He had supplementary work lined up at the *Brazil Herald,* Rio's English-language daily paper, and within a couple of months, his girlfriend of three years, Sandy Conklin, flew down to shack up with him. Sandy arrived just days before Thompson's trip to Paraguay and Uruguay. When he came back at the end of November, the two of them moved into a tiny and kitchenless apartment in the beachside neighborhood of Copacabana, the center of a soon-to-be-famous expatriate scene that was just then getting off the ground.

"If you talked to people back then," Bob Bone told me, "maybe they went to Europe, but they didn't go to South America all that much." I talked to Bone via Skype while sitting on a flea-ridden bunk bed in the cheapest hostel in Rio—also in Copacabana and, by sheer coincidence, within a few blocks of Thompson's old apartment building. Bone was in Rio in 1962 running an English-language business magazine for the American Chamber of Commerce. He stayed there until 1963 as well, after which he went on to a long career as a travel writer and photographer. Now in his eighties, he lives in the San Francisco Bay Area and is still an active contributor to a number of travel publications.

Back then, Bone said, Rio de Janeiro didn't yet have its worldwide reputation as a beach-blanket paradise. There were Americans and Europeans floating around, of course, many of them connected to the embassy and various English-language media, and yeah, the Copacabana Palace Hotel had been a storied celebrity hangout since the 1920s. But the idealized image of sunny, seductive, sophisticated Rio only cemented itself in the American imagination with the wide-spread export of bossa nova music a few years later. Bossa nova was the catalyst for the worldwide Rio "brand," and even in Brazil the swinging, jazzy take on the samba was still a new phenomenon in 1962 (the phrase means "new trend" in Portuguese). The nightclub district on Copaca-bana Beach was the happening heart of the nascent bossa nova scene. In fact, a month before Thompson arrived, in a club just blocks from his soon-to-be apartment, an audience of hip students and artists heard the very first rendition of a song called "The Girl from Ipanema," which would do more to define the sultry Brazilian mystique than all of the string bikinis and cocoa butter on the Atlantic coast.

What's more, Brazil in 1962 wasn't yet the stable, affluent world power that it's since become. Back then, the largest country in South America was in many ways a microcosm of the continent as a whole, characterized by sporadic vio-lence, a roller-coaster economy, and a vast gulf between the powerful and the powerless. Thompson wrote five *Observer* articles about Brazil. Four of them covered the country's unstable political situation, which was rapidly deteriorating as hyperinflation prompted a crisis of confidence in Brazil's leftist, labor-aligned president, João Goulart—popularly known as "Jango."

Is there anything sexier than hyperinflation? For all of the city's sultry appeal, I spent my first couple of days in Rio looking into Brazil's decidedly unsexy history of serial currency replacement. Before I left for South America, my grandmother had given me a five-cruzeiro bill, a piece of Brazilian paper money that she'd somehow picked up during the 1950s or 1960s. "Maybe you can use this?" she'd asked in a note. The bill was in pretty good shape. On its front was a mustachioed nineteenth-century diplomat named José Paranhos. On the reverse was a scene from the conquest of the Amazon. It's a bill that was in circulation when Thompson was based in Brazil. I like to think that he was the one who brought this bill back to the States, where it somehow circulated and eventually ended up among my grandma's keepsakes. At the time, a five-cruzeiro bill would have been worth approximately one-half of one cent. And it was dropping fast.

Brazil's toilet-bowl spiral of inflation began in the 1950s, when government spending surged with the large-scale effort to modernize Brazilian infrastructure and industry. When Brazil financed the ground-up construction of its shiny new capital, Brasília, it did so primarily by simply printing more money. That worked well enough that the government went ahead and printed some more money to pay off its foreign debts. Later, when the state-owned railroad started losing money hand over fist, Brazil just kept on printing it in order to keep the company afloat, and when the worldwide price of coffee (then Brazil's main export) tanked around 1959, the government made up the slack by—you guessed it— continuing to print more and more money.

These days, the only place in Rio to find a bill like the one my grandma gave me is at the National Histori- cal Museum. I shared a subway car on my way there with an easygoing Oregonian kid who worked night shifts at my trashy hostel in exchange for room and board. Clean and uncrowded, Rio's subways are a delight—even the usual two-toned "doors closing" chime is replaced by a couple of mellow notes strummed bossa nova–style on an acoustic guitar. The Oregonian was off to meet a Brazilian girlfriend downtown. I told him I had big plans to check out the museum's numismatic collection, and he looked at me like he was waiting for a punch line.

"You know, currency," I said lamely. "Brazil has a really fascinating monetary history."

"Nu-mis-matic collection?" he repeated, chewing on the words like they were soggy vegetables.

"Like coin collectors," I told him. "There are a lot of people out there who take currency pretty seriously."

He shrugged and let his hand slide down the silver subway pole. "Yeah, I guess so," he said with obvious disinterest. "After all, they're always killing each other over it."

At the museum, the glass displays full of glinting coins are spread chronologically throughout the main exhibit so that visitors can follow the evolution of Brazilian currency over time. The first case I saw was filled with dullish, rough-hewn silver tokens that clinked in colonial cash registers during the sixteenth century. Many of them, said the object label, were minted in Potosí. Over the decades, they got a bit more polished and symmetrical. Eventually, they were joined by paper money, but it wasn't until 1942 that all numismatic hell started breaking loose. That was the year that the value of Brazil's historic currency, the real, disintegrated to the point that a new one was necessary to replace it. Thus was born the cruzeiro that my grandmother gave me, at a value of 1,000 reales to 1 cruzeiro.

And here begins what Thompson in 1963 called "one of

the worst inflationary spirals in the world," a monetary sink-hole that just kept deepening for three decades after he left. The new cruzeiro hung in there until 1967, at which point the story starts sounding a little like an Old Testament ge-nealogy passage. The cruzeiro begat the cruzeiro novo, at a rate of 1,000 to 1. The cruzeiro novo begat the cruzado, at 1,000:1 yet again. The cruzado begat the cruzado novo, once more worth 1,000 times its predecessor, and the cruzeiro real came after that, its value magnified once again by 1,000.

Finally, in 1994, Brazil reverted to using the real, but this time a brand-new one with a fixed value linked to the dollar. The new real was valued at 2,750 cruzeiro reales. Which means that if you fight your way back through the whole ridiculous half-century equation, a Brazilian real in the mid-1990s was worth 2.75 *quintillion* of its 1941 self. No calculator of mine is up to the task of divining the value of that bill from my grandma, but suffice it to say that if she'd given me about a quadrillion of them, I might have been able to afford my subway ride back to Copacabana.

To me, the modern history of Brazilian currency nicely illustrates the fundamental nonreality of money—the act of pure invention that is ultimately the assigning and reas-signing of value. But as Thompson points out, there are real-world consequences to the fluctuation of even imaginary things. In January, Thompson made the *Observer*'s front page with a story that foretold Jango's downfall. The year before, he explained, the cost of living in Brazil had soared by 60 percent, and even the president's allies were frustrated by the government's inability to halt inflation. Thompson speculated in his story that Jango wouldn't last through the end of his term.

"A revolution, even without shooting, probably would come from within the armed forces," he predicted. "Further, it would probably succeed; the president doesn't have enough of the military on his side to survive a showdown."

Which is pretty much exactly how things played out the following year. On April 1, 1964, Brazil's army generals led a march on Rio de Janeiro, where the presidential palace and several government ministries were still located. Jango fled in exile, and the triumphant generals promised free elections within two years. Instead, the coup kicked off twenty-one years of an oppressive military dictatorship.

Needless to say, this was not the "new trend" that the young *bossanovistas* had anticipated.

III

"At that time, Hunter was the best reporter we had."

So explained Bill Williamson over Skype one afternoon, the former editor and managing partner of the *Brazil Herald* from 1959 to 1979. Williamson, now in his eighties and living in Florida, hired Thompson on Bob Bone's recommendation, just days after Thompson's arrival in Rio. "Our correspondence showed me that he was a bit, um, flaky in some areas, but there was no question in my mind that he was a good journalist."

The office tower that once housed the *Brazil Herald* is a painfully nondescript stone building across from the US consulate in downtown Rio. I got a look at it one afternoon on my way to the National Library, where I went to leaf through a few old issues of Williamson's now-defunct newspaper. From an office window on the fifteenth floor, Thompson could have looked out on the spot where I was standing—a small green plaza called Praça 4 de Julho, or Fourth of July Square. He would have seen a bronze statue of a woman holding some laurel leaves, with an inlaid bust of George Washington below, commemorating the friendship between Brazil and the United States. Maybe, I thought, he would have looked at it and thought of home.

Thompson had written to Williamson several months earlier, asking about a job, and the editor told him what he often told the stream of itinerant foreign journalists who wrote to him back in the day: The pay's not much, but we might be able to use you—stop by when you get into town. At the time, the *Brazil Herald* had a circulation of about 7,000, mostly around Rio and São Paulo. The newsroom was run by a motley crew of a half dozen expatriates: an Austrian PhD, a couple of Russians, a British society writer. The *Herald* also leased space to CBS and a young Latin American bureau chief named Charles Kuralt, later famous for his folksy road-tripping segments on the network's nightly news, inspired by Steinbeck's *Travels with Charley*. Williamson took a look at Thompson's *Observer* clips, and he was impressed enough to hire the young writer as his primary reporter, a gig that paid $100 a month. It was a respectable sum, considering Thompson's apartment with Sandy cost only $30 a month and the *Observer* was shelling out $175 per story. During his first few months in Brazil, Thompson was living comparatively large.

"Right now," he wrote in October of 1962, "I have more money than I can reasonably waste."

In the periodicals room of Brazil's National Library, I flipped through several giant bound volumes of the *Brazil Herald*. The pages had a musty, grassy smell. The *Herald* didn't look so different from any American newspaper of its day. I spotted *Peanuts* cartoons and *Dear Abby* columns, cigarette ads and movie showtimes. The vast majority of the news stories were written without a byline. Strikes seemed to garner a lot of ink. There were pieces on police strikes, transit strikes, and rice-growers' strikes. One issue began with an apology for a three-day lull in publication, caused by a printers' strike. There was also a society column covering parties and receptions for Americans and other expats. The column had a slightly glib, above-it-all tone, and I imagined it appealing to people like the British rooftop golfer and his well-connected chums. I even saw an ad promoting "lands in the Mato Grosso," inviting *Brazil Herald* readers to invest in real estate "in the most prosperous agricultural colony, with good watering places and rich in hardwoods."

I read several stories about Cuba, a few on the Alliance for Progress, and a handful more covering the problem of Brazilian inflation. Thompson, I realized, might have written any of them, but they were all pretty dry, just straightforward examples of no-frills news reporting. Only one article I saw really showed a glimmer of Thompson's caustic humor and no-bullshit style, and that one had his byline on it. It was also the article that ended Thompson's brief career at the *Brazil Herald*.

At the end of October 1962, Williamson left Rio for a conference in Chile. In his absence, he told me, he put Thompson in charge of the newsroom. That week, Thompson covered a Chamber of Commerce luncheon where a pair of visiting US senators were the guests of honor. Both of them were conservative, segregationist "Dixiecrats"— Herman Talmadge of Georgia and A. Willis Robertson of Virginia (father of batshit-crazy televangelist Pat Robertson). They were also rabid anti-Soviet alarmists and establishment relics from the Eisenhower era. On page 2 of the *Herald*'s October 23 edition, I saw a grainy black-and-white photo showing a dour-looking Senator Robertson speaking into a microphone, flanked by three identically flat-topped men in suits, ties, and thick-framed glasses. The image was practically a caricature of 1950s Cold War conformity.

Without an editor to rein him in, Thompson couldn't resist taking pot shots at such easy targets, and he seeded his article with belittling jabs at both the senators and the president of Rio's Chamber of Commerce. As each of them took turns condemning the various popular movements around South America—movements that, unlike Thompson, they had not witnessed firsthand—Thompson countered with subtle mockery:

> Talmadge admitted that "great social change is taking place (in South America) and will continue . . . but if the people move faster than their governments it will benefit nobody but Moscow." Not all observers were quite sure just what he meant by this, but all agreed that it had an ominous ring.

When the chamber president denounced the anti-business stance of Brazil's leftist government, voicing concerns about the country's "present climate," Thompson noted wryly, "It was generally agreed that Mr. Fallon was not talking about the recent rainy spell." The president went on to request that Senator Robertson "throw some light" on the issue of American businessmen operating in Brazil, but Thompson scoffed that "Sen. Robertson's light was none too revealing." Thompson painted Talmadge as a loudmouth who "delivered his address in such a way as to render the mike obsolete," and he ended with a cheap shot at the chamber's windbag president:

In closing, Mr. Fallon tossed in an analogy of
obscure and indeterminate import. He noted that
when Yankee Stadium was constructed in 1923,
it was decided that seats of from 17 to 19 inches
wide would be adequate for the average spectator.
But when the new stadium was constructed last
year in Washington DC, it was deemed necessary
to install seats of 20 to 23 inches in width.

At least one spectator interpreted this to
mean that if Brazilians refrain from harassing
American businesses, Rio's man in the street will
be three inches fatter 40 years hence.

"It was pretty irreverent," remembered Williamson.
"Fortunately, I didn't get much blame for it because I was
out of the country." Williamson admired Thompson's clev-
erness, but the Chamber of Commerce and several major
advertisers did not. The editor had to phase out Thompson
as a reporter. He might have contributed a few more stories
after that, Williamson told me, but Thompson's byline never
appeared again in the *Brazil Herald*.

"It upset a number of the powers that be," said Williamson, "but I still laugh every time I read it."

IV

For all of Rio's sun and sand, Bob Bone said that he,
Thompson, Sandy, and their friends were really just "sit-
around-and-talk people." Sure, they'd hit the beach every so

often. Maybe they'd go for a quick swim, then lie around on their towels sipping liters of Brahma Chopp, the watery lager that's still the de facto national beer of Brazil. More often than not, though, they pulled up a table at some dark bar and talked long into the night—about current events, mostly, but also about books, politics, ambitions. Wherever the conversation led. Drugs were out, of course. If there was a drug scene among Rio's expats back in the day, Bone said they didn't know about it. At that point in his life, even Thompson had only ever dabbled in drugs.

"He would put down drug people, in fact," said Bone. "Called them 'hopheads' and things like that."

Bone mentioned a bar called the Kilt Club, where the group used to hang out. Apparently Thompson didn't care much for the place, but it was close to his apartment, and there were cheap drinks, girls, and dancing. I saw an ad for it in an old *Brazil Herald* ("Whisky a Gogo—Come Enjoy Yourself with International Singer Jean Pierre!"), and I scribbled down the address. The former Kilt Club turned out to be just a few blocks from my hostel, on a single-block cobblestone pedestrian street called Rua Carvalho de Mendonça.

A little Googling told me that Rua Carvalho de Mendonça used to be a happening nightlife strip during the early days of bossa nova, with a number of small clubs that helped incubate the new sound. It's not a leisure spot anymore, despite being just two blocks from the beach and the grand Copacabana Palace Hotel. I strolled the block one drizzly Saturday morning, passing a hardware store and a grungy-looking dry cleaner. The address that used to be the Kilt Club was now a bakery. There was only one bar on the whole block—an open-fronted affair with a blue awning, a sandwich board, and a few simple wooden tables spilling out onto the sidewalk. I walked inside and took a seat.

It was early, and the place was empty. On the wall nearest me was a tacky airbrushed mural of a liquor bottle exploding its contents, announcing that I was the sole patron of the Orgasmo Bar. Classy, I thought. So much for International Singer Jean Pierre. In the back of the room, a wide-gutted guy in his fifties looked up from the cooler he was stocking. When he strolled out to my table, I asked in fumbling Portuguese whether he had any coffee.

"I'm sorry," he said kindly. "We don't serve coffee during lunch."

I parsed this statement without making much sense of it. It was ten a.m. The alternative was either a sweet *caipirinha* cocktail or a tall liter bottle of beer. So I surrendered to fate, ordered a Brahma Chopp, and settled in for some morningtime drinking.

The Orgasmo had a television in the corner, and a Brazilian morning news show was showing pictures of President Obama standing in front of a pair of armed humvees. The voiceover was in Portuguese, but I gathered he had made a surprise trip to Afghanistan. Briefly, the screen flashed a picture of Obama meeting with Brazilian president Dilma Rousseff a few weeks before, followed by a quick shot of a waving Mitt Romney, and I thought of how far away the whole shrill American news circus seemed. Election coverage had hardly begun when I'd left. By now, I thought, the commentators and pundits would be at full froth. The segment ended, and the news show cut back to its coanchors, a short-haired blond woman wearing an ear microphone, and what seemed to be a large green animatronic parrot. They exchanged a few observations, the parrot's voice a kind of sarcastic half squawk. Then they moved on to a cooking segment.

For Thompson and his friends, the biggest news story for cocktail chatter down at the Kilt Club would undoubtedly have been the Cuban Missile Crisis. Even as Thompson was subbing in as newsroom director at the *Brazil Herald* in October of '62, twenty Soviet ships were streaming toward the US naval blockade around Cuba, possibly containing missiles capable of deploying nuclear warheads. The very night that he wrote his offending Chamber of Commerce piece, President Kennedy was on TV back home, announcing the discovery of missile bases in Cuba and warning that any attacks launched from Castro's island would incur "a full retaliatory response upon the Soviet Union." The Cold War that Thompson had followed to South America was arguably reaching its apex. The possibility of all-out nuclear war had never seemed so real.

Thompson described the moment in his book *Kingdom of Fear,* published in 2003, just two years before his suicide. The crisis felt real despite the distance, he wrote. He was living well in Rio at the time, but feeling burned out from "a long year on a very savage road, mainly along the spine of the South American *cordillera*, working undercover in utterly foreign countries in the grip of bloody revolutions and counterrevolutions." It must have been a hell of a thing, I thought, to have spent the year trying to make sense of South America's violent power struggles only to settle in Rio just in time to see the United States poised on the brink of the greatest violence of all. It was a moment, Thompson wrote, "when expatriate Americans all over the world glanced around them in places like Warsaw and Kowloon or Tripoli and realized that life was going to be very different from now on."

Absorbing the news of your homeland while traveling

abroad is like watching a car accident from a hot air balloon. On the one hand, the perspective is disorienting. You miss the vivid details that make rubbernecking so deeply satisfying, and your vantage point depends entirely on the prevailing winds. On the other hand, the picture you get is wider in scope. You're undistracted by noise, heat, and light, and your bird's-eye view imparts a kind of clarity and serenity that drivers and passengers on the ground can't touch.

Back in 2000, I watched from Scotland with increasing dissociation as the United States spent thirty-six days trying to hash out who had just won the presidency. News sources in the UK covered the event with very little sensationalism, even less partisanship, and just the slightest dusting of sarcastic faux-amazement—a subtle tone that seemed to say, "What *will* those crazy Yanks do next?" My interest gradually shifted from impassioned to detached. I watched the story unfold as if I were watching the movie that I knew would inevitably be made from it. Which is not to say that I was disinterested—far from it. I still couldn't wait to see how things played out, but the election's outcome felt less like something to pull for than something to puzzle over, to analyze in the way that a film critic breaks down a movie in search of its themes. I learned some things I had never known about the Electoral College and the judicial process, and when the crisis ended with a result other than the one I'd first hoped for, I came back to the United States feeling a kind of enlightened disengagement that it would have been easy to mistake for cynicism. It was like I'd taken some kind of existentialist civics class; I felt a deeper understanding of the political forces that had brought about the whole fiasco, even while those forces had lost their gravity for me, even as they'd come to seem trivial and untethered.

I don't mean to say that watching from Scotland allowed

me to take a more objective view of the election. It didn't. What it did was to expose the myth that there ever was such a thing as an objective view for me to take. It was a radical unmooring, a slow-burn realization that everyone is watching everything *from* somewhere, that there is simply no alternative to perspective.

I imagine a similar process playing out for Thompson toward the end of 1962. In his "Anti-Gringo Winds" piece, he declared that "objectivity is the first casualty of culture shock," and for a writer who so famously scorned objectivity in his later work, this amounts to a pretty ringing endorsement of travel. It's a backward way of saying that radical perspectivism is the first benefit of leaving home, and I wondered how much of Thompson's enthusiastic embrace of subjective journalism was informed by his perspective-jarring experiences in South America. It must have been surreal to watch the Cuban Missile Crisis unfold from the sunny, carefree environs of Copacabana. I looked up at the blond lady and her parrot and imagined them replaced by the grim black-and-white footage of missile silos, the shots of battleships lined up in the Atlantic, and behind it all a lilting bossa nova soundtrack, the clink of kissing bottles, the warm beach breezes rustling the palms.

"All things considered," Thompson wrote in *Kingdom of Fear,* "Rio was pretty close to the best place in the world to be lost and stranded forever when the World finally shut down."

V

Of course, the world didn't shut down, and Thompson and his friends went right on living the expat life in South

America's burgeoning expat capital. I went back to the Orgasmo for an occasional beer over the next few days, which
I mostly spent interviewing modern-day expatriates around
town, trying to tease out the common threads in their experience. I was curious to know how the lifestyle has evolved
since Thompson, his girlfriend, and Bob Bone passed
through fifty years ago. I met a wayward Texan drawn by
Brazil's burgeoning oil industry, an American concert cellist
who'd once worked as a reporter for the *Brazil Herald* in the
1970s, and a pair of gorgeous thirtysomething chapter hostesses for a networking organization of young internationals.
All of them agreed that certain places in the world simply
have a magnetic pull, and that Rio is one of them.

"Rio and Brazil are like quicksand," said the cellist, a
former New Yorker named Harold. He'd come to play in
the Brazilian Symphony in 1973, started moonlighting as a
journalist shortly thereafter, married a Brazilian in '77, and
simply never left. These days, his only strong connection to
New York is his accent. Brazil allowed Harold to live out ambitions that would have been unlikely at home. Growing up,
he'd dreamed of playing in the New York Philharmonic or
writing for the *New York Times,* and at best, his odds were
long. But in Rio, he'd not only played with the national or-
chestra, he'd been a staffer at one of the national papers of
record (for English-speakers, anyway). He remembered
the *Brazil Herald* newsroom as a "beer-on-the-table kind
of place," a haven for both eccentric vagabonds and serious
writers. Thanks in part to his connections there, he'd met
visiting diplomats and even royalty. As an American abroad,
Harold explained, he'd rubbed shoulders with "a different
strata of people" than he ever would have met back home. He
had access to better doctors in Rio, his money went farther,
and he was more likely to know the right people in a pinch.

"The life I have here," he said, "I could never give up."

For the Texan, though, one of the main draws of Rio was that the social rift between locals and foreigners seemed comparatively narrow. He'd worked for years in Southeast Asia and grown tired of his conspicuous (and privileged) outsider status. In Brazil, he said over beers one night, the income gap was less pronounced than in Asia or even the Andes, and having pale skin didn't immediately confer prestige. Gringos and Cariocas were on more equal footing, he explained, in part because of their shared passion for what he simply called "the Brazil lifestyle."

"There's definitely a kind of mysticism about *a vida boa,*" the girls from the expat organization told me the next night. "People from abroad just have this idea that 'in Brazil, I will find the good life.'"

One of the networking hostesses was Portuguese and the other a Brazilian who'd spent time living in England. The Texan was right, they said. The barriers between Brazilians and expats are definitely porous, but they also cautioned that the seemingly uninhibited Cariocas can actually be quite hard to get to know. Rio's exuberant beachgoers might warmly invite a stranger to join their volleyball game, but they have a reputation for being guarded when it comes to close friendships. For an outsider, the girls explained, Rio can be weirdly alienating in that way. One cliché holds that residents are a lot like their famous Christ the Redeemer statue: their arms are wide open, but they never close in an embrace.

What everyone agreed about is that Brazil right now is a land of opportunity, a place where an outsider with some ambition can write his or her own ticket. The Texan called it "a country that's on the way up," and not one of my correspondents failed to mention Brazil's role as host of the 2014 World Cup and 2016 Summer Olympics—widely viewed as validation of the country's increasing global prominence. Thompson had called Brazil a "semi-dormant nation," but it is dormant no more. Socially, politically, and economically, the country has come a long way since the currency crisis and the fall of Jango. The military government that replaced him stayed in power until 1985—staunchly anti-communist, but increasingly oppressive, violent, and indifferent to human rights. Even after its transition back to democracy, Brazil struggled well into the '90s with corruption, inflation, and debt.

Ironically, it wasn't until the country pivoted *back* to the left that it morphed into a global powerhouse. Under labor hero Luiz Inácio da Silva, elected in 2002, Brazil made huge strides against poverty and became the world's eighth-largest economy. "Lula" is a former head of the steelworkers' union, once jailed for leading strikes in the 1970s. His generous social spending helped create a new Brazilian middle class, and his tight regulation of banks minimized fallout from the global recession. This prompted big-time foreign investment, much of it in the country's booming oil industry. Brazil today still struggles with corruption and the cost of living, but economically it's riding high, and current president Dilma Rousseff is Lula's handpicked successor, a former Marxist agitator herself who was also jailed and tortured by the military regime.

As an indication of the country's rapid progress, everyone I spoke with referenced the ongoing "pacification" of the favelas—Rio's famously crowded and violent hillside slums. Since 2008, heavily armed squadrons of military and police have been systematically invading the city's most plagued neighborhoods, seizing weapons, expelling gangs and militias, arresting drug lords, and establishing a permanent police presence in areas that have long been essentially lawless. With dozens of favelas now patrolled for the first time in decades, murders and robberies have decreased, and basic services are reaching many areas that were formerly off-limits. The pacification campaign arguably reached its pinnacle in November of 2010, when the Brazilian military took control of a sector called Complexo do Alemão, the city's largest network of favelas and one of its most impregnable. When I was in Rio, the Brazilian Army had only just relinquished control of the area to civilian police.

I went to Complexo do Alemão on an overcast day during my last week in town. Since the moment I'd stepped off the plane in Barranquilla, the experience of profound poverty had been such a common thread across South America, I had almost become desensitized to it. Notably, I'm not sure you can say the same thing about Thompson. His vivid and affected descriptions of the "fear & rot in the streets" color his writing right up through his final dispatches from the continent. The favelas would have been conspicuous during his time in Rio, having swelled considerably over the previous decade as country-dwellers flocked to the city seeking jobs in the ballooning industrial sector. In 1950, there were 58 favelas on Rio's hilly outskirts. By 1962, there were about 150, and one in every ten Cariocas lived somewhere in the city's sloping shantytowns.

In an effort to stem the tide of squatters, the Alliance for Progress funded vast residential developments on the city's outskirts, but in many cases, these simply devolved into new slums. Just months before Thompson's visit, thousands of favela dwellers had been "resettled" out of Rio's affluent south and into new, Alliance-funded developments on the city's western edge. By the time I showed up, neighborhoods like "Vila Aliança" and "Vila Kennedy" were among the most brutally violent on the continent, high on the list for future pacification.

There are close to 1,000 favelas in Rio today, tightly packed pop-up communities that house a third of the city's population. Some 400,000 people live in Complexo do Alemão alone, a network of adjacent favelas filling up neighboring hillsides in the city's Zona Norte. Each one is set progressively farther from Rio's main roads and transit corridors, and until pacification, it took residents hours just to reach the city proper. Then, in 2011, the city unveiled an aerial tramway that links Complexo do Alemão to Rio's train system, soaring above the district's chaotic tangle of single-lane roads and M. C. Escher staircases. I bought my ticket at the connecting station and climbed into a tram car alone.

From the air, Complexo do Alemão is actually pretty breathtaking, a geometric chaos of rectangles upon rectangles. The colorful, flat-roofed houses are stacked on top of one another like matchboxes, and they look about as sturdy. I stared out the windows at the narrow streets and footpaths that spidered through the neighborhoods and marveled that these seemed to be the only undeveloped patches for miles. There were no green spaces and no parking lots—just an uninterrupted slag pile of housing. At first glance, Complexo do Alemão doesn't necessarily look any poorer or more dangerous than similar slums in Bogotá, Lima, or La Paz, but the sheer density of the place set my head spinning.

I got off at the last tram stop, but I didn't wander far. The visible presence of policemen toting M-16s was in some ways reassuring, but I worried about getting lost on the nonsensically snaking streets. I walked down a long and steep staircase, through a claustrophobic corridor of houses. Most of them were brick and about the size of a train car; others were tiled on the outside like bathroom walls or slapped together with a polychrome of scrap wood. Laundry lines stretched across the rooftops like prayer flags in some jumbled Tibetan monastery. Occasionally, an alleyway stretched between the houses, and I waved to the kids I saw playing there, barefoot and clutching naked dolls.

The stairway ended at a dirt road lined with trash piles and graffitied storefronts, where I picked a direction at random and started walking. The street was empty, but from inside the darkened bodegas, unsmiling men looked out at me with vacant eyes. Their gazes betrayed nothing—not curiosity or irritation or welcome. It was uncomfortable, and I looked away. I thought sadly of T. S. Eliot's famous poem "The Hollow Men," about the "eyes I dare not meet in dreams." The street kept winding along, silent except for the occasional mongrel dog rifling through the trash. On either side was a row of slab-concrete houses behind crumbling brick walls. I followed the road, curving this way and that for all of ten minutes, just long enough to get confused about which direction I'd come from. Then I turned around and retraced my steps.

Heading back up the long stairway to the tram, I slowed up behind a young girl and her father, who were trudging toward the station with agonizing slowness. The girl seemed to have some severe physical handicaps—muscular dystrophy, I guessed—and her father watched her silently from behind as she made her way up, one gasping step at a time. Of course, medical facilities in Complexo do Alemão are sparse to nonexistent, and I couldn't imagine how this girl managed to navigate the crumbling cubist landscape of the favela each day. When her father heard me coming up behind, he gently tugged on his daughter's sleeve. I thanked them quietly as I walked past, and I ascended the rest of the staircase feeling the weight of their misfortune.

I t is a testament to Thompson's moral core that the misery of places like Rio's favelas seemed to weigh on him as well. As I rode the slow tram back over the clutter of Complexo do Alemão, I felt that just maybe I had finally zeroed in on the foremost way in which South America changed Thompson's outlook on things. In the early months of 1963, having lost his *Brazil Herald* gig, Thompson saw his initial affluence fade, and his enthusiasm for Rio faded with it. His later articles and letters from Brazil give a vague sense that something in him is about to crack. In a letter from early April, Thompson warned his editor at the *Observer* that he was starting to come undone:

> It's the goddamn awful reality of life down here. I can't shrug it off. I can't avoid it. . . . Christ, I have to live like the rest of these poor bastards— harassed, badgered & put upon from morning till night for no good reason at all. I wouldn't blame them if they revolted against just about everything—and in the name of whatever party or Ism that supplied the means of revolt.

I find this passage to be one of the most poignant in all of Thompson's writing. Not only because it shows the genuine vulnerability of a young writer who was once so eager to "sink his teeth" into South America. And not only because it illustrates an empathy for society's castaways that would stick with Thompson in the years to come. It also contains the sad, implicit admission that struggle and revolt are nothing more than cathartic rituals for the "harassed, badgered & put upon" masses: a kind of pressure-release valve that masquerades as ideology and fosters little change. As Thompson watched, again and again, the Sisyphean struggles of the South American underclass, he felt inside of him a growing tension, a vague and nameless friction between political idealism and tragicomic nihilism. Before long, that tension that would manifest itself as something called "gonzo journalism."

In a year of South American travel, Thompson had seen the left revolt against the right, the right revolt against the left, the powerful putting down the people, and the people dispensing with the powerful. And yet everywhere, he still encountered the same urban beggars, the same starving miners, the same illiterate Indians and destitute *campesinos*. If Thompson's year abroad showed him why the United States would never be "what it could have been, or at least tried to be," maybe it's because he looked homeward and saw just how much of the American project in the twentieth century had become the unchallenged domain of parties, movements, and isms—and he had come to suspect their futility. The goal of the Alliance for Progress, Kennedy had said, was to "lift people up from poverty, ignorance, and despair," but in South America, Thompson saw how the Alliance's pro-growth, anti-communist aims left it hopelessly mired in empty isms and fruitless uprisings. From where he stood in Rio, the poverty and ignorance and despair seemed entrenched in ways that none of these mechanisms could touch.

A year after returning to the States, Thompson wrote a book review in the *Observer,* noting that "the difficulties thus far confronting the Alliance for Progress should be a good indication of how easily a fine and noble idea can get bogged down in unforeseen realities." It's exactly the kind of language he would later adopt to describe both the counter-culture and the American Dream. This dichotomy—of noble illusions versus grim realities—would become a recurring theme in much of Thompson's work. In the end, he couldn't buy into the supposed "good life" of the South American expat, but for years after leaving the continent, the lessons he learned there still continued to shape his work. In 1970, in a campaign ad from his quixotic run for sheriff of Aspen, Colorado, Thompson might have been channeling the frustrated hopes of the Indians, miners, and *campesinos* when he wrote:

> The twisted realities of the world we are trying
> to live in have somehow combined to make us feel
> like freaks. We argue, we protest, we petition—
> but nothing changes.

VI

It is pure speculation on my part, but one final event in February of 1963 may have further jangled Thompson's nerves and soured him on life in Rio. On the first of that month, about an hour before dawn, Thompson woke to a frantic phone call from a friend. The Army was killing people right outside of a Copacabana nightclub, the voice shouted, at a place called the Domino. The caller was locked inside a nearby club, watching the violence play out in the street. Over his tinny connection, the still-groggy Thompson heard his unnamed friend yelling that he needed to get down to the nightclub district and see what was going on, and he needed to go *now*.

The Domino, it turned out, was on the very same cobble-stone nightclub strip as the Kilt Club. By the time Thompson pulled up in a cab, the shooting had stopped and the soldiers moved on. The sidewalk was littered with slug casings and broken glass. In front of the club, an unexploded hand grenade lay ominously in the street, and blood pooled on the asphalt where a doorman had been killed. Medics were loading an injured bartender and several patrons into ambulances, and bystanders were still milling about in the road, stunned and inspecting the damage. Thompson walked among them, passing right outside the bar where he liked to drink and talk politics, and his observations formed the basis for a powerful article that the *Observer* ran ten days later. The headline read DAYBREAK AT THE DOMINO: BRAZILIAN SOLDIERS STAGE A RAID IN REVENGE.

Rereading the piece in my grungy hostel one afternoon, I just about fell off my bunk when I realized that the Domino Club had also been on tiny Rua Carvalho de Mendonça, just blocks away from where I was sitting. A half hour later, I was back down at the Orgasmo, where the beer-bellied proprietor smiled to see me coming. With help from my Portuguese phrasebook, I managed to ask him whether he knew anything about the story of the ambushed club.

"*Doh-mee-nah, doooh-me-nah*," Dom Orgasmo said, stroking his chin. He shook his head vigorously and stepped out onto the sidewalk, leaving his bar unattended and motioning for me to follow. "*Vem comigo*," he said. Come with me.

The violence at the Domino was a major news story at the time. The renegade soldiers were avenging the death of a sergeant who'd been killed there weeks before, beaten to death when a fight broke out over his bill. "The establishment was completely wrecked," according to the *Brazil*

Herald's coverage the next day. The culprits were a "para-trooper detail with blackened faces" who barricaded the street before firing tear gas and machine guns into the crowd. For Brazilians, the shooting at the Domino was an ominous reminder that, more and more, the military was acting with impunity. In retrospect, it seemed to foreshadow the country's impending military takeover. As Thompson pointed out, "The basic problem is hardly unique to Brazil: Where civil authority is weak and often corrupt, the military gets power by default."

Friendly Dom Orgasmo took me up and down the street, asking various shop owners and roustabouts whether they remembered the place. It seemed to strike everyone as vaguely familiar, and each shopkeeper referred us to someone else down the block who might know more. The guy at the hardware store pointed across the street to the liquor-store guy. The liquor-store guy suggested we talk to the kitchen-store owner. The kitchen-store owner's wife pointed out a balding man with a salt-and-pepper mustache, loitering in front of the Laundromat next to the Orgasmo.

"Doh-mee-nah?" repeated the mustache man, crinkling his forehead. Then, all at once, his eyes lit up and he let out a rapid stream of unintelligible Portuguese. With his hands, he made the universal double-point-and-shake gesture of a machine gun.

"That's right!" I said in English.

"Exatamente!" Dom Orgasmo said, slapping us both on the back.

The mustache guy's name was João, and for the next few minutes, he spoke to me in what must have been painfully slow Portuguese, with a lot of hand gestures and a bit of supplementary Spanish. João was just a boy in 1963, but he lived in an apartment building at the end of the block, and he remembered how the soldiers had closed down both ends of the street. "There and there," he said, pointing. It was very loud, he said, and he made the machine gun motion several more times. Afterward, he remembered, the block was full of people, all walking around slowly, many of them in shock. How strange, I thought, to know that Hunter S. Thompson had been one of them.

"And where was it?" I asked, gesturing around at the block.

João made a humming sound and furrowed his eyebrows. "Definitely on this side of the street," he said. He was quiet for a minute, looking up and down the block. Then he looked straight at the Orgasmo.

"I think it was here," he said, sounding a bit surprised. "Or maybe there," he added, pointing at the dry cleaner. Or maybe both. It was big, João said, maybe three whole store-fronts, but it was definitely right about here.

I thanked him profusely, and we shook hands before he walked away. What were the odds, I wondered, that of all the bars in Rio de Janeiro, I'd been drinking all week at the former Domino Club without knowing it? I inspected the cobblestones at my feet, half expecting to see crimson bloodstains from the assassinated doorman. My hands were trembling. For a second, I felt uncomfortably engulfed by history, at the center of the relentless, invisible crush of everything that has ever happened.

I sat back down in the Orgasmo and ordered a Brahma Chopp, thanking the ebullient owner for his help. When I'd finished my beer, he brought me another and waved off my attempts to pay for it. It was, he insisted, a *saideira,* and he clapped me on the back once more. When he had gone, I looked up the word in my phrasebook. "One for the road," it meant.

———

The road. Hunter S. Thompson was on it for a year, almost to the day, and for him, that was long enough. Not too long after the Domino incident, he started making plans to get out of Rio. He flew to Lima in April, intending at first to pick up the trail once more for the *National Observer*. He put his girlfriend on a plane to New York, and he planned to meet her there after a long swing back through the Andes and into Central America. With his editor, he discussed story ideas about the Panama Canal, earthquakes in Costa Rica, and communism in Baja. But his heart wasn't in it, and he told his editor as much. Latin America was burning him out, and he was eager to turn his attention to the United States.

"We will have to get together on my return," he wrote to the editor, "so I can tell you how I'm going to write what America means."

Then, in Lima, arguably his least favorite city on the continent, Thompson snapped. By then, he was stone broke again—in debt to the *Observer,* in fact, which had been paying in advance for articles he hadn't yet written. His and Sandy's plane tickets had sapped him dry. The jackboots were still running the show in Peru, where a new general had overthrown the old general who'd invalidated the election the year before. What's more, Lima's winter fog was settling in, heralding a six-month end to sunshine in the City of Kings. "I wish to jesus I had never seen this continent," Thompson wrote on April 28.

The next day, he wrote his editor again, describing a total meltdown—"violent shouting, destruction, tears, the whole works." Was he exaggerating? There is no way to know. What is certain is that Thompson was back in New York within days.

And this is the way the Hunter S. Thompson Trail ends: not with a bang but a whimper.

My last day in South America was simple and beautiful. I woke up at Rio's cheapest hostel to find little trios of bite marks decorating my hands and forehead, a telltale sign of bedbugs. So that part wasn't great. But it was sunny and it was Saturday, when the Cariocas traditionally prepare the slow-cooked bean, beef, and pork stew they call feijoada. All over Copacabana, sidewalk diners were camped out at large tables with their families and friends, enjoying multi-hour lunches of the rich, heavy dish. I picked a café where they served me a giant, steaming crock of it, with sides of clingy white rice, fragrant collard greens, and orange slices. Next to my plate, the waiter set a dish of bright red hot sauce and a shot of cachaça rum—to settle the stomach, I suppose. I ate in a perfectly contented silence for almost two hours, shamelessly ogling the beautiful people of Rio de Janeiro.

In the afternoon, I strolled the beach, and before sunset, I set out to hike up Morro da Urca, the smaller wooded hill that rises in front of Rio's famous Sugarloaf Mountain. After Machu Picchu, the oblong haystack of Sugarloaf may be the continent's most recognizable landmark, a dramatic rock set idyllically against the Rio cityscape and the perfect blue of Guanabara Bay. From Morro da Urca, a cable car runs to the top, and I crammed inside with forty other camera-toting tourists to take in the famed sunset views.

They did not disappoint. Rio's nickname is "o Cidade Maravilhosa" (the Marvelous City), and it really is a marvel how the sparkling disarray of the metro weaves itself in and around the green curves of the coastal mountains. The city spills like a flood out of every open valley and creeps up tentatively into the gentler folds between hillsides. As the sun sank behind the hills, the horizontal light stretched out across the bay, where a surging mob of white apartment towers stops short against the coastline. On a twin butte opposite Sugarloaf stood Christ the Redeemer, whose arms never close, looking down over the whole weird mess.

I stood there for a while, poised on the edge of the continent and looking back. Then, as the sun's last rays disappeared, I shuffled with the rest of the crowd back into the cable car. A bossa nova trio had started up at the patio café on Morro da Urca, and the music drifted across the hillside like a warm breeze. I sat down, ordered a *caipirinha,* and stared out across the city of Rio, just another thirsty foreigner looking for the good life.

EPILOGUE

Un Paseño

Back in the low-barometer loony bin that is La Paz, the local beer of choice is a pale golden lager called Paceña, which they brew up there at 12,000 feet and sell in the tall liter bottles that I'm accustomed to calling "bombers." One night at the hostel, my twentysomething German roommate had offered me a pull from the bottle he was nursing. It wasn't too bad, he said, and he added that he was Bavarian, so he should know. Did I want to know the etymology of the brand name?

"It comes from the word *pasado*," he said sagely, displaying the label to me like a waiter with a fine Bordeaux. "This is Spanish for 'the past,' you see. So a *paceña* is a person who is tied to the past, yes? Or a person who is obsessed with the past, someone who is living in it."

That sounded *muy romantico,* I said, and I thanked him for the swig. Unfortunately, this is a bullshit explanation. Like beers all across Bolivia, Paceña takes its name from the demonym for its hometown—a *paceño* or a *paceña* is simply a citizen of sky-high La Paz. Likewise, the Santa Cruz–dwellers are called *cruceños,* and Cruceña is their beloved local brew. Down in Potosí, it's warm cans of Potosina that all those miners are tipping back underground.

Still, I think the young Bavarian was on to something, and I kind of wish his definition were true. The closest word for what he was describing would probably be *paseño,* a made-up piece of pseudo-Spanish that nonetheless pretty nicely describes what I felt like during my six months of travel in South America. I was a wandering *paseño,* with one foot in the here and now and another alongside Hunter Thompson in the early '60s.

I am increasingly convinced that this is the only way to travel. Maybe the only way to live. Another famous *paseño,* Thompson's hero William Faulkner, probably put it best when he wrote, "The past is never dead. It's not even past." South America is a full-on, sensory manifestation of this idea, its historical sites both durable and distinct, presenting travelers with regular, visual reminders that the consequences of what happened yesterday are still acting on us today. Of course, this is equally true in the absence of pre-Columbian ruins or the colorful ziggurats of the conquistadors. The people and ideas and events of history are not something we can pave over or leave behind. They are always right there with us, even if only we real good *paseños* can see them.

I f the Hunter S. Thompson Trail traces the author's ideological journey as much as his geographic one, then in a sense, its real terminus isn't Rio de Janeiro but a spot on Elm Street in downtown Dallas, in front of the former Texas School Book Depository. I visited the city a few months after I came home from South America, and I spent a quiet Sunday afternoon there wandering the grassy Dealey Plaza and the surrounding landmarks associated with the Kennedy assassination.

The president's murder in November of 1963 served as a kind of coda to Thompson's evolution from budding novelist and rebel without a cause to acerbic, hard-charging journalist. Kennedy was the closest thing to a travel companion that Thompson had in South America. Nearly all of his *Observer* stories from the continent at least mentioned the president, and half of them dealt directly with fallout from Kennedy's foreign policy. It wasn't a set of policies that Thompson always agreed with, but in Kennedy he saw a striver, a bulwark against both the warmongers and the golf-balls-off-the-balcony mentality of greed and indifference. The assassination, he wrote, was "a triumph of lunacy, of rottenness . . .

the death of reason." It validated the dread that had crept up on him all across South America, that gnawing sense that the deck was stacked against the strivers.

Life moved pretty quickly for Thompson after he got back to the States. In May, he was invited to speak at the National Press Club in DC about his *Observer* reportage, which had turned some heads among American media bigwigs. By the end of the month, he and Sandy were married. By August, he was considering writing a book on Latin American politics—an idea sadly abandoned—and by September, he and Sandy had moved to Woody Creek, Colorado, a rural enclave outside Aspen. Thompson would call Woody Creek home for the remaining forty-two years of his life.

Then, on November 22, Thompson heard from a neighbor that Kennedy had been shot and killed in Dallas. He immediately went into Aspen, where there was radio and TV, and that night, he wrote to his friend and fellow author William Kennedy. He was done with fiction, he said, done with nostalgia for the days of Fitzgerald and Hemingway. For the foreseeable future, politics and social struggle were the only things that mattered. Describing his disgust at the assassination, Thompson coined what would become his trademark phrase. "There is no human being within 500 miles to whom I can communicate anything," he wrote, "much less the fear and loathing that is on me after today's murder."

As I walked through Dealey Plaza, a man with a megaphone shouted at passersby, urging them to board a bright red "JFK Assassination Trolley." Dads with camera phones posed their kids like snipers on top of the grassy knoll. The marquee ticket, though, is the museum on the sixth floor of the old depository, where an exhibit pathway leads visitors past the window from which Lee Harvey Oswald fired down into the president's convertible. I bought a $16 ticket from a grandmotherly attendant who twice called me "sugar," and I rode the elevator up with a troop of camera-toting Chinese tourists.

The first third of the exhibit recaps Kennedy's three years in office. I looked around until I found a black-and-white photo of the president in Bogotá in 1961, posing at a cornerstone-dedication ceremony on the edge of the city. He's grinning at a crowd of onlookers and TV cameras, unveiling a plaque at the future site of an Alliance-funded housing project called Ciudad Techo—soon to be renamed Ciudad Kennedy, in memoriam. Jackie stands off to the side in her pea coat and pillbox hat, and the backdrop is a jagged tableau of forested peaks. It made me nostalgic for Colombia.

The text accompanying the image mentions the success of the Peace Corps, then offers a short, blunt assessment of the Latin American development plan that Thompson traveled so many miles to cover: "The Alianza para el Progreso, a massive ten-year economic and social program for Latin America, was less successful and did not live up to expectations."

Today, historians widely consider the Alliance to have been a flop. It limped along for another decade after Kennedy, doing little to curb poverty and mostly serving to shore up US-friendly, anti-communist governments. In fact, looking back on my time along the Thompson Trail, it's hard to ignore just how much of South America today seems to represent exactly those scenarios that the US policies of Thompson's day had been drawn up to prevent. The populist left now has a firm foothold on the continent. The poorest haven't much improved their lot. And a not-small percentage of the populace still views the United States with a kind of weary, conflicted resentment.

Still, what you don't find in South America is the resulting nightmare scenario that many in Thompson's era might have predicted. Had you described to officials in the Kennedy administration, for instance, a Brazil led for twelve years by a popular unionist and a former left-wing militant, they would probably have gone into fits. But far from being a downtrodden socialist dystopia, Brazil has one of the continent's strongest democracies—and one of the world's largest and most decidedly capitalist economies.

Despite the slums and the favelas and the hard-luck villages, the South America that I saw only spottily resembled the bleak, dependent purgatory that Thompson often described. What I found instead was a vibrant and endlessly striving continent, proud of its identity and working to meet its own challenges. Is it chaotic? Yes. Drastically unequal? Absolutely. Is it sometimes economically unstable and other times plagued by seemingly overwhelming ideological conflict? Yes and yes again.

But I can think of at least one other sprawling society that fits every one of these descriptions. In fact, it's ironic to suppose that in many ways, the United States has probably become more like South America in the last fifty years than South America has become like the United States.

Thompson left the continent—fled it, really—with a sense of dark foreboding. But beneath all that frustration and cynicism, he seemed to have retained a few kernels of optimism for both continents. A couple of months in the United States helped to calm him down. Returning to the American West, he later wrote, gave him "a sense of renewing," and he wrote to his editor that, despite his criticisms of the Alliance, he believed the program's ideals were still obtainable. The United States and Latin America could still work together to foster peace, fight poverty, and ensure dignity across the hemisphere, Thompson said, but only if the United States avoided paternalism and self-interest, "only so far as we believe in ourselves, and only as long as we keep proving, over and over again, that we are not as mean and greedy as were our forefathers."

As for me, I'm hesitant to say whether my time along the Thompson Trail incited any profound personal revelations. It's fashionable for writers of travel books to declare this kind of thing, and if I'm honest, it's partly what I'd hoped for when I first packed my rucksack all those months ago. The truth, though, is that I came home pretty much the same guy I was before I left—albeit with bedbugs and a more nuanced understanding of how historical forces and US interests continue to shape life in South America.

The thing is, I think Thompson might have said the same thing. He may have even chided me for confusing personal metamorphosis with simple, hard-knock lessons about the way the world works. After all, if Thompson was a different writer for the time he spent on the continent, it isn't because he was mystically reborn along the way. He had no moment of transcendental conversion—South America just gave him an education. All along, I'd been thinking of travel as a sweat lodge when I should have been thinking of it as a classroom. Travel doesn't change who you are. At its best, it just presents you with new information, and how you act on it is up to you. Sure, Thompson could be pretty grandiloquent about suddenly understanding why his own country had failed to live up to its promise, but if South America had simply conferred on him some bleak enlightenment, opening his third eye to the utter pointlessness of it all, Thompson would have spent the next forty-two years sitting cross-legged in an ashram. Or maybe passed out on a barstool.

Instead, he was out there chasing that promise down. Which means that his trip left him just as conflicted and unenlightened as mine. Which means that it left him with hope.

After the museum, I walked a few blocks to the JFK Memorial Plaza, where the city erected a sort of walk-in, symbolic tomb in 1970. It's an imposing thirty-foot cube made of white concrete columns, surrounding a courtyard the size of a small apartment. I was alone at the plaza, and when I walked inside, the monument's innards echoed dully with the sound of my footsteps. The only thing in there was a black granite square with the words "John Fitzgerald Kennedy" inscribed in gold. It was low to the ground in the center of the roofless chamber, a sort of ankle-high podium on which someone had strewn half a dozen red roses. A loose breeze swept stray petals around in tiny, aimless swirls. I looked around at the white walls and black altar. The sky above me was the color of old newsprint, and I spent a few long minutes just pacing around the memorial, looking up at it. Then a JFK assassination Segway tour pulled up, and I figured it was time for me to move on.

Author's Note

While researching and writing this book, I sometimes wondered how Thompson's earliest stories might be different if he were writing them now, at a time when writers have far less liberty to embellish or exaggerate. The mechanisms of journalistic fact-checking have come a long way since 1962, and writers today face scrutiny from media watchdogs that the young Thompson simply never would have confronted. His published correspondence from South America shows him to be a meticulous gatherer of data and a stickler for details. At no point during my research did I come across any serious claims from Thompson's letters or articles that I found to be outright falsehoods. Still, he does set up some suspiciously perfect scenes (the golfer in the penthouse, for example) that would have been difficult to verify. Here and there, quotes attributed only to anonymous bystanders sound an awful lot like something Thompson himself might have said.

My admiration for Thompson as a writer and reporter runs deep, but it has never been my goal to emulate his writing style. Indeed, who could? Thompson's confessed fondness—in his later career, anyway—for blending fact with fiction makes for some great storytelling, but it's not an affection I share. I have, however, relied on some basic time-compression, filtering, and other stock literary techniques in this book, which I'd like to spell out here.

I performed the bulk of my research over a three-year period, during which time I made three trips to South America to travel what I've called the Hunter S. Thompson Trail. The first was a five-week trip to Colombia in 2009 and the second a two-week trip to Lima, Peru, in 2011. The majority of the action in the book occurred during the third and longest of these trips, four months in 2012, beginning in Colombia and ending in Rio de Janeiro, but portions of the book took place during the previous trips as well.

In a few instances, I've recounted stories in an order other than that in which they occurred. Sometimes I did this to relay segments of my journey in a way that better mimicked the segments of Thompson's. Other times it was simply for the sake of narrative simplicity. For example, I met Julio and his coworkers near the bridge in Barranquilla, Colombia, before leaving for the Guajira Peninsula, although I don't describe this encounter until the following chapter. For the most part, however, the events of the book are laid out in broadly chronological order.

All of the book's dialogue comes from my notes, occasional recorded interviews, and in rare occasions, memory alone. I have made every effort to faithfully translate conversations held in Spanish, although many of the conversations I had during my travels were conducted in English or some kind of weird Spanglish amalgam. I've not consciously changed any names or identifying features of the people I met, nor has anyone been combined into composite characters.

I am emphatically not an expert on Latin America, although damn if I'm not pretty fond of those parts that I've visited. What I know about the culture, ecology, and history of these places is drawn from many books, articles, and historical documents written by people with more knowledge than me—although any mistakes are mine alone. I certainly don't hope to present this book as a comprehensive account of how the Cold War issues of Thompson's day shaped the places that he visited, although I would be pleased if it serves for some readers as a kind of primer.

When I began writing this book, I lived in western Montana, which I (affectionately) refer to as home throughout. By the time I finished writing it, I had moved to coastal Maine. Where I will be when you read this is anyone's guess.

BRIAN KEVIN
Damariscotta, Maine
October 23, 2013

Acknowledgments

Anything good about this book owes to the kindness of a small army of friends, acquaintances, contacts, and correspondents, who somehow lent a hand before, during, or after my travels: Benjamin González; Bernie José; Ivan Romero Herrera; Ricardo Cerquera; Mauricio Gomez; Joshua Barr; Diana Ojeda; Wes Carrington, Lisa Swenarski, Jennifer Lawson, Elizabeth Mayberry, and the staff of the PAS at the American embassy in Quito; Lara Devries and the staff of the Light and Leadership Initiative; Jon Jared and Don Montagne of the South American Explorers Club; Stephanie Smith, Finn Tollefson, and the weird people of the Secret Garden; Dr. Alejandro Argumedo; Bianca Crousillat, Joe Levitan, and the staff of the Sacred Valley Project; Elda Cantú, Julio Villanueva Chang, and the staff of *Etiqueta Negra;* Dario Kenner; Ken Davis; Fathers Steve Judd and Ray Finch of the Maryknoll Mission in Cochabamba; George and Sylvia Ritz, Dr. Laurel Parker, Cessar Fernandez, and the staff of the Andrea Ritz Clinics; Sean Conway; Joe Lochridge; Bob Bone; Bill Williamson; Vera Sardinha and Barbara Butland of Internations in Rio; Adam Parry; Jamil Roberts; Jack Epstein; Rory Feehan; Douglas Brinkley; Matthew Fishbane; Andrew Zimmern; Mark Sundeen; Peter Stark; Karen Chen; Bryan DiSalvatore; Deirdre McNamer; and Judy Blunt.

To anyone I've overlooked, please accept this as evidence of nitwittedness and not ingratitude.

I owe far more than thanks to Sky Gilbar and Reid Wilson, who did far more than lend a hand.

My thanks also to Kyle Cassidy of *Wend,* Steve Hawk of *Sierra,* Joe Keohane of *Hemispheres,* Alisa Opar of *Audubon,* and Neely Harris of *Mental Floss,* assignments from whom kept me in bus fare and antibiotic money while on the road.

Thanks as well to the Mesa Refuge (where I wrote the proposal for this book, although I told them I was working on something else) and to the President's Office at the University of Montana, which helped fund my initial trip to Colombia in 2009.

I'm indebted to Carrie Braman, Lauren Hamlin, Maria Simpson, and Liv LiaBraaten, four swanlike women who offered invaluable feedback on early drafts of the book.

My sincere thanks to John Talbot of the Talbot Fortune Agency for helping make this project a reality. Thanks also to Charlie Conrad for his initial interest and guiding hand.

My editor at Broadway Books, Meagan Stacey, is a phenomenal talent and an extremely patient person. Every page of this book benefits from her insight. Thanks to her and Kim Silverton at Broadway. Rachelle Mandik is a rock star of copyediting.

Finally, this book wouldn't exist if not for the peerless reportage of that old footloose American Hunter S. Thompson. It's been a pleasure traveling with you, Hunter.